DEALEY PLAZA
DALLAS, TEXAS
November 22, 1963

TRIPLE UNDERPASS

STOCKADE FENCE

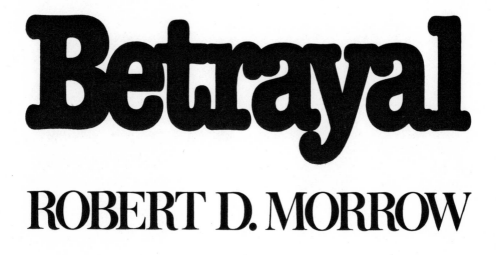

Betrayal

ROBERT D. MORROW

Henry Regnery Company
Chicago

Library of Congress Cataloging in Publication Data

Morrow, Robert D.
    Betrayal.

    1. Kennedy, John Fitzgerald, Pres. U.S., 1917-1963—
Assassination.   2. Morrow, Robert D.   I. Title.
E842.9.M64   1976   973.922′092′4   75-32980
ISBN 0-8092-8092-2

Published by Henry Regnery Company
180 North Michigan Avenue, Chicago, Illinois 60601
Manufactured in the United States of America
Library of Congress Catalog Card Number: 75-32980
International Standard Book Number: 0-8092-8092-2

Published simultaneously in Canada by
Beaverbooks
953 Dillingham Road
Pickering, Ontario L1W 1Z7
Canada

To Mario Garcia Kohly, Sr., friend and comrade,
who struggled until death to free his country,
and to his wife, Doris, who still carries on.

Acknowledgments

To my wife and children, who kept asking where Daddy was; to Cecily, who had the patience; to Zal and Richard, who made it possible for me to finish the book; and, last but not least, to Hap, who did so much of the work—thank you all.

"The people will recognize that the CIA was behaving during those years like a rogue elephant rampaging out of control. . . ."

The Hon. Frank Church
Chairman, U.S. Senate Select Committee on Intelligence
quoted in the *Baltimore Sun*, July 16, 1975

Author's Note

I have written this reconstruction because I feel obligated to supply, despite the hazards of doing so, some significant missing pieces to the puzzle of John F. Kennedy's assassination. They reveal, for the first time, the motive for that tragic act and the identity of the elements responsible for it.

In early 1960, while working as a consulting engineer, I was introduced to Mario Garcia Kohly, who later became the de facto Cuban president-in-exile. Kohly impressed me greatly, and we developed a strong and enduring rapport; ultimately I became his technical advisor. It was, I suspect, this close relationship with Kohly, whose Cuban underground was indispensable to the anti-Castro efforts of the Central Intelligence Agency, coupled with my technical training and experience, that led the CIA to recruit me in early 1961. I am certain that the access I had to top people in the CIA during the eighteen months immediately preceding President Kennedy's assassination—as well as the candor with which these same people discussed in my presence such officials as the president, his brother Robert, Vice-president Lyndon B. Johnson, CIA Director Allen Dulles, and others—was due to the CIA's need and desire to exploit the confidential relationship I had with Kohly.

For more than a decade, handcuffed by the secrecy agreement required of everyone directly or indirectly on the payroll of the Central Intelligence Agency, I lived with what I knew. Even today, despite the many sensational revelations about covert intelligence operations of the United States government, there are risks inherent in divulging the facts about my own experiences. Among other things, the mortality rate of the witnesses to JFK's assassination is inordinately high; that of the probable assassins is remarkably low.

This book is based upon my experiences, on events related to me at the time and subsequently by close associates, and on evidence available in public testimony. All of the characters in the book are real and, for the most part, have been identified with their real names. In those cases where it has been necessary to use fictitious names—out of consideration for survivors, or to protect the cover of agents who are still alive, or for other reasons—that fact is noted in the epilogue.

In a few cases dates and places have been altered, for the same reasons. And to help the reader grasp the complex plot and the motives behind it, some dialogue has been improvised and certain events reconstructed. Occasionally, I have even attempted to surmise the thoughts that, under great tension, must have raced through the minds of some of the more important figures in the book. Nevertheless, in its salient features I believe this book to be a valid reconstruction of a series of major events that would, if verified by an appropriate government body, answer most of the questions that still disturb the world about the assassination and bring the real assassins to justice.

I devoted several years of my life to the nation's clandestine intelligence operations because I believed them to be essential to the preservation of a free society here at home and elsewhere in the world. That view has not changed. However, I am now convinced that our ability to maintain effective intelligence services is threatened less by enemies of the CIA than by misguided individuals in that Agency and related ones, whose efforts to cover up their shortcomings have virtually destroyed the credibility of all U.S. intelligence operations.

That is why much of the information in this book has already been supplied to the U.S. Senate Select Committee on Intelligence. That is why I have offered to reveal in secret testimony before that committee additional information that I could not in good conscience include here. The committee must judge the extent to which that testimony can be revealed without jeopardy to the security of the United States.

Robert D. Morrow
January 15, 1976

Foreword

In October of 1960 a clandestine meeting was held on the links of suburban Washington's Burning Tree Club between Richard Milhous Nixon, then vice-president of the United States, and the Cuban exile leader, Mario Garcia Kohly. At that time it appeared that Nixon would be the next president of the United States. After twice winning the vice-presidency on the Eisenhower ticket, he was expected to snatch an easy victory from the young Massachusetts senator, John Fitzgerald Kennedy.

Kohly, until 1959, had been a highly successful Havana businessman and financier. His father had been Cuba's ambassador to Spain throughout the presidency of Carlos Prio Socarras, a good friend of the Kohly family. As he watched Castro's communist government take shape, Kohly attempted to warn the Cuban people of the consequences. He was arrested and sentenced to be shot. Only a bizarre act of sheer bravado enabled him to escape Castro's death chambers. For several years thereafter, Castro maintained a $100,000 reward for his capture, dead or alive.

Also present at Burning Tree that day were two high-ranking officials of the Central Intelligence Agency, who were introduced to Kohly only as "Ed" and "Chuck." The one known as "Chuck" was later identified by Kohly as Air Force General Charles P. Cabell, then deputy director of the CIA, who would one day call Jack Kennedy a traitor for not supplying the air cover for the Bay of Pigs invasion. Ironically, General Cabell's brother, Earl, would be mayor of Dallas on the day President Kennedy was assassinated. The true identity of "Ed" was never revealed to Kohly, but he was to be the first case officer in Kohly's collaboration with the covert arm of the CIA. He appears in this book under the code name "Ed Kendricks."

That secret meeting, arranged by Washington attorney Marshall Diggs, would weld the destinies of Richard Milhous Nixon and Mario Garcia Kohly in a bond that would eventually destroy them both. It was at this meeting that Nixon chose Kohly's invasion plan and domestic program to restore Cuba to a democracy once it had been liberated by a CIA-sponsored invasion,* which Nixon, as White House Action Officer, would persuade the Eisenhower Administration to sanction.

During the 1960 presidential campaign, Kennedy and Nixon were far apart in their views on how to deal with Fidel Castro. Cuba became a hotly debated issue between the two candidates on national TV.

Nixon, in the spring of 1959, had spoken personally to Fidel Castro for three hours, after which he wrote an extensive confidential memorandum to the CIA, the State Department, and the White House. He said that he was convinced that Castro was "either incredibly naive about communism or under communist discipline." He urged that Castro be dealt with accordingly and prescribed a "stronger policy within Administration councils," such as direct military action if the occasion called for it. His view up until November 8, 1960, was shared by the CIA conservatives but opposed by the State Department.

Throughout 1960 Kohly made several trips to Cuba to unite

---

*Kohly, in 1959, developed "Operation Lake," a plan to invade Cuba. The author has the original document in his possession. The code name was changed during the Kennedy administration to "Operation Pluto."

the underground, preparing more than 40,000 men throughout the island to rise up at his command. He also controlled a strike force of 300 men in the Escambrey mountains, the old stronghold of Fidel Castro, and he had pledged these men to Nixon for use in any future invasion. In addition, he assured the vice-president that the underground would rise up to create chaos at his direction.

When Kennedy won the election, the conservative forces inside the CIA ran for cover, expecting the young, new president to be diametrically opposed to the former vice-president's views. They were correct. By the time John F. Kennedy took office on January 20, 1961, liberal factions inside the Agency had aligned with José Miro Cardoña and Dr. Manuel Francisco Artime, former Castro officials, on the recommendation of the liberal wing of the State Department.

Mario Garcia Kohly, who was identified with the Nixon camp, was termed *persona non grata* by the new administration, and his warnings of the communist activities in Cuba described in this book were rejected or concealed by the White House from 1961 through 1963. But though Kohly was out of favor he was not without power, and his underground network inside Cuba was still of vital importance to the CIA. Consequently, a tenuous liaison between the Agency and Kohly was maintained.

The extent of Kohly's control of the Cuban underground was recognized when, after Kennedy reneged on his promise to supply air cover for the Bay of Pigs invasion, Kohly ordered the underground to withdraw its support as well. Impressed by this demonstration of Kohly's power, and ostensibly to provide him with future support, the president asked his special military advisor, General Maxwell Taylor, to arrange a meeting in an effort to subvert Kohly and get control of his forces.

Taylor told Kohly that if he could unite all the splinter Cuban groups in the U.S., the president would support and recognize a Cuban government in exile headed by Kohly. Taking the presidential advisor at his word, Kohly by late summer had united 115 of the Cuban exile factions in the U.S. under the banner of the United Organizations for the Liberation of Cuba, incorporated in Florida September 5, 1961. During this period

Kohly also adopted a plan to undermine the economy of Cuba with bogus currency.

By this time, however, because he had not been able to control the CIA, Kennedy was in a running battle with the Agency. He had replaced its director, Allen Dulles, with John McCone, and General Cabell with General Marshall "Pat" Carter. Maxwell Taylor was out of the picture, having been appointed Chairman of the Joint Chiefs of Staff.

The promise made to Kohly by Taylor was never kept, and Kohly found himself totally estranged from the administration at a time when his organization represented ninety per cent of the underground forces inside Cuba and virtually all of the Cuban exile groups in the U.S.

Thus, this book begins in early 1961 when all these dramatic events were developing and Kohly's underground had reported activities in the heart of Cuba's central Camaguey mountain district that were potentially disastrous to the United States. It is a story of a betrayal, both political and personal, that eventually led to a conspiracy—a conspiracy that still haunts us today.

Betrayal

Chapter One

When General Charles P. Cabell, deputy director of the Central Intelligence Agency, plucked my résumé from a personnel computer in April 1961, neither of us knew that his action would involve me in events that ultimately would lead to the assassination of President John F. Kennedy. 4/61

My introduction to Cabell came after I had been recruited for a special mission by a man who introduced himself to me as "Ed Kendricks," although that was not his real name. Like most of the senior people in the covert arm (Section C) of "The Company," Ed used a cover name in all of his CIA operations. He had supplied me with one, too, and the ID card in my wallet read: Robert Porter; sex, male; hair, brown; eyes, blue; height, 6'0"; weight, 176 lbs.; age, 26; employer, Comcor, Inc.

Kendricks said that Cabell had picked me for the mission because of my association with the major Cuban exile leader, Mario Garcia Kohly, Sr., and because of my experience as an electronics expert in the aerospace industry, including the CIA-sponsored Comcor firm. He didn't tell me that my skills, those of an engineering specialist in jamming and coding techniques, were to be employed in circumstances vastly different from any with which I had ever before been involved.

When Ed finally introduced me to Cabell it was at the general's lavishly appointed quarters in the Foggy Bottom section of Washington, D.C. That was an awesome experience for me because the much-decorated Westpointer had had an almost legendary Air Force career. He had even been with FDR at Yalta.

What impressed me most at that first meeting, however, was not the general but the elevator we used to reach his study. It was a commercial "Otis" type set unobtrusively into the rear of the classic three-story townhouse. The control panel indicated seven levels, four of them below ground.

Cabell had the steel-gray hair and rugged features of a model in a Marlboro ad. Although he lived with his wife and three children in the officer's compound at Bolling Air Force Base, he devoted most of his waking hours to the Central Intelligence Agency. As deputy director he had the major responsibility for covert operations, supervising a vast network of agents and contract employees whose activities did not exclude fighting undeclared wars or committing political assassinations.

Kendricks and I were joined at the briefing that day by a pilot named Dave Ferrie, who would fly the mission I was to undertake. Standing in front of a large wall map, Cabell spoke to us in a tone so matter-of-fact that it was almost monotonous. But his message was electrifying.

"Your destination will be the Camaguey mountains, where you will be met by some of your friend Mario Kohly's guerrillas. You will fly due south from the mouth of the Caloosahatchee River at an airspeed of 160 knots for fifteen minutes, then onto a heading of 128°, at which time, if you are in your proper position, you should pick up the Key West beacon twenty-five miles to your left at 222°. At your altitude, Key West will not be visible. Maintain your 128° heading for another ten to fifteen minutes; then you should pick up the guerrilla radio beacon located on the beach. If you don't pick it up within eighteen minutes, scrub the mission and return home. You'll be flying beneath the range of Castro's radar, as well as ours at Guantanamo, if you don't exceed an altitude of 100 feet. Frequency for the guerrilla locator beacon will be given you just before you take off. Needless to say, you must maintain complete radio silence.

"Now comes the clincher. It's likely that no one will detect you, because we have arranged a sizable diversion. Two guerrilla assault forces, one staged and launched from Central America and the other from the Florida Keys, will be going ashore about an hour before you take off. One will land approximately fifty miles south of your beacon location, across the island at a place called Bahia Cochinos—the Bay of Pigs. The other will land near Guantanamo at Pinar del Rió. If all goes as planned, this affair should keep the Cubans busy while you complete your mission, pick up a passenger, turn tail, and get the hell out."

When neither Ferrie nor I said anything, he continued, watching us intently to be sure we were reading him, "Once you have passed over the locator beacon, it will be turned off. You should then spot an arrow-shaped line of smudge pots, which will give you your first overland heading.

"Your checkpoints, if not full arrows, will be groups of smudge pots spaced every seven to ten miles. The number of pots will give you your altitude; or, if they manage an arrow, separate pots off to one side will indicate what your minimum altitude should be in hundreds of feet. For example, if three pots are lit, you should fly at an altitude of 300 feet or more; four, 400; and so on. You should maintain an airspeed of ninety knots once you have crossed over the beach. Your landing strip will be about forty-five miles inland. It will be marked on each side by a row of electric lanterns. I don't know how long the strip will be; but we're making sure it'll be more than enough."

Ferrie interrupted. "How much is enough, General?"

I can still hear Cabell's little chuckle as he replied, "We'll try to give you 1800 feet. Remember, you've got a new Super G model with tricycle gear."

"Hooray!" Ferrie burst out sarcastically.

Awed by the risks of the flight, I was annoyed by his nonchalance. Cabel ignored it and came to the point.

"The purpose of your mission is twofold. For some time Guantanamo has been monitoring unusual pulse transmissions that appear to be coming from the Camaguey. They are too

weak to be identified by Guantanamo, but we suspect they are
the sort associated with guidance systems for drone aircraft
and similar devices.

"Your job, Robert, will be to try to record or analyze those
transmissions and identify their precise function and, hopefully,
their source. You will also bring out one of Mario Kohly's principal lieutenants, Manuel Rodriguez, who may have some additional information."

The reassuring drone of the Pratt and Whitney engines pene-
trated the soundproofing of the twin Beech's cockpit, and the
red glow from the instrument panel confirmed that all was in
order. From the right-hand seat I could barely discern the dark
outline of the Florida coast off to my left. The moonlight, break
ing through a rift in the clouds, revealed the dancing whitecaps
of the Gulf of Mexico as they flashed by less than 50 feet below.

We had held a steady course 180° due south since the plane
had slipped away in darkness from Buckingham Field, an abandoned World War II airstrip 20 miles southeast of Ft. Myers,
Florida. My calendar watch read 3:45 A.M., April 17, 1961. It
occurred to me that in the rush of events I had forgotten
my mother's birthday; I would remedy that oversight when
I got home.

Dave Ferrie, a contract employee of the CIA, was at the
controls of the Beech. In civilian life he was an Eastern Airlines
pilot, but there was no FAA-approved flight plan for the mission
we were on. We had now been airborne for about fifteen minutes, and he concentrated on recaging the gyro compass before
taking a 128° heading.

The coast of Florida had disappeared in the blackness of a sky
that was completely overcast, and we were skimming the surface of the Gulf without lights. Only the blue-white exhausts
from the powerful engines were visible. As we banked to the
left, I tuned the ADF (Automatic Radio Direction Finder) to
check the Key West beacon approximately 45° to my left. The
indicator arrow swung directly to 222° as the gyro compass
came around, indicating a heading of 128°. My shoulders
twitched with apprehension; our new course would take us

directly to the center of Cuba.

"We'll hold this course for another fifteen minutes until we pick up the guerrilla beacon on the ADF," Ferrie said, breaking a long silence. "It should be close to the beach." He reached over and retuned to a new frequency.

"I suppose that's meant to be reassuring," I replied, "but what if it isn't where it's supposed to be?"

"It will be. But if you really want something to be nervous about, remember Cabell's instructions. We go VFR after that."

I knew that Ferrie was a top-notch pilot. After God knows how many clandestine missions he was still alive, so he had to be. Yet I couldn't recall our instructions without misgivings. Enough CIA men had been wiped out by Castro that I knew the middle of Cuba was no place for an American to be.

Furthermore, the flight plan itself, however intimidating, was only the beginning. In the cabin behind me was a custom-built, battery-operated Tektronix spectrum analyzer with a Polaroid camera attachment. I also had a portable instrumentation tape recorder with a frequency capability to record most electronic control pulses. I had used this gear before, but never under these conditions.

Soon, as I stared out the cockpit window, I began to see the phosphorescent glow of surf breaking along the beach about seven miles in front of us. Off to our right, and barely discernible on the horizon, I could detect tiny, flashing pinpoints of light, indicating that our covering assault force was already engaged and probably encountering stiff opposition. I was grateful not to be one of those poor devils sloshing through the water toward hostile guns on the beach at the Bay of Pigs.

Focusing on the instrument panel, I saw that we were almost over the locator beacon. The luminous indicator needle of the ADF began fluctuating wildly, then stopped; the beacon had apparently been turned off. As we flashed low over the narrow strip of sand, blackness again engulfed us. Without changing power settings, Ferrie pulled up the nose of the Beech and took us to 250 feet. Leveling off, we spotted—slightly to the right of our nose—the faint glow of flickering lights in the distance. Soon we swept over a crude arrow made up of about twenty smudge pots, pointing approximately thirty degrees to our left. As Ferrie executed the sharp left bank, the lights disappeared beneath our wings and were promptly extinguished.

As we flew inland, we repeatedly spotted other groups of smudge pots, just as they had been described by Cabell. We had changed our heading four times and were now flying at an altitude of 1150 feet—but still only 100 feet above the increasingly rough terrain below. We crossed over arrow number five. Dave slowly eased the throttles back, and the heavy twin began to lose airspeed. At seventy-five knots, he lowered the flaps to thirty degrees and extended the landing gear. Two minutes later, out of nowhere, about forty powerful lantern beams drilled the darkness, feebly lighting up a flat area approximately a thousand feet in length. It was a quarter of a mile ahead and no more than a hundred feet below. At the far end of a makeshift runway, the headlights of a small vehicle suddenly flashed on, the beams making a crisscross pattern with the lanterns. In another thirty seconds we were on the ground, the lanterns blinking out as we rolled past them. Dave cut the power, and we rolled 800 feet to a gentle stop. He had made it seem as simple as a landing at National Airport.

Within seconds we were surrounded by a group of bearded men in battle fatigues, all with Thompson submachine guns slung over their shoulders. For a wild moment, I thought they might be Castro forces. Then Ferrie shouted anxiously out his open window, "For God's sake, Pepe, keep them back till the props stop."

"O.K., amigo."

Pepe was a short, tough-looking Cuban, distinguished from the others only by a pair of captain's bars pinned casually to the collar of his fatigues. I was to learn that Pepe Arnez, a Cuban-born American citizen, had held the rank of U.S. Marine captain during the Korean War but had left the corps to go back to his homeland when Batista was ousted. He had been one of Fidel Castro's most trusted aides until three months before, when a chain of events ending in the torture death of his wife had brought him into Mario Kohly's revolutionary camp.

The whine of the dying gyros reminded me that I had survived at least the first half of this wild exercise.

"You get the hatch," Ferrie said, "and I'll start unloading the cargo. We'll have to move to be out of here before daybreak."

It was only 4:25 A.M.; we had taken off from Florida less than one hour before. As I squeezed past him in the crowded cabin, Dave began unstrapping my gear, which was lashed to the rings on the floor. The hatch swung down to form the stair ramp. Before I could exit, Pepe Arnez reached up, grabbed my hand, and announced with great dignity, "Welcome to Cuba, compadre. I take it you're the electronics expert the chief sent."

"Right, Sir. My name's Bob Porter."

"Pepe Arnez, here. No relation to Desi, I'm sorry to say. And call me Pepe."

He appeared to be about thirty-five, but with his smoothly trimmed beard I couldn't be sure. His eyes were black in the dim light, now that all but a few lanterns near the Beech had been extinguished. Ferrie reached past me and shook Pepe's hand vigorously.

"Glad to see you," he said. "We don't have much time, so you and Bob had better get moving."

Pepe and I loaded my gear into a World War II-vintage jeep and began a grinding ride, without lights, up the mountainside. At the top of the ridge, we reached a level plateau. Pepe cut the engine, jumped out, and began unloading my gear. While I opened the first container, he took a pair of night infra-red binoculars from the jeep and surveyed the countryside. Then he pointed to a flat rock that could serve as a working surface. "It's best you set up here," he said. "We should be good for at least another forty-five minutes."

I worked feverishly to set up the sophisticated electronics gear. A few minutes later, the first signals appeared on the screen of the spectrum-analyzing oscilloscope. After sweeping the lower frequencies with negative results, I shifted to a higher range. Within ten more minutes I had locked onto a very unusual pulse transmission. I knew at once that it was useless to attempt a tape recording because the response of the recorder was far below what I was receiving.

But what surprised me most was the intensity of the signal. It had to be originating nearby. None of the reports from our naval base at Guantanamo, about 175 miles southeast of us, had indicated that we could expect to find signals of this magnitude. Fascinated, I took photographs of the high- and low-frequency segments of the pulses appearing on the oscilloscope screen, snapping the shutter as rapidly as I could. I was so engrossed that I didn't notice that Pepe, lying beside me peering through his night binoculars, had spotted something far down the canyon, near the top of the opposite slope.

"Madre de Dios!" he muttered under his breath as he tapped me on the shoulder. "I think we may have been discovered."

Pointing in the direction we had come, he whispered, "I can see a line of men moving down into the canyon about three miles from your plane. They must be government troops garrisoned at Puerto Marah. Probably heard the plane and took the mountain highway toward Victoria de las Tunas, hoping to spot something."

"How far is the highway?"

Pepe said softly, "Uno momento." He concentrated on his binoculars. "On second thought, they never would have had time to get here. It's at least thirty miles to Puerto Marah by air and twenty miles from here to the highway. They must be from the construction site about seven miles east of here."

I was startled. "Construction site? Would it be more southeast of here?"

"Si. That would be right. It is more southeast from this point. How did you know?"

"Watch this," I replied. As I slowly turned the little antenna on top of the spectrum analyzer, the train of pulses, which had filled the height of the screen, contracted. As I continued to turn it through a full 360° circle, the screen was again filled with the unusual pulse train. I explained, "When the screen is full, the direction arrow on the base of the antenna points to where the signals are coming from, just like the old radio direction finders. Then you check the arrow in relation to your compass, and it gives you the heading."

He nodded. "Now," he said, "if you have enough data to work

with, let's vamos out of here as fast as we can. If those troops get between us and the plane, you can kiss your ass goodbye."

I began shutting everything down. "What time is sunrise around here?" I asked.

"About six o'clock, but it will be light before then."

It was just a few minutes after 5 o'clock. We should take off within half an hour, to be sure of clearing the coast by sunrise. If not, we could get nailed by one of Castro's new armed jet trainers.

Pepe suggested that to save time we abandon the gear and the jeep and climb down the side of the canyon. That made sense, so I shoved the exposed film into the pockets of my leather jacket and we charged off through the brush.

When we reached the top of the ridge just above the plane we could see no lights but I could make out the white top of the fuselage and wings. Fortunately, the wind had shifted and Ferrie had turned the Beech around to face into it, so we would not have to take off over the troops and expose ourselves to small arms fire.

Pepe and I hit the bottom of the canyon less than fifteen minutes after leaving the jeep, unscathed except for our brush-burned hands and faces. As we stopped to catch our breath, I saw Ferrie standing next to the Beech, looking at his watch. I didn't blame him for being restless; it was twenty-five minutes to six and the sky was beginning to brighten overhead. As we approached the plane, I saw that the truck and the three soldiers had disappeared and that a stranger was waiting with Ferrie.

Pepe said, "Good, Manuel made it," and I was quickly introduced to Manuel Rodriguez, one of Mario Kohly's principal lieutenants. He was halfway through his forties and in the predawn light his dark blue eyes seemed almost unreal.

Ferrie asked, "Did you get the data you went for?"

"I sure did," I told him. "It appears that the transmissions are coming from very near here. Pepe says there is some type of construction going on about seven miles southeast. Do you have any idea what it is?"

"No," Ferrie said. "Let's get out of here, and Kendricks can fill you in when we get home."

We quickly said our goodbyes, scrambled into the plane, and strapped Rodriguez into the single bucket seat just behind the pilot's cabin.

When Ferrie hit the starter the starboard engine kicked over almost immediately, but the port engine wouldn't catch. As the starter labored, Pepe, who had been standing about twenty feet away looking skyward with his binoculars, suddenly lowered them and gestured wildly, then stretched his arms straight out to emulate an airplane.

"Mother in heaven, that's all we need!" Ferrie yelled. "This engine picked one hell of a time not to start. You start pumping the fuel pressure pump. I'm going to put the starboard engine up to 1500 revs and hope the generator will juice up the starter enough to crank the livin' bejesus out of it! We must have fouled a plug, with the high manifold pressure and rich mixture coming in."

The engine ground over, and a moment later the powerful roar of a 2500-horsepower Bristol Centaures engine streaked by overhead. Before it turned and disappeared over the rim of the canyon, I could see that it was one of Castro's old World War II British Sea Fury fighters.

"Jesus," I thought. With a jet we might have had a chance, but it was not likely against the slower, more maneuverable prop fighter.

"He must have seen us." I could barely hear Dave over the roar of our starboard engine and the starter, still relentlessly grinding away.

"It's unbelievable," I said. "Why didn't he fire?"

Ferrie yelled back, "He probably saw we're in trouble and he's setting us up like a sitting duck."

With that, the port engine sputtered into life for a few seconds, then died.

"Damn! Damn! Damn!" Ferrie roared.

"We've got to gamble," I said. "We're pointing into the wind. Can we take off with one engine?"

"We'll have to," Ferrie replied. "I don't want to die here!"

Now the fighter reappeared, flying down the canyon toward

us at a much reduced airspeed. We could see him clearly against the lightening sky, preparing to make a strafing pass. When he was within 200 yards, he dropped the fighter's nose slightly and loosed a volley of .303-calibers. Terrified, I could see the lattice trace along the ground in tiny puffs of dust as the bullets swept up to the front of the Beech and suddenly seemed to stop. Miraculous, I thought. My eyes followed the plane as it circled off to the left and then banked sharply out of the canyon.

Turning back to Dave, I noticed that his hand was no longer on the starter switch but was grasping his left shoulder. He was gritting his teeth and swearing under his breath. One of the heavy slugs had evidently ricocheted off a rock right through his open window. Now I really started to panic, and as I began to get out of my seat Ferrie yelled, "Sit your ass down, Porter, and do what I tell you. Start cranking that engine over. That will give you enough oil pressure to feather it. Unless you want to die in this miserable valley, you're going to take us out of here with the one engine." With that he closed his eyes and fainted.

"Oh, Christ," I thought, "I've never flown one of these from the right-hand seat." Then, instinctively, I reached over and hit the starter switch for the port engine. It half-sputtered into life. Quickly adjusting the mixture to medium-lean, I started easing the throttle up. The engine kept running half-heartedly. Pushing hard on the toe brakes, I gave her a hard right rudder and got the engines up to their maximum, 2600 rpm on the starboard and a sad 1700 on the port. I knew that I must be well up over the thirty-one-inch red danger line on the starboard engine, but it was the only chance we had.

Now the port engine was developing some power, and as I released the brakes we began moving down the canyon. As we rolled toward the end of the short airstrip, I realized that I had forgotten to put down the flaps and reached down to shove the flap control to fifteen degrees. The airspeed indicator showed that we were now rolling along at fifty knots, and we had already used up most of the runway.

The plane felt extremely light to me, and my confidence rose as I recalled that we had unloaded all of my gear and that we carried only enough fuel to make it comfortably back to Florida. Rodriguez, our passenger in the cabin behind me, was a featherweight, so we'd have at least a chance, if I could somehow avoid the Sea Fury that now must be setting itself up to shoot off our tail.

The airspeed indicator read sixty-five knots, and I had used up the runway when I eased back the wheel. The Beech lifted off but veered sharply to the left, and I gave her a hard right rudder to straighten her out. Once in the air, I raised the flaps, then reached down and pulled up the landing gear lever. At fifty feet we already had an airspeed of better than ninety knots and I had no intention of going any higher as long as that Sea Fury was in the vicinity. I eased back the throttle of the starboard engine to twenty-five inches and held the port at seventeen. Although we were vibrating severely, there was no way to synchronize the props.

Keeping well below the rim of the canyon, I estimated we had gone about thirty-five miles when the Sea Fury suddenly reappeared about two miles ahead. He had evidently lost us after our takeoff but was now coming directly at us. Within seconds, at slightly less than a hundred yards, he pulled up sharply, passing above us at tremendous speed. He was so close I could see the smile on his young face. He obviously intended to attack from the rear to prevent the possibility of our ramming him.

About a mile ahead the valley narrowed again into a deep ravine that dead-ended into another fairly wide valley, running obliquely. I figured that it was here we had crossed over our first heading arrow after leaving the guerrilla beacon. This meant that the sea and the beach must be only a few miles off, about 30° to our right. God knows what was to our left.

In another ten to fifteen seconds, the Sea Fury would be making mincemeat of us. I had to make a choice.

Once out of the narrow canyon, if we turned right, we could be shot down at leisure. If I gambled by making a 330° left turn, the Castro pilot might be sufficiently surprised to try to follow me. When he had passed overhead, a few minutes before, he must have been flying at maximum power. And now, anxious to make the kill, he wouldn't have cut it back any. The Beech was traveling at less than half his speed and, if I timed it just right, we might be able to make the sharp maneuver. If he made the turn with me at that velocity, the Sea Fury would be smeared all over the hillside before he realized what had happened.

I decided to risk it. I put the nose down, gained airspeed, and dropped down to about a hundred feet off the canyon floor, well below its rim. To get a shot at us, the Cuban would have to follow. Waiting until the last possible minute, knowing that he was hurtling down behind me, I feigned a slight right turn by dropping my right wing slightly. Then, swiftly, I kicked the left rudder pedal hard and brought the right wing up close to a 45° angle. In combination with the superior power of the starboard engine, the maneuver practically tore the wings off the Beech as it went into a sharp left bank, slipping a few feet in altitude. For a wild moment, I thought my left wing was going to touch the ground. Obviously confused, the young Cuban held his fire and started to turn after me. As he hurtled past our tail, he tried desperately to execute a climbing right-hand turn. His speed must have been in excess of 300 knots. I heard the explosion behind me as the Sea Fury buried itself in the hillside.

Flying up the rapidly narrowing valley, I had just about given up trying to gain altitude when the port engine coughed once, then regained full power. I had all I could do to compensate for it, but it relieved the burden on its badly overheated mate. I pulled the manifold pressure of both engines back to twenty-four inches, set the mixtures, synchronized the props, and started the Beech into a tight vertical climb. Within less than a minute, we pulled out over the top of the valley, now bathed in the first light of a magnificent sunrise. Executing a 180° turn, I could see the white beach and the blue of the Straits of Florida less than five miles ahead. Off to the left, not quite a hundred feet from the top of the hill, a tall column of thick smoke rose from the funeral pyre of the downed fighter. Dropping into the valley, I followed it directly out to the sea. I set the autopilot on a course of 308° as we flashed over the beach and headed for home at an altitude of seventy-five feet.

14

Soon the sun's rays, glistening on the sands of Sanibel Island, told me that I could gain some altitude and fly inland over the swamp to the abandoned government strip we had left a few hours before.

When we touched down at 6:42 A.M., a waiting CIA crew rushed Ferrie to Lee Memorial Hospital in nearby Fort Myers. I was told later that a splinter of rock over three-eighths of an inch in diameter had been removed from his upper left shoulder, just a fraction of an inch below his neck. The doctor in the emergency room accepted the explanation that the splinter had been kicked up by a passing truck along the Tamiami Trail.

With Ferrie incapacitated, I was the one who climbed aboard a National Airlines jet for Washington with the pulse train film taped to my belly. I also had, courtesy of the agents who had met us, a new Walther PPK automatic in a spring holster tucked under my left armpit.

Chapter Two

The dashboard clock read 11:30 A.M. as I pointed my XK-150 Jag convertible onto the Baltimore-Washington Parkway from the Fort Meade interchange. I've always been a nut about sports cars, and just driving the Jag gave me a thrill. But today I was more excited about the luncheon meeting with Ed Kendricks and Mario Kohly at the Golden Parrot, a new and sophisticated retreat catering to the unlimited expense accounts of corporate salesmen and influence peddlers who dealt with the DOD, the CAB, and other alphabetical benefactors of Washington reps. Situated near the corner of R Street and Connecticut Avenue, across the street from the gaily colorful carts of itinerant flower peddlers, the restaurant was affectionately referred to by the CIA brass on Nebraska Avenue as the Dirty Bird.

Holding the Jag to a steady seventy miles an hour down the blistering parkway, I was curious about the conclusions that had been reached by the experts who had studied the electronic data I had brought back from Cuba. I wondered if they had confirmed my initial suspicions that what I had observed were computer pulses designed to trim and guide some sort of high-speed space vehicle. If so, what was such sophisticated technology doing in Cuba? I still hadn't put any of the pieces together when I pulled into the Parrot's parking lot half an hour later. I locked the car, even though I knew that, in this heat, it would be an inferno when I returned.

As I opened the ornate double door of the converted brownstone mansion, I praised God for air conditioning. Kendricks and Kohly were waiting for me in the lobby. Mario Garcia Kohly, a short and wiry man, did not have the physical stature to match his reputation, but I knew from my own association with him that he was one of the most determined and controversial anti-Castro leaders in the United States, and I knew he was tough and fearless.

Studying the menu, I asked Kendricks, "What did the experts make of my pulse train photos?"

"What I'm sure you suspected," he replied. "Castro and the Russians are operating a control center in the Camaguey. The pulse trains you photographed indicate computer-controlled digital signals of the kind used to give inertial guidance direction to space vehicles and ballistic missiles. But we have more evidence than that."

Kendricks' eyes darted observantly around the room. Then he reached into his inside coat pocket and drew out a small stack of 5 x 7 photographs. He handed them to me.

For a few moments, what I was looking at didn't register; the photos were dim and slightly blurred. Then I realized that they probably had been taken at night with an infra-red camera. Now what I saw, I didn't believe. Each of the six shots was obviously of the same subject, taken from a different angle and position. They were photos of launching facilities for intermediate or long-range ballistic missiles.

"Jesus!" I exclaimed. "These are in Cuba?"

"Less than seven miles from where you were standing," Kohly replied.

Stunned, I asked, "Who knows about this? How long have they been in place? What's going on?"

Ed interrupted me. "Take it easy, Bob. Other than Chuck

Cabell, the Director, and the three of us at this table, the only other person who's been briefed is President Kennedy. Cabell informed him of our suspicions in early March. When the underground informed Mario that they had these pictures the first week in April, we sent you in to secure the electronic data and bring Rodriguez out with the pictures. We thought we might need him as a witness."

I thought for a moment about how close we had come to not getting back at all; then Kendricks went on. "And now you should know the clincher. At the end of March, JFK ordered us to drop the entire matter."

"Drop the matter?" I blurted, appalled.

Kendricks continued: "In fact, as of 10 A.M. today he ordered all our intelligence data, photos, the report on your findings, and any other documents pertaining to the site, turned over to the attorney general. He then asked that the names of all our personnel who have been working on the project be turned over to a new agency for transfer, the DIA."

"DIA?" I asked. "What's that?"

"If you hadn't been so buried in electronic gear for the past several weeks, you would know that the president ordered McNamara to set up a counterpart to the Agency. It's called the Defense Intelligence Agency, and it is under his direct control."

I was incredulous. "Are you two telling me that the White House knows that there are IRBMs or ICBMs located less than 100 miles from continental American soil and that they want the information turned over to this new agency to hush it up?"

"As near as we can tell, they want to bury it."

"But why? Sooner or later one of the U-2 overflies is going to detect it and the whole military establishment will know about it."

"This missile site could take a year to detect from 90,000 feet. Pepe Arnez had to take an infra-red camera to within 200 yards to penetrate the heavy camouflage. Of course, the administration's action this morning could be strictly political. Our operation at the Bay of Pigs turned out rather badly for the Kennedy image and the president isn't apt to forgive us for it, but it was absolutely necessary for us to insure the success of your mission."

"Poor bastards," I interjected. I really felt for them. "They sure caught hell."

"Yes, but we had no choice," Kendricks continued. "If the diversion had been less extensive, we might not have gotten close enough to that site to collect the electronic data. That was a risk we couldn't afford to take. We had heard rumors about the building of that site for several months, but, as I said, it wasn't until the first week in April that we could get any hard evidence to substantiate our suspicions. Then we had to be absolutely certain they were for missiles by virtue of their guidance system. That was the data you got. Tracking systems, as you know, are almost impossible to identify positively unless you are right on top of them."

"That's for sure," I replied, handing the photos back. "But all those men lost at the Bay of Pigs. Surely it didn't require that big an operation?"

"You're absolutely right, of course. But because of the time element, we elected to advance a planned invasion operation composed of Cuban exiles who had been training for months under the CIA's direction—in fact, since long before the missile business came up. The invasion wasn't supposed to take place until late this month, but it was easier to advance it than to create another diversion. When we were notified by Mario's underground that they had hard evidence of the site's existence in their hands, we had to act swiftly. That was the first week in April. But when Cabell called on Kennedy to brief him on the situation, he was ordered to make no further moves, at least none relating to missile intelligence."

"You mean that the president, knowing that there might be missiles in Cuba, gave specific orders for us not to go there to get the information? Why?" I asked.*

"At that point in time we could only assume he wanted the situation to be completely under his control. Thus you have the ultimate reason for setting up the DIA. It may sound far-

---

*This event occurred more than eighteen months before the public was told there were Soviet missiles in Cuba.

fetched, but it's our opinion that he wants to be able to use the missile info for some future political advantage. It's even possible that he could suppress the information long enough to use it as a lever to swing next year's Congressional elections. You know, 'don't switch horses in the middle of a crisis.' That sort of crap. FDR was a past master of it."

"So we went anyway?"

"Damn it, we had to. From the information we got through the underground, we estimated that that site was far enough advanced to be operational within six months. And, I might add, that's less than three months from now. Then we began to hear rumors, after Cabell's April briefing, that Kennedy had given some incredible instructions to Secretary McNamara regarding the Agency. These instructions were, in effect, to inform all the Cuban leaders who were to participate in the invasion that they should ignore Agency directives in the event we accelerated the tentative June date. They were told to notify the White House immediately if such orders were issued."

Kendricks looked at Mario Kohly, who appeared to be occupied with other thoughts until a nod of his head indicated that he was listening.

Kendricks continued, "In fact, we had been so undermined by the White House that on Saturday afternoon, the 15th, we called an organization meeting of the Cuban leaders favored by the Kennedy administration. Once they had all arrived at the Lexington Hotel in New York, we transported them to a safe house at Opa-Locka where they were placed under close surveillance to keep any word of our plans from reaching the White House. Unfortunately, one of the leaders, Tony Varona, managed to escape through a bathroom window and called Washington. When the president found out we had scheduled the invasion for the next day, he ordered the Navy to withhold the fighter support he had formerly pledged to cover the B-26's supplied by the CIA."

Bitterly, Kohly took up the story, speaking in the cautious English of one not using his native tongue. "This, in effect, caused a slaughter, with nothing except a few ancient B-26 bombers to try to fend off Castro's jets. Madre de Dios, how many of the assault troops died!"

As he went on, I began to feel sick.

"I found out about the president's treachery after the troops had already sailed. It was too late to stop them but, obviously, without air support I could not commit the members of my underground and my few forces on the island. Without any outside help, they would all have been slaughtered. As it was, one of my underground leaders, Rogelio Gonzales Corso, known as Francisco, was picked up by Castro and executed the night the invasion forces went in. But even now, with all these men having been sacrificed to get the evidence, your president apparently intends to do nothing about it." His voice cracked, but in a controlled rage he continued. "Now, by God, your president is risking the very existence of America, possibly the free world, for some purpose unknown to us."

My emotions were playing tricks with my hands; as I downed my martini, they were shaking perceptibly.

"You should also be aware," Kendricks said, "that the Company has asked Mario to commit his underground in an attempt to liberate the survivors of the 2506 Brigade captured at the Bay of Pigs. Obviously, the president and his brother have no knowledge of this. Mario agreed, but insisted that he have a free hand to operate as he sees fits with no interference. I don't think that will be acceptable."

Kendricks paused, grunted quietly, and changed the subject. "How about another shooter, then let's get Uncle to feed us one hell of a good lunch. Eat hearty, my lad, because you are in for another shock after lunch."

When we arrived at Cabell's quarters Kendricks and I left Kohly in a small reception room just inside the front door reading *Newsweek* magazine. We entered the elevator and after a short descent the doors slid open to reveal a small room with a mirrored panel set into the far wall. There were no apparent openings or doors, but Kendricks motioned for me to enter and then followed as the elevator doors shut quietly behind him. The room was brightly lit by several fluorescent fixtures recessed into a very high ceiling.

A large section of the wall to our left slid open, revealing a short corridor with two doors. Two of them were marked "Gentle-men" and "Ladies." Some things never change, I thought. These johns had to be some of the most expensive pieces of real estate in D.C.

Kendricks walked to the door at the end of the hall, pushed a card into a chrome slot, and the door opened into what appeared to be an operations room. As we stepped inside, I caught my breath at its dimensions: at least 50 by 100 feet.

This layout looked like a movie set, but it was for real. On one wall were large plate glass double doors and several large plate glass windows. Through them, I could see a computer, one of the new IBM 360 models I knew were to be introduced shortly. Dominating the far wall was a map of the U.S. projected on a twenty- by eight-foot screen. Beneath it stood three program consoles manned by military personnel. The room was crammed with communications gear of all types, including a radar display of Washington. "Where the hell is the antenna for this baby?" I wondered—and then saw the octagonal outline of the Penta-gon painted on the screen's center. To the right of the entrance were several video displays set in long consoles. They were being monitored intensely by green-garbed young civilian technicians.

Amused by my obvious astonishment, Kendricks said, "Fol-low me," turned, and walked through a door I hadn't noticed before, next to the entrance.

I followed him into a large, spartan office. Behind a massive desk with a long conference table forming a "T" in front of it, sat General Cabell. Standing, he greeted Kendricks and then me. "I trust you had a pleasant lunch," he said and, without waiting for a reply, gestured for us to be seated.

"Have you brought Bob up-to-date?" he asked.

"Yes, Sir," Ed replied.

"Well, young man, I assume Kendricks has told you about the Agency's feud with the White House."

"Yes, Sir, I'm afraid he did; and I know it must place you in a difficult position."

Cabell glanced at Kendricks, then said, "Of course, we're all concerned. It isn't every day that we are forced to act independently—only in what could be termed a crucial situation."

"But, Sir, even against the express wishes of the president?" I asked.

"In this case, yes. But before you make any rash assumptions, take a look at this." Reaching into his top desk drawer he took out a large legal file folder and handed it to me.

The first item I removed from the folder was a memorandum handwritten on stationery headed "Office of the Vice-President of the United States." The salutation read, "My dear Charles:"

It is nearly fifteen years since I read it, but I will never forget its tone and its message. After a number of critical, self-serving comments about the intention of the president and his brothers to build a Kennedy dynasty in the White House, Lyndon Johnson got to the guts of his message.

The vice-president said that he had learned, "strictly by accident," that the secretary of defense had been secretly ordered to use any means at his disposal to control the activities of the CIA in order to render it powerless. The vice-president reported that McNamara had been authorized to set up the Defense Intelligence Agency for this purpose. Finally, he told of a meeting between the president and the chairman of the Senate Appropriations Committee in which the president intimated misuse of power by the CIA and asked the chairman to institute an investigation that would severely limit the Agency's unvouchered funds and place all U.S. intelligence activities under DIA control.

Beneath the handwriting were the initials "LBJ"; there was no date.

I looked up with a queasy feeling. Cabell was watching me intently.

"Read the next report," he said. "It was handed to us by one of the president's Secret Service bodyguards."

I opened the file folder. On top of a stack of reports was a carbon of a handwritten memo. It was short, and I can remember almost the precise words.

> Memorandum to the Attorney General:
> If possible, try to apprehend all Cuban and
> American personnel currently engaged in manu-

facturing bogus Cuban currency. As you know, in its efforts to overthrow the Castro regime, the CIA has disregarded our direct orders and placed us in a politically embarrassing position. The names of all the parties involved in the conspiracy should be in the Agency's file.

Also, you might consider leaking to the Cuban authorities that a massive counterfeiting scheme may be launched against them that could jeopardize the Cuban economy.

The memorandum was signed "Jack."

"When did you receive this?" I asked. "In some circles this could be considered tantamount to treason."

"Not necessarily. It perhaps could be justified as part of a diplomatic strategy. But continue reading; there's a lot more."

During the next half-hour, I read through numerous reports dealing with everything from unsavory campaign tactics authorized by the president to surveillance reports on how he occupied many of his nights.

When I finished, I whistled in amazement and asked, "What now?"

"Well, young man," Cabell said, "this afternoon we have arranged for our friend Mario Kohly to confront the attorney general with the photos of the missile site and your electronic data report. If he reacts negatively, Kohly will give a television interview and break the story. That should flush them out and force them to admit the site's existence. I'm telling you this because your position in Section C has been changed to contract status.* Kendricks will talk to you later about compensation and you'll also have a reasonable expense account."

I thanked him for his confidence.

"Now," he said, "we had enough warning to stop the arrests for counterfeiting, and in the past two days we have moved the

---

*A contract employee of the CIA is one who is hired as an independent contractor, usually through one of the armed services. Mine was with the Army, but payment for services was made by a cashier's or treasurer's check with a coded contract number to identify it.

operation to Baltimore. But the attorney general appears to have been successful in leaking the information to Castro. Our agents in Havana notified us this morning that the premier has just ordered new currency printed in Czechoslovakia.

"After it's delivered, Cubans will be required to trade in their currency. Any cash not converted within thirty days will no longer be redeemable. That means that a number of banks trading in Cuban currency, as well as thousands of Cuban refugees, will be wiped out. It will also have cost us two years' time and God knows how many lives those bogus pesos could have bought out of Castro's torture chambers. So now we start over, and it'll be the fall of 1963 before we can start dealing with the new stuff."

"Why so long?" I asked.

"We anticipate it'll be next spring before the changeover can be completed and the new bills put into circulation. By the time we get the samples and make the plates, it will take a year. The job has to be done to perfection in order to fool the Banco Nacionale de Cuba's new Russian currency validators. Three denominations have to be made, and making the plates for each will take several months. Then the printing operation begins. My guess is it'll be September of 1963 before we'll have enough currency printed for any sizable operation."

"What if the president or attorney general finds out?" I asked. I was still shaken to learn that the CIA would defy a direct presidential order.

"Who's going to tell them?" he asked sarcastically. "We want Cuba's economy broken before they discover what hit them. Then we deal with Fidel on our terms, missiles or no missiles. This time we will plan it so that no one will know anything of the currency operation except me, Mario, Kendricks, and the personnel directly involved in its manufacture."

When he paused, I asked, "Not to change the subject, but when is the meeting between Mario and Bobby Kennedy to take place?"

"Kendricks will drive him over in the next few minutes. If all goes well Kohly will simply cancel his TV interview."

He reached into his top drawer again, drew out a green identification badge, and handed it to me. "Put this on." Then he turned to Ed. "You'd better get going or you may be caught in the Monday afternoon traffic."

"Will do," Kendricks replied. "Bob, I'll pick you up later, depending on what happens. Your distinctive car has been taken back to the 'Bird's' parking lot."

"My car! How?...." I stopped short as he waved a set of keys in my face and chuckled. "For any car, Robert. You could be equipped with a set of your own before you leave." Then, waving to us, he said, "See you later," and walked out the door.

Cabell got up from his desk. "Come on, I'll introduce you to the crew."

I clipped on my badge and followed him into the operations room. Standing just outside Cabell's office, talking to one of the green-suited technicians, was a man I judged to be about my age, perhaps a few years older. Cabell introduced us.

"Bob Dalton, meet Bob Porter. You two could be working together quite a bit in the next few months." As we shook hands, I saw Dalton's eyebrows lift when he noticed my green badge. The red one he wore apparently bore a lower classification.

Cabell said, "You show Robert our setup and introduce him around. I've got some work to do and then I'd like to see both of you in my office, say in about an hour. I'll page you."

Dalton's tour lasted well over an hour. As we went from level to level, I was dumbfounded at the facilities crammed into the underground complex. Several third-level rooms were filled with jamming and anti-jamming equipment. There was also a sealed room accessible only through a huge safe door. Dalton told me that it contained the Agency's cryptographic gear and that the only persons admitted to this room were green badge holders; he knew of only six others. Why Cabell gave me one, I don't know to this day. The second level housed the administrative operations; here, he said, all unvouchered funds for the Agency's covert operations were handled and distributed. I assumed that everything tied into the master computer I had seen on the lower level, just off the master control room.

The master control, or operations, room fascinated me more than any other area. Dalton explained that half of its twenty video screens monitored the complete spectrum of electronic signals across the short wave bands. If a technician noted something of special interest, he could push a button next to the screen and activate a video tape recorder to transcribe it. He said that the complex housed a recorder for each of these ten consoles. The others, he added, were used for personal surveillance. He left it at that.

As we entered his office, Cabell was talking excitedly on the phone, his face livid and his hands shaking. He slammed down the phone, turned to me, and ordered, "Porter, get over to the TV studio. I want you standing by outside when Kohly finishes his interview."

It was obvious that the meeting with the attorney general had gone badly, although Cabell didn't say so. "It's five now, so Kendricks and Mario are driving directly to the station from downtown. Kendricks will fill you in on Kohly's meeting with Bobby. When you get to the studio, stay clear of any direct contact with Kohly or Kendricks. Let them come to you. After he arrives at the station Kendricks will call me, and I'll tell him that you're on your way and will be waiting in the parking lot. Leave your car parked at the 'Bird' and take mine. It looks nondescript, a standard Buick convertible."

"Do you think we'll have any trouble?"

"I hope not, but be prepared for it. Kendricks told me that the attorney general was so mad he almost hit Kohly. Now, here's where I've got to count on you. After his interview, I want you to fly Mario to Florida. We have a brand new 400-horsepower Comanche hangared in the Butler terminal at Friendship Airport."

He hesitated and, reading his thoughts, I said, "If there's trouble, I'll have a rough time getting to Friendship, especially in rush hour traffic and having to backtrack through town."

"You're right. I'll have the Comanche shuttled over to Montgomery County Airport at Gaithersburg. Here's a set of keys for the plane and my car. I'll have the tanks topped off. And remember, this bird's special. It's got a 1200-mile range. Now, unless something changes, you will take Kohly directly to Gaithersburg and from there into Opa-Locka Airport just north of Miami. When you arrive, have the plane refueled. When you land you will get further instructions from Manuel Rodriguez, the man you flew back from the Camaguey. Incidentally, don't file a flight plan. All the latest weather reports and a recommended VFR routing will be on the front seat of the Comanche. But remember, we can't plan everything. If the weather's good, you should make it in just under four hours. Now, get cracking." Smiling, he added, "Good luck!"

"Thank you, Sir."

"Dalton will show you the Buick," he said. As I was halfway through the door, he asked, "By the way, are you carrying a gun?"

I nodded and closed the door behind me.

As the elevator doors opened at the street floor, I spotted Dalton on a phone next to the front door, presumably talking with Cabell. He beckoned to me as he hung up. "Come on," he said. "You get the boss's souped-up model."

"Souped-up how?"

"Well, for openers, she's got a supercharged 300-horsepower overhead cam V-8, the individual coil springs have been replaced with torsion bars, and the Dynaflow drive train has been replaced with a four-speed box and dual-speed rear axle."

"Jesus! Why didn't you just buy a Ferrari and be done with it?"

"Simple," he replied. "Everyone knows that a sports car has all that gear, but who would expect a dynaslush Buick with its soft coil springs to be a tiger? Takes everyone by surprise. We have three just like it, two down south and the one Cabell uses here."

As we stepped outside, he pointed up the street and said, "There she is."

The yellow Buick looked just like any other '61 model until you got inside. A panel of instruments just beneath the dash sported an electronic tachometer, a Rootes blower pressure gauge complete with engaging switch, and other goodies. The speedometer indicated up to 160. The biggest surprise came when I started the engine; it didn't make any of the familiar noises I would have expected of a supercharged job. In fact, it sounded like any other piece of Detroit iron.

Although the normally light Monday traffic had not hit its peak, it still took me the better part of an hour to get to the studio parking lot. As I pulled into one of the visitor slots farthest from the studio entrance, Kendricks, who must have spotted me from inside, walked over to the car and slid in. Wiping his brow with a large handkerchief, he said, "All hell's broken loose. Just after you left, Cabell got a call from the attorney general. He has issued orders to have Kohly picked up. Cabell refused to tell him where Mario was, but there's always the chance that we may have been followed."

"What happened at the meeting?"

"The attorney general called Mario an unmitigated liar and accused him of making up the whole story about the missile site, even to faking the photos."

"But the data on the pulse trains can't be denied."

"Robert, you know it and I know it. Something mighty queer is going on. My major concern right now is Mario. As soon as he finishes, get him the hell out of here. Cabell told me what your instructions were. I'll try to keep the bastards off your back long enough for you to get away. Damn, you would think we were in an enemy country."

With that Kendricks jumped out of the car. Then, leaning in through the window, he said, "You probably won't see me again. I'll go out the back door. If anyone was following us, he'll expect that kind of maneuver and maybe he'll tail me instead of you. Wait here for ten minutes and then pull up in front of the entrance. Leave your engine running, and when you're in position I'll send Mario out fast so he can jump in. Then dig out. If anyone follows you, you should be able to lose them in this bomb. So long."

Before I could reply, he had disappeared between two parked cars. A moment later I saw him entering a side door of the studio building. I backed the Buick into a spot directly opposite the studio entrance; then I put the top down. It was a full fifteen minutes before I spotted Kohly just inside the glass doors. Putting her into low gear, I swung the powerful car out of the slot fast and pulled up to the front steps.

As I screeched to a halt, a black Ford sedan surged out of another slot three cars down and cut in front of me, blocking the drive. Instinctively, I threw the Buick into reverse, backed fast into the slot I had just vacated, cut the wheels hard, and headed out in the opposite direction. Fortunately, Mario had spotted what was happening. The little guy lunged headlong into the back seat as I gunned the Buick down the studio drive. For the next ten minutes, heading away from Gaithersburg to avoid revealing our intended destination, the Ford and the Buick played tag, the two-way traffic being just heavy enough to deny either car an advantage.

Finally I spotted a short gap in the oncoming traffic. I engaged the blower switch, floored the accelerator, and pulled around the next three cars. Now it only took a fraction of a mile to lose our pursuers by running a yellow traffic light. The signal and the intervening autos tied them up long enough to enable us to get out of sight and cut into a side road.

A half hour later we rejoined the slow-moving northbound traffic and arrived at the Montgomery County Airport at Gaithersburg within twenty-five minutes. As we entered the parking lot, I spotted the Comanche on the ramp in front of the fuel pumps of Freestate Aviation. I pulled the Buick into a crowded rear section marked "employees only," and we walked casually to the plane.

I had flown a lot of Comanches, but this lady was special. Her nose was a good foot longer than her sisters', making her look more like an ME 108 than a civilian plane. She had wing-tip fuel tanks to supplement the four standard ones in the wings, and in front of her supercharged 8-cylinder power plant sat a three-bladed Hartzel prop. I unlocked the door and slid in to take a look. The engine time recorder registered a pure eleven hours.

As I was climbing out to preflight the ship, a young pump attendant presented me with a fuel bill. It was made out to one of the many companies that Cabell used as covers. I signed it, asked him to pull the chocks from the wheels, and proceeded to preflight the plane while Mario bought some sandwiches and a quart of milk in the terminal building. It was 7:30 P.M. and the sun was low in the west as I finished running up the engine and pulled onto runway 24. With less than half the runway gone, we rose swiftly into the darkening sky. If all went well, I judged our ETA at Opa-Locka to be approximately 11 P.M.

Chapter Three

Casa Verde was one of the newer and more exclusive Fort Lauderdale motels catering to the extravagant northern executive wife. Mario Kohly and Manuel Rodriguez were standing at the picture window of my suite looking at a seemingly endless expanse of carefully manicured lawn. Beyond the palm trees and the thousands of exotic flowers was the sand, white under a full moon.

Rodriguez had joined us at Opa-Locka for the tedious trip across North Miami and up Biscayne Boulevard. As he turned from the view, his dark blue eyes snapped.

"Mario is going to have to get out of the country to avoid being arrested," he said, crossing the large room to the bamboo bar where I was mixing myself a nightcap of light rum and orange juice. "So far, Mr. Porter, you're lucky. From what Kendricks said on the phone, the Kennedy brothers don't know who you are yet, but they sure as hell will when they run a make on your picture."

"Oh? How did they get my picture?" I asked, more curious than surprised.

"They photograph everyone going in and out of Cabell's house, Kendricks told me."

Mario chuckled from the massive chaise longue in a darkened corner of the room. But he spoke with quiet venom. "The bastards may force me out of the country, but they will regret the day they sold out the American people."

Rodriguez, fixing himself a rum and coke, grinned at me. "I think we had better get the old man out of the country fast, before he does something rash."

"Don't worry about me, amigo," Mario retorted. "I can take care of myself. Did Kendricks say anything about the weapons we were promised?"

"Ah, yes, I was coming to that. Sometime early tomorrow funds will be transferred from Mexico to your numbered bank account in Bimini. Someone could probably catch a flight over late tomorrow afternoon and come back the following morning."

"Excellent. Excellent. Now, Roberto, I am going to have to borrow your services, at least for another week or two."

Surprised, I replied, "I don't know whether my orders cover working directly for your organization, particularly down here."

"Nonsense. I'll get Kendricks to verify it in the morning. In fact, now that we have the use of the plane, you can be the one to fly to Bimini." Reaching inside his shirt, he unstrapped a large money belt, brought it over, and put it on my night table. "I certainly can't make the trip. I don't hold a U.S. passport and, with the brothers after me, I would be deported immediately into the loving arms of Fidel. If that happened, I wouldn't last an hour in one of his torture chambers."

"I'm sorry, I meant no offense. What precisely would I have to do in Bimini?"

"You will be picking up a package of between 250 and 350 thousand U.S. dollars, all in relatively small denominations."

"Quite a package," I replied.

"You won't have it long. The next step will be to fly back here, deposit the cash with Manuel at Miami International, and fly down to the Homestead Airport to pick me up. Together we will head for a little town called Peterboro, Ontario. There we will meet a Canadian friend of ours who flies a DC-4 for Cubana Airlines. He will be carrying the samples of Fidel's new currency that have been approved by the finance minister. Cubana operates between Mexico and Canada regularly, and anything going to or coming from Europe is flown via Canada. If we can intercept the approved samples before they get back to the printers in Czechoslovakia, we can save considerable time in setting up our new counterfeiting operations. Only a few hours are needed to take scaled photographs and duplicate samples of the color tones. Then when the proofs come back from Europe for final approval, we can again intercept them and make the necessary corrections. With any luck at all, we can be in production almost simultaneously with Castro's Czech friends."

Manuel had finished his first drink and was now fixing himself another. "You know," he chortled, "it hadn't occurred to me before, but when Fidel finds out about this one, he'll think the Russians have sold him out."

"Not to be vulgar," I thought aloud, "but he'll have a shit hemorrhage."

That seemed to strike the right note; it broke them both up. Then Mario said, "By the way, Roberto, the cash you'll be bringing from Bimini will be used to buy weapons, medical supplies, and communications equipment. When you get back from Canada you could be off to Europe to complete that transaction. Kendricks will have to give you the itinerary."

The clock on the far wall said 2:30 A.M., and I was wondering if I could keep my eyes open another ten minutes when Mario said, "Gentlemen, I think we had all better get some sleep."

Kendricks, ever attentive to details, had told Manuel on the phone that we were without luggage and had given him our approximate sizes; the Cuban had bought each of us a pair of pajamas, a sport shirt, slacks, and some underwear. I was damn grateful to be able to shed my sweat-stained summer suit.

As they left the room, Manuel said, "Pleasant dreams and hasta la vista. If you want us, we're just down the hall."

"Thanks," I said, too tired to ask the number of their room. I fell into bed without even bothering to turn out the lights.

The phone rang at 7 A.M. The operator reported that long

distance was calling me and in a second I heard Kendricks' booming voice: "I've got news for you. Don't say anything about it to our friends, but late last night one of our overflies disappeared off the radar screen in the vicinity of that missile control center in the Camaguey. To make matters worse, it was one of our top-secret D model RB-57's, especially outfitted for infra-red night reconnaissance work."

"Jesus, that's a medium bomber."

"She's now overdue six and a half hours. We've got to presume the plane is down or has landed somewhere, whether intentionally or otherwise."

"How about the U-2's?"

"No problem there. However, as we both know, they can't carry the equipment for a surveillance job of this sort, particularly with the sophisticated camouflage used by the Russions. We frankly suspect that it was a deliberate act on the part of the crew."

"It couldn't be another Francis Gary Powers incident?"

"I don't think so. This has a more sinister look. Somehow the president knew about it as soon as we did—maybe sooner—and ordered the cancellation of all B-57 reconnaissance flights over Cuba." He paused, then mused, "The whole thing seems too damn pat."

I was stunned by the obvious inference. Kendricks apparently suspected that the president had arranged the disappearance of the plane to create an excuse for halting aerial reconnaissance before the Air Force also discovered the missiles.

"Your job," I heard him continue, "is now more important than ever. Mario needs that package you're to pick up in Bimini. He'll use some of the money to buy supplies and equipment for his guerrilla group to go in and take some prisoners. We've got to know what the hell is going on down there."

"I'll buy that," I said. "Damn it, Ed, we know the exact location of the missile complex. Isn't there any chance for a U-2 overfly to get some immediate dope?"

"No. They don't carry the gear, and, anyway, until we are sure of the reason for the B-57's disappearance, the CIA is also restricting all its flights over Cuba."

"So all that's left is Mario's underground?"

"That's all," Kendricks replied. "Now get your tail in gear. Tell Mario that the package he was expecting from Mexico arrived in Bimini about an hour ago and will be available at the bank by 10 A.M. With any luck at all, you'll be back by nightfall.

"I have one last piece of advice. You're going to have to come back through customs at Miami International Airport. File a flight plan once you're airborne from Bimini so you'll have no problem getting back in. When you land, a customs officer by the name of Murphy will be assigned to you and your plane. He's one of our men and knows what to do. Once you are released, fly directly to Homestead General, as Kohly requested. He'll meet you there. I understand he wants you to fly him to Canada. But in a single-engine bird, you won't be permitted to enter Canada until daylight, so Kohly will make arrangements for you to stay in Coral Gables, probably at his son's house. At any rate, don't check out of the Casa Verde. That way, nobody will really know you're gone or what your plans are. In the morning, file a flight plan for Rochester before flying on to Canada. Tell them you are meeting friends for a fishing trip at Stony Lake, Ontario. I understand you own an island there."

"But where do I land in Canada?"

"Fly to Lakefront Airport in downtown Toronto. A PA-22 with floats has been reserved for you. You do know how to fly a float plane, don't you?"

"Oh, hell yes, just like that! What's a PA-22?"

"Sorry, old buddy. It's known as a Tri-Pacer when it has wheels."

"No sweat. I'll indicate in my logbook that I know all about float planes."

Kendricks snorted. "Robert, be serious. I know you've had some time in seaplanes. This is the easiest of them all."

"Sorry, Ed. But you keep springing these damn surprises on me."

"Speaking of surprises, tell Mario his attorney called me. Mario has been asked to meet with Maxwell Taylor, Kennedy's military advisor. I frankly don't know what they have up their sleeves, but apparently the president has calmed down brother

Bobby. Call me in Washington if you run into any trouble."

"O.K. I will."

There was a moment of silence, then, "Buddy, take care," and Kendricks hung up.

I could feel the adrenaline pumping through me; then I remembered that the 150 dollars I was carrying wouldn't take me very far. I needed a credit card before I took off for Canada. Thank God I didn't have to check out of the Casa Verde; the tariff had to be seventy-five dollars a day if it was a cent, and there was still the Comanche. As economical as it was, those 400 horses did eat up fuel.

As I put the receiver on its cradle, I noticed for the first time what a magnificent day it would be for flying.

Mario and Manuel arrived just as I finished dressing. It was Kohly who asked, "So what's new, compadre?"

"Well, I heard from Kendricks. The money will be available in Bimini at 10 A.M. I have been assigned to the ranks of the infamous; I'm part of your group, at least temporarily, and I've been instructed to fly to Bimini to pick up the cash."

"Great, chico," Mario exclaimed. "I'm sure we couldn't have a better man. Now, we can give 'em hell!"

"Uhh . . . hhuh, Mario," I said, as I realized it would be necessary to put my role in perspective. "Let me put it to you this way: I really hadn't intended to do any fighting. I'm the original chicken."

"No fights. No fights. But maybe a little scrap here and there. O.K.?"

Manuel interrupted, "For God's sake, Mario, knock it off. You'll scare the hell out of him."

I decided to change the subject. "Mario, now hold on to your hat. Kendricks just informed me that the president has called off his dogs, for the moment at least. A meeting is being arranged, through your Washington attorney, with Maxwell Taylor."

Mario was stunned and looked it momentarily. Then a smile crossed his face. "The son of a bitch has decided he needs my underground."

"If you want my opinion," Manuel said, "I think the Director finally got to him and gave him the facts of life. However, I wouldn't trust anything either of the Kennedys did, to save my soul."

"I agree, chico, but it will be most interesting to see what General Taylor has to say. When did they propose this meeting?"

"Kendricks didn't say but I would assume sometime soon. Now, let's get some breakfast. I've got to get going, if I'm going to get everything done by this afternoon. Also, before I forget, you'd better give me the documentation I'll be needing in Bimini."

Minutes after leaving the coast of Florida, I was on final approach for South Bimini Airport. I covered the sixty-three miles in about sixteen minutes, being careful to stay in sight of land; even the most seasoned pilot gets an uneasy feeling at being over nothing but water in a single-engine airplane.

On my final approach to the Bimini airport I passed over the estate of the island's most notorious citizen, New York Congressman Adam Clayton Powell. Too bad I can't stop for a long weekend, I thought.

I touched down on the 5,000-foot Bimini runway. After clearing immigration and customs, I rode into town in the most dilapidated taxi I'd ever seen, a Ford Anglia of uncertain vintage. The ride gave me a moment to sit back and enjoy the beauty of this quiet little island that sits, as they say, like a pearl at the end of the Bahamian chain.

Ten minutes later, the Anglia creaked to a stop in front of the Island Bank in the center of town. At ten o'clock, Bimini was barely awake. I went in and asked to see the manager.

Alexander Westwood was nattily British in his white linen suit and light blue shirt, bisected by a deep red tie. The carnation in his buttonhole would have made the managing director in London beam with approval.

"Mr. Kohly?" he said hesitantly.

"No, Sir. My name's Porter, Robert Porter. I'm here on Mr. Kohly's behalf."

"Fine," he replied as we shook hands. "I have been advised by our main office that a transfer was made to Mr. Kohly's numbered account from the Banco Nacionale de Mexico. I presume you have the proper identification, along with a signed authorization to withdraw, of course. May I see it, please?"

"Certainly." Reaching into my wallet, I pulled out a sheet of onionskin paper, which had been carefully folded between two sheets of plastic, and presented it to him.

After unfolding the paper, he opened the top drawer of his desk and removed a large manila envelope with what I assumed was the account number printed at the top. After carefully checking each number, he opened the folder to compare signatures. Then he said, "All seems to be in order. We'll have to count the currency in accordance with the instructions. I would like you to count it with us. We wish to avoid any problem at the other end."

"Thank you. I appreciate that."

"Excellent. Let's get on with it then. I have everything set up back in the vault."

As we walked out of his office, I saw him give a little nod to one of the girls seated near the entrance. She picked up a telephone as we walked toward the vault. In the next hour, we counted out 320 thousand U.S. dollars—in twenties, fifties, and hundreds—which I then carefully placed in the money belt Mario had given me. After signing the receipt, I said goodbye to Westwood and left the bank.

On my arrival I had spotted a taxi stand half a block away. Walking toward it now I could sense someone following me. Suddenly I felt very naked without my Walther, which would have been impossible to conceal under a loose sport shirt with no jacket. As I approached the cab stand, the first of the three taxis pulled out and the others moved forward.

I stopped to look into a shop window that displayed several parakeets and other tropical birds. The angled plate glass reflected a small, shabbily dressed man in a white cotton jacket and torn trousers watching me from across the street, less than fifty feet away. He held a newspaper in front of his face as if he were reading it. I was ready to dash for the cabs when I caught the menacing reflection of two other swarthy men who stepped out of a doorway between me and the taxi stand. I was about to panic when I noticed, in the narrow alley next to the shop, a rusty rack containing three bicycles and a BSA motorcycle with its ignition switch unlocked. The owner probably thought no one in his right mind would steal a motorcycle, or any other vehicle for that matter, on an island you could drive across in ten minutes. It was a straight shot to the airport, and I figured that with any luck at all I could be halfway there before my shadows could crank either of the rickety cabs into motion.

I turned and started to walk back toward the bank, causing my shadow across the street to turn away so that he was not directly facing me. Then I made a quick about-face, ran into the alley, and pulled the motorcycle off the stand. Two quick kicks and the engine came alive. I roared out of the alley, careening across the sidewalk, over the curb, and into the street, heading out the airport road.

Riding along, I wondered who was paying the three characters I had just shaken. Presumably no one except Kohly's immediate group and Cabell's staff knew of my intended trip. Yet somebody must have tipped off Castro's boys. That could only be someone with knowledge that a large transfer had been made to Kohly from the Banco Nacionale de Mexico. That had to be it: The three men must be on Castro's payroll, and for that matter, so must a bank officer.

As I approached the airport, I began to feel a little better, until, speeding past the fence parallel to the taxiway, I spotted four men in uniform waiting next to the Comanche. One of them appeared to be the customs and immigration man who had checked me in upon my arrival, and the other three were definitely colonial police. I wondered what in God's name was happening. Everything indicated we had been betrayed—probably by someone in the Mexican bank or the one on Bimini—and that Castro's people would try to get the money and keep me from leaving the island alive.

I knew there was one possible sanctuary nearby, one place where an Agency employee should be safe, and I headed for it at full speed. About a mile past the airport entrance, the road came to an end. I pulled the bike to a halt about twenty-five feet from the entrance of Congressman Powell's estate.

Getting off, I wheeled the bike through the gates and up a winding, white-graveled drive to the doorway of a sprawling, tropically modern house. Off to its right was an expansive green lawn flanking a terrace, where I could see flashing black and white bodies and hear the sound of laughter and splashing water.

I rang the bell, and in a moment the door was opened by a gorgeous bronze-skinned girl who wore a brief halter and a very short skirt.

"Good morning, Sir," she said. "Can I help you?"

"I hope so," I replied. "My name is Robert Porter. I've had some trouble and would like to use your telephone." At that moment, my only thought was to let Kendricks know what was happening.

"I assume you are an American," she said. I nodded. "Do you know whose residence this is?"

"I do indeed," I replied, "and if the congressman is here I wonder if I might speak with him. You might tell him I'm a friend of General Cabell."

After a short pause, staring at me all the while, she said, "If you will wait here for a moment I will ask whether he will see you."

When she returned, she said, "If you will follow me I will take you to the congressman. He is having lunch by the pool." Then, almost as an afterthought: "My name, incidentally, is Françoise Manet."

As sometimes is the case, I found myself torn between my appreciation of beauty and my regard for food. The mention of lunch stirred pangs of hunger. I had not eaten for more than twelve hours and hoped I might be invited to join the congressman. I had been admiring the handsome foyer of his palatial home, but now, as I followed Françoise to the terrace, I could hardly take my eyes off her. The congressman certainly had superb taste.

Although all the windows and doors were open the place was surprisingly cool, but as we reached the terrace I felt the heat of the sun again. Powell was seated at a yellow-canopied table that was covered with white Irish linen and set with sparkling silverware. Just across a broad expanse of beach was a brilliantly green and blue Carribbean. On the other side of the terrace was a kidney-shaped, Olympic-size pool where the congressman's guests frolicked.

Powell did not rise to greet me, but when I offered my hand he shook it briefly and pointed to the white wicker chair opposite him. Without looking at Françoise he said, "Leave us, and make sure that we are not disturbed."

"Yes, Sir," she said dutifully, and walked back toward the house. I watched her retreating figure as long as I thought I should and then looked back at my host. He had an amused smile.

"Françoise is a lovely child, twenty-six and thoroughly corruptible. You may be my guest as long as you are my guest." I felt chagrined that I had been so obvious. "But no one need be lonely here," he continued, waving toward the pool. "As you can see, we have a bountiful supply of companions for our Washington guests."

For the first time I focused my attention on the group in the pool and recognized, at the shallow end, two United States senators, one in his late forties and the other in his early sixties.

"Now, what brings you to Bimini, and what, if anything, can I do to help you? I presume there was a message in your reference to Chuck Cabell."

Suddenly, I became uncomfortably aware of the $320,000 in the money belt around my waist. Getting it back to Mario, and getting off Bimini, became the two most important things in the world. At the airport I had made a split-second decision that Powell might well be the only individual on the island willing and able to get me out alive. I decided to level with him.

In the next five minutes I gave him a full report on who I was, who I worked for, and what I had gone through on Bimini. He listened attentively, commended my frankness, and said, "Now, while you're having some lunch I'll see what I can do. When you have finished, Françoise will show you to some quarters where you can relax, or, if you wish, join the group at the pool."

He left the table and in a moment Françoise reappeared with a servant who brought a feast that matched the surroundings— avocados stuffed with crabmeat and lobster topped with a creamy garlic sauce; for dessert, cherries jubilee and Viennese coffee. When I had finished, Françoise, wearing a matching bikini swimsuit and short skirt, escorted me to a cool, spacious bedroom dominated by a huge canopy bed. She said, "You'll find robes and swimming attire laid out in the bath, Sir, unless you would prefer to take a nap. I'll try to have a fresh suit for you soon. If there is anything else you need, please call me. The phone is beside your bed and my intercom number is seven."

I took a hot bath, put the money belt under the pillow, and tumbled into bed. The last thing I remember thinking about before falling into a deep sleep was the hell Kendricks was going to give me for not being back in Miami this afternoon.

When I awoke, it was to the strains of soft music coming from the patio beneath my window and a cool hand lightly caressing my cheek. It was early evening.

Françoise, taking her hand from my cheek, said, "My, you're going to need a shave." Her hair, which earlier had been piled on top of her head, was now down around her shoulders, a thick, soft, and wavy chestnut. She wore a superb long white sheath dress, cut to reveal her figure.

"My God, you're beautiful."

"You're not so bad yourself, chérie. I've laid your things out." Then, hesitantly, "I've been told that you are going back to Miami tonight; the congressman has arranged everything. But before you leave you will be having cocktails and dinner with him. If you'd care to escort me, I've been invited to attend . . . with you."

I reached up and took her hand. "It will be my pleasure, mademoiselle."

"Thank you, Robert. I'll wait downstairs for you until you're ready. The guests are already having cocktails, but we probably won't eat dinner much before nine o'clock."

"I don't have my watch on. What time is it now?"

"Why, it's not quite 7:15. I'll be waiting."

With that she went out, closing the door quietly.

As I swung out of bed, I noticed that my money belt was missing. Frantic, I looked around in the subdued light and sighed with relief when I saw it lying beside a pile of fresh linen, next to an unfamiliar white linen suit and shirt on a hanger.

Françoise probably had removed the belt. I checked the contents; it seemed to be as thick with bills as when Westwood and I had filled it that morning.

I quickly showered, shaved, and dressed. The suit fit. That was no surprise because I was a perfect size forty-two, but even the cuffs were the right length. I took a quick look in the mirror and walked down a long corridor to where the cocktail party was in full swing. The congressman did things right; the music I had been hearing was not from a stereo but from a small orchestra playing on the terrace.

Françoise appeared at the doorway of the library, a glass in each hand. Smiling, she handed one to me, then put her lips to my ear and whispered, "It's nonalcoholic. You're going to fly the senators back to the mainland tonight, so I don't want anything happening to you." The warm, moist tip of her tongue darted into my ear.

I took the glass and kissed her lightly.

Arm in arm, we walked through the library to the softly lighted terrace. The empty pool glowed with a blue fluorescence.

"Let me fill you in," Françoise said. "You'll be meeting Major Hamilton, who is commissioner of the Colonial Police. He is in charge of immigration for Bimini as well as the rest of the Bahamas. You will be introduced as Senator _____'s administrative assistant. Commissioner Hamilton has already released your plane into the congressman's custody."

"Great," I said. "Can we see each other again?" I asked.

"I wish we could. But it would be unwise for you to return to Bimini."

"Do you ever get to the mainland?"

Her eyes brightened and she said, "Of course, how stupid of me. I'll be in Miami with the congressman for the next few days. He is meeting with some constituents who are attending a convention and wants me to go along to assist."

"Can you get away while you're there?"

"Probably. I usually do some shopping while I'm on the mainland. It may even be possible to get away overnight." The implication was overwhelming. I pulled her close and kissed her.

The moment was broken by a harsh voice. Powell was standing in the doorway to the veranda, speaking loudly to an officer in formal dress.

"It appears that Senator _____'s administrative assistant has found a friend on our little island."

Startled, Françoise jumped away from me and said, "I'm sorry, Sir." Then, with a quick glance at me, she hurried into the library.

When she had gone, Powell introduced me to Major Hamilton. "I've explained to the commissioner that an irate employee of Falcon Aeronautics abandoned one of their planes on the island and that you have offered to fly it back to the mainland," he said.

"Why, yes," I said, my mind racing, "if that's all right, I'm more than happy to." The commissioner was looking dubiously at the glass in my hand. "Only fruit juice, Major," I added.

He smiled and said, "Of course, I should have known. At any rate, the keys to the aircraft have been turned over to Congressman Powell and you may depart at any time."

"Right, Robert," Powell interjected, "but not before dinner, eh? There's a marvelous feast awaiting. In fact, the senators are probably gorging themselves at this very moment. So why don't you join them? When you're finished, you'll all be driven to the airport."

"Thanks, I think I will. Nice meeting you, Commissioner. If I don't see you before I leave, thank you again."

"You're quite welcome. Any friend of the congressman is a friend of mine."

I left them and walked through the library into the crowded dining room, where a large buffet was spread. I looked through the forty or fifty people, unable to find Françoise, and had just finished dinner when a servant told me that the senators were ready to leave for the mainland. I asked if he would tell Miss Manet that I had to leave.

"I believe that Miss Manet is waiting in the car with the two gentlemen, Sir. She will drive you to the airdrome. First, however, the congressman wishes to see you in his private study."

He escorted me to the room where Powell was waiting.

"Well, I guess this is it," I said. "Goodbye, and thanks again for everything. I'll return the suit."

"Forget it," Powell laughingly retorted as he shook my hand. "I was happy to help."

A Lincoln convertible, its top up, was at the entrance with its engine running, Françoise at the wheel, and the two senators in the rear seat. I got in beside her. As we started down the drive, she turned on the radio and set the controls so that music would come only from the rear speakers, preventing our passengers from hearing our conversation.

"If all goes well, I'll meet you in Miami tomorrow night. The senators will be staying at the Kenilworth and the congressman and I at the Fontainebleau. We can meet there."

"That's fine," I said. "I have a suite at the Casa Verde in Lauderdale, but with the traffic and construction it takes an hour to get from there to Miami Beach."

"In that case, I'd better call you sometime in the afternoon. If you're out, I'll tell the desk at the Casa Verde what time I'll be free and where you can meet me. Until then, you can believe I want you as much as you want me."

Getting back to Miami looked better all the time.

The airport came into view over a small rise, and no one was in sight as the Lincoln sped down the access road to where the private aircraft were hangared. When we reached the Comanche I opened the door, but Françoise put her hand on my arm and I waited until the two senators got out. "I'll see you tomorrow night, mon amour," she said.

I touched her fingers to my lips. By the time I had helped the senators strap themselves into the rear seat of the Comanche, the Lincoln had disappeared.

The panel clock indicated that just over thirteen hours had elapsed since I had touched down on Bimini.

Chapter Four

Kendricks was waiting at the customs ramp at Miami International Airport when I returned from Bimini. Murphy, the customs officer on the CIA payroll, rushed us through the formalities, then found a taxi for the senators and sent them off to their hotel.

After the Comanche was released from customs, I taxied it over to the L. B. Smith executive terminal and tied it down. Kendricks, meanwhile, drove the car around to meet me, and on our way to the Casa Verde I filled him in.

Kendricks listened intently. "Well, I never thought I'd say it, but thank God for Powell. We're meeting Manuel Rodriguez and Mario Kohly back at the Casa Verde. When they didn't hear from you, they got in touch with me. That's why I came down. I had orders from the general to go find you if you didn't show up by tomorrow."

"It's reassuring to know he cared," I said.

"Now, our plans have changed somewhat. Another of our men met the Cubana pilot on his way through Canada. You will meet him in Toronto on his trip home. He'll arrange to have

47

some engine trouble that will hold him over as long as necessary. If all goes well, we expect that to be sometime day after tomorrow. So, until then, you might as well enjoy the Florida sunshine, particularly if Françoise is coming in from Bimini."

I was shocked, indignant. "My God, is nothing sacred? Everybody in this outfit seems to know everybody else's business, no matter what."

"Don't ever forget it, Robert. That's the name of the game," Kendricks said, as the car headed up Biscayne Boulevard toward Fort Lauderdale.

An hour later Ed and I joined the two Cuban leaders at the Casa Verde. I turned over Mario's money belt and we carefully counted its contents. By the time we finished it was after midnight and time for a nightcap.

The next morning, Kendricks gave me the keys to the car he had been using, a Buick convertible equipped like the one I had driven in Washington. He left, assuring me that he would check back that evening.

Meanwhile, Rodriguez and Kohly had taken off in a rented car for Coral Gables, to visit Mario's son. I sat around the pool watching the flurry of beach bunnies until just after lunch, when a call came from Françoise. She told me that she was in Powell's suite at the Fontainebleau, and that it would be available until late the following afternoon. Powell had been invited on an overnight fishing excursion.

I wasted no time getting to the Fontainebleau and made it in just under an hour. After an afternoon of shopping and swimming in the surf, Françoise and I showered together and made love. Then we went dancing and had dinner in the hotel's lavish supper club. Shortly after midnight we returned to the suite and made love again. It was everything both of us had expected it to be, and by 3 A.M. we were exhausted and soon fast asleep.

It was three o'clock in the morning when the four bearded Cubans, in dark green fatigues, slipped over the side of the grimy cruiser into a battered dinghy and silently rowed toward the shore. There was no moon, and only a few lights shone from the Casa Verde. Within minutes they had pulled through the mild surf to the motel beach. They drew the boat into a clump of palms and, from waterproof bags, removed five Thompson submachine guns and a number of spare clips.

They were joined by a fifth man who had appeared from the undergrowth. The leader handed him the spare submachine gun, turned, and they all moved quietly toward the building, moving through a row of palms growing along the perimeter of the Casa Verde property.

The night desk man at the Brecken Security Service office was just returning to his desk with a cup of coffee when the telephone rang.

The caller was the night manager of the Sand Castle condominium complex, adjacent to the Casa Verde, reporting that he had just noticed a small boat heading toward the beach between the two motels. The security man promised to send a car around to investigate.

Just as the Cuban gunmen were slipping into the hall entrance of the Casa Verde, patrol car number two was pulling to a stop in the parking lot of the Sand Castle next door. The security officer switched off the lights, grabbed the flashlight from the seat beside him, and stepped out of the car.

He had walked about fifty feet toward the beach when, somewhere off to his left, he heard the staccato bark of several automatic weapons. He ran back to the car and reached under the front seat for his heavy Colt .45 service automatic. He would need something heavier than his light .38 police positive.

Grabbing the radio mike, he tried to call his headquarters, but got no response. Cursing, he tossed the mike onto the seat, cocked a round into the chamber of the .45, and ran toward the Casa Verde. Pausing in the shadows near the building, he could scarcely believe what was happening. The rooms were being systematically raked by the Thompsons, and orders were being shouted in Spanish.

Kendricks had snapped awake when he heard the first volleys being fired and realized at once that there were several men shouting in Spanish to each other and firing automatic weapons in the rooms adjacent to his. He concluded quickly that they must be after Kohly and Rodriguez, who fortunately weren't there. Sensing that there could be no adequate defense, he dashed into the bathroom. Quickly he climbed up on the sink and pushed up one of the ceiling drop panels. Fortunately it was next to a supporting joist, and he hoisted himself through the opening, replacing the panel beneath him. With luck, the assailants would conclude that his suite, like the others, was empty.

The Brecken Security man was about to make a run into the building when he spotted the man guarding the patio, holding a submachine gun. Steadying himself against a palm tree, he took careful aim with both hands and fired directly into the small of the Cuban's back. The man convulsed in an arch and crumpled, his spine broken by the huge .45 slug. The others failed to hear the shot over the racket they were making.

The security officer shoved the .45 into his belt and ran to the dead Cuban, scooping up his Thompson. Hugging the wall, he edged toward the door to the inner hallway and peered through its small glass panel. At that moment the firing stopped. In the center of the hall, less than fifteen feet from where he was standing, three men with submachine guns were conversing rapidly in Spanish.

Checking the Thompson, he made sure that it was cocked and that the safety was off. Taking a deep breath, he flipped the door inward with his foot, holding it against the automatic door closer, and opened fire at point blank range.

As they fell he continued to fire, emptying the full clip of fifteen rounds. Then he dropped the empty Thompson, pulled the .45 from his belt, and proceeded cautiously down the hall.

The fifth man and leader of the group had been checking Kendricks' room thoroughly, having noted the unmade bed and the personal effects on the dresser. Hearing the new burst of firing and the screams of his partners, he went to the patio door and slid it open. Cautiously he looked out, spotted his dead comrade, and ran toward the beach. He tossed his weapon into the dinghy and pushed it through the surf with the strength of desperation.

The security man, satisfied that there were no intruders left, put the .45 back in his belt. He could hear sirens racing toward the motel. As he was checking the last room, he nearly had a heart attack when Kendricks dropped through the ceiling and said, "I thought you'd never come."

Within moments, the Casa Verde was swarming with men from both the police and sheriff's office. For nearly an hour, Kendricks worked to make certain that there would be no publicity about the episode that would compromise the Agency. Then he began to worry about the man who had been in his room, the one who apparently had gotten away.

The distraught manager of the Casa Verde reluctantly gave him a suite in another section of the building, and he placed a call to the Fontainebleau. After ten rings, the hotel operator came back on the line saying, "I'm sorry, Sir, but the congressman's suite does not answer."

"Did you try all the bedrooms?"

"Yes, Sir," she replied.

"Thank you," he said and hung up. Looking at the clock radio, he saw that it was 4:10 A.M. He did not guess that I had shoved the telephone into a drawer in the nightstand so that neither Françoise nor I, in our deep slumber, heard it ring. He decided to get hold of Kohly and Rodriguez and have them check out the Fontainebleau, just on the off chance. . . .*

It was 5:30 A.M. when the Dodge van backed up to the Fontainebleau's loading dock. In the rear of the truck, the two regular drivers, gagged and bound, were lying side by side under a pile of dirty linen on the floor. Replacing them this morning were Capitan Juan Rojas and Lt. Felipe Callas, two of Fidel Castro's most notorious butchers.

---

*The Cuban who escaped from the Casa Verde was later apprehended by Kohly's people. The account was reconstructed from his description of the incident, given to Kohly, and the account given me by Kendricks. —*Author's note.*

Getting out of the truck, they went around to the rear, opened the doors, and rolled out two large laundry hampers. The dock attendant responded to the bell by sliding open the large overhead door. Waving them through, as he did every morning, he observed that these two were not the men who usually drove the truck. But, then, with the influx of Cuban refugees, the turnover rate in Miami had been high.

Rojas and Callas rolled their heavy hampers to the freight elevator at the end of the long corridor. When the door slid open, they rolled the hampers in, pressed the button for the ninth floor where Powell's suite was situated, and began the slow ascent.

It wasn't until 5:30 that Kendricks reached Kohly at his son's house in Coral Gables. After he had recounted the events at the Casa Verde and expressed his concern about me, Kohly agreed that he and Rodriguez should go at once to the Fontainebleau. It was possible that I had been followed and that Castro's agents were aware of my presence there with Françoise. After my trip to Bimini, they could also have tied me to Powell.

"You should be able to get over there in less than half an hour. Let me know what you find. I'll hold down this end and get instructions from Washington as soon as they open up shop."

The doors of the freight elevator clanked open and the two Cubans pushed their hampers into the ninth floor service lobby. As the doors closed behind them, Rojas silently cracked open the door leading to the main hotel corridor. Observing that all was quiet, he motioned to his partner. Callas reached into one of the laundry carts, extracted two submachine guns, and handed one to Rojas. A minute later Rojas picked the lock on the door to Powell's suite. He stepped quickly inside and Callas followed, closing the door.

After glancing quickly around the living room, Callas began checking the rooms on the right side of the suite and Rojas the ones on the left. In a few moments Rojas found Callas and motioned to him to follow. They entered the bedroom where Françoise and I lay sleeping.

Rojas waited until Callas got into position next to the bed, then he reached carefully under the pillow and removed my Walther. He flipped a switch and, as the overhead lights flooded the room, he snarled, "Wake up, you filthy Yankee pigs. I wish to have a little talk with you."

I had sensed the Cuban's presence before he spoke and awoke with a start, instinctively reaching under the pillow for my gun. Then I saw the Walther in Callas's hand, pointed directly at me.

Françoise moaned, covered her eyes, and turned over on her stomach. Callas's eyes narrowed as he looked at her naked body.

"What the hell is going on here?"

"We will ask the questions," Rojas replied. "Get up."

Françoise, stirring, turned over again and I put my hand over her mouth to stifle her scream.

"Watch her," Rojas ordered his partner. "Porter, I'll talk with you in the other room. My friend here will entertain the girl."

"You can go to hell! If that son of a bitch lays a finger on her, I'll kill him. And you along with him!"

Callas turned to his superior and laughed, "He talks big for a Yankee swine. Particularly a naked, unarmed one."

Rojas picked up the negligee Françoise had left on a chair and tossed it to her.

"There, niña. Put this on. Callas will not harm you if your amante tells us what we want to know."

"Robert, Robert, don't let them . . ."

Rojas cut her short. "Shut up, or I'll turn you over to my friend. And you, Porter, get in the other room." He turned to Callas. "Do not touch her. We have work to do. Comprende?"

"Sí, Capitan."

"When she is dressed, tie her to the bed and come out. I may need your help."

With his gun at my back, Rojas forced me toward an open-back chair in the spacious parlor. "I have no intention of killing you or the girl," he said, "unless I absolutely have to."

"What do I know that could interest you?" I asked, trying to sound convincing.

"Nothing, amigo. Nothing at all. But perhaps you could explain what you planned to do with the three hundred thousand dollars you picked up for your friend Kohly, who is a convicted traitor. Perhaps you could reveal the whereabouts of the criminal and his lieutenant, Manuel Rodriguez. And, most important, you might tell me what your Central Intelligence Agency was doing in the Camaguey on the night the traitors attempted to invade our homeland at the Bay of Pigs." He looked at me with hatred and contempt. "As you Yankees would say, how is that for openers?"

I wondered how they had already learned so much, but I had to play out the string, although I knew it was futile. They obviously intended to kill us both when they had the information they sought. "What makes you think that I know anything about these things?"

"Don't be foolish, Porter," Rojas said with confidence. "You're working with Kohly and we know it. You're his link to the CIA. We know about your flight to the Camaguey, and the money you picked up in Bimini. We know these things, but tonight I am going to find out what you know that we don't know."

He slapped me so hard that it knocked me semiconscious. When I recovered I could feel my bare legs being tied together just below the knees, and my arms being bound behind me to the chair. In a half daze, with one of my front teeth loose and my mouth bleeding profusely, I heard Rojas shout, "Hurry up in there, Callas. I need you to help persuade this Americano pig that we are serious."

Rojas propped a coffee table under my legs as Callas entered the room. Then he shoved the heel of his palm under my nose so I couldn't breathe, forcing my mouth open, and Callas, standing behind me, pulled a twisted towel tightly between my teeth, almost gagging me.

With my head held tightly by Callas and unable to make a sound, I watched with hypnotic fascination, as though I were seeing the episode on a stage, as Rojas took a cigar lighter from his pocket and admired the flame. I knew what he meant to do with it. I bit fiercely on the towel and closed my eyes. Almost immediately I felt an excruciating pain in the toes of my left leg. When the stink of burning flesh hit my nostrils, the pain became five times as bad. I tried to scream, but with the towel pressed against my tongue, gagging me, I passed out.

Callas revived me with a bucket of half-melted ice water and I once more experienced the incredible agony, this time all the way up my left shin. Through a haze of pain, I heard Rojas ask, "Tell me, now, what I want to know; and we will leave you and your whore."

Callas released the pressure on the towel in my mouth. The pain in my leg was so agonizing that I was tempted to talk, but I knew that I would live only until they knew what they wanted to know. So I told them to do something anatomically impossible. At that point, Callas pulled the towel tight again and Rojas flicked on the lighter and started on my right leg. Fortunately, before the pain became unbearable, I passed out again.

When I regained consciousness the room was full of people, among them Kohly and Rodriguez.

My tormentor, Rojas, was lying in the doorway of the bedroom where I had last seen Françoise. His belly had been sliced open and his intestines were hanging out; he had died trying to stuff them back in. I vaguely remembered what had been done to me, but felt no pain and realized that a doctor was working on my legs. The needle in his hand had administered novocaine to the charred flesh.

"You'll be in a hospital shortly, my friend," Kohly said. "The doctor has given you a shot so you will soon be asleep."

"Françoise. Is she all right? What's happened?"

"Don't worry about it now. I've taken care of everything. I will explain later."

I wanted an answer, but the darkness came and I floated quietly away.

A day later I awoke to find Kendricks at my side in a strange and sterile room. The pain in my legs took me back to the Fontainebleau, and I asked, "Where am I and how did I get here?"

"You're in a private clinic in Coral Gables, guarded by a couple dozen loyal Cubans."

I thought about that for a moment and then asked, "Françoise?"

Ed hesitated. Then he looked at me intently. There was compassion in his voice. "You'll have to know sometime . . . she's dead."

My stomach whipped into knots. "They killed her. . . . Oh, my God, I killed her. If she hadn't been with me, she'd be alive."

Kendricks said, "Don't be a damn fool. They nailed you by following her."

"But if we hadn't been together, they'd have had no reason to kill her. How did she die?"

Kendricks sighed resignedly. "I'll fill you in, but first there are things I must know because other lives are at stake. What did you tell them? Or, rather, what did they torture out of you? Manuel got Rojas, but his partner got away with whatever he learned."

"That was nothing, Ed. I didn't tell him anything he didn't already know. He asked me about the three hundred thousand and I told him I didn't know what he was talking about. Then he asked me about that night in the Camaguey and I played dumb on that, too. Then, with his torch working on my legs, I guess I passed out."

Kendricks pursed his lips. "I guess that's when they started working on the girl."

"But, Ed, she couldn't tell them anything. She didn't know anything."

"No, but they didn't know that. They worked her over pretty thoroughly."

I pressed him for details, but he ignored me. "I've told the nurse to put you back to sleep because I'm going to need you for some flying in a few days, even with those legs." When he left the room, a nurse entered almost immediately and gave me a shot. In moments I was out again.

I finally forced it out of Manuel. With a towel knotted in

Françoise's mouth to keep her from screaming, Rojas had begun by burning the nipples off her breasts with the cute little toy he had used on me. When she couldn't tell him anything, he raped her with a ten-inch knife, allowing her to die an excruciating death. But he had paid the supreme price. Manuel had shot him in the knee and then, after seeing what he had done to Françoise, he had sliced open Rojas' belly with the knife he removed from the dead girl. Writhing in agony from his smashed kneecap, Rojas had died watching his own disembowelment.

Callas had fled into the hall and apparently escaped in the laundry truck. Days later the truck was found, abandoned, in central Miami. The two bound drivers each had a bullet in the back of the head.

Chapter Five

I spent two days in the Coral Gables clinic, but when I left my burned feet and legs were still giving me hell. Kendricks, who had returned to Washington with Mario's money belt, had telephoned twice, apologetically pressing me to return to the capital as soon as possible.

I assumed that he was concerned about Mario's Canadian appointment with the Cubana pilot, who was probably finding it difficult to maintain the fiction that something was wrong with his aircraft. I finally checked out of the clinic and, armed with a bottle of codeine tablets, picked up the Comanche at the Miami airport.

The weather was fine and I flew VFR to Savannah, where I landed to refuel. Despite the clear skies, I couldn't be sure about the weather in Baltimore, and I like to have a little margin for error. When I touched down the tower turned me over to ground control and I was directed to Butler Aviation for refueling. I was also told to call the control tower for a message.

While the ground crew refueled the Comanche at the Butler ramp, I dialed the tower, wondering how Washington had tracked me down. To my surprise, the tower gave me a Miami call-back number. I found a pay phone, gave the operator my credit card number, and placed the call. After two rings, I was talking to Manuel Rodriguez.

"Roberto!" he exclaimed. "Madre de Dios, I found you! I left a message at three airports hoping you would stop at one of them. Are you all right?"

"Sure," I replied, "but calm down a bit. What's got you so upset?"

"I have some information that Castro's men are still after you, and a report from Mario that something may have been done to your plane. You had better double check it before you take off again."

"Well, thanks for your concern," I replied, "but everything seemed O.K. on the way up here. I'll take a good look anyway, just to be sure."

I hung up and went back to the Comanche, which the ground crew had already refueled. They were going to wonder why I was fooling around with the aircraft when I had told them I was in such a hurry to get out of there, but that couldn't be helped.

It took me fifteen minutes to find the explosive, adroitly rigged with a thermal fuse and barometric pressure switch. The insulated caulking around the engine cowl had been carefully removed and replaced with plastic explosive. The two substances are almost identical in color and texture, and I would never have found the explosive except for the thermal fuse buried in one end.

It was an ingenious rig. The pressure switch would activate when the plane had reached a specific altitude, directing electrical current into the thermal fuse. But one thing made it clear that the mechanic who did it was a real pro: He had connected the devices to the glide slope circuit. That, combined with the pressure switch, provided absolute insurance that the plane would be destroyed in the air and not on the ground. Even a preflight check wouldn't set off the charge because the pressure switch wouldn't function except at higher altitudes.

If conditions were minimal or I was making a night landing,

I would normally turn on the glide slope on final approach, placing me several miles from the end of the runway when the explosive blew. The FAA would, in all probability, assume that something in the fuel system had malfunctioned, and write it off as a routine accident. Flying VFR, I had had no need for the glide slope going into Savannah, but chances are I would have used it after dark at Friendship.

Making sure the master switch was turned off, I gingerly removed the wires from the thermal fuse and gently worked it out with my fingers. Plastic explosive of this type is generally as harmless as clay, unless it is ignited electrically by this special type of fuse. Once the electrical circuitry was disconnected I began the tedious process of removing the explosive with a screwdriver and my fingernails.

This took me about forty-five minutes and, as expected, the attendants were obviously wondering what I was up to. But I couldn't worry about that. I bought some plastic caulking and refilled the channel from which I had removed the explosive. I put the explosive in an empty coffee container and then took the thermal fuse, pressure sensor, and connecting wires and put them in a separate bag. I went into the men's room, molded the explosive into pellets, and flushed these down the john. Then, gently pulling the wires out of the thermal fuse, I sent it down with another flush. A trash can took care of the rest.

The ground crew was becoming increasingly curious and I was glad to climb back into the Comanche and leave them with the mystery. The good weather held and I again flew VFR, staying close to the coast until I reached Chesapeake Bay, and followed the bay all the way to Friendship Airport in Baltimore. Approach control cleared for me a landing on runway 15. I taxied to Hinson Aviation at the South terminal, where I left instructions for refueling and called a cab. We made the trip through the new Baltimore Harbor Tunnel to my apartment in just under half an hour.

I was surprised to see my XK-150 in front of the building, with Ed Kendricks in the driver's seat. As I paid the cab driver he grabbed my suitcase and preceded me into the building, where he let me into the apartment with my own key.

"I thought you'd appreciate getting your keys and car back," he said.

With mock indignation I protested, "Christ, can't I ever get rid of you? I expected to have some peace and quiet tonight." Then, expressing what I really felt, I added, "Actually, Ed, I'm glad you're here. I'd forgotten that my car was in D.C. It would have been inconvenient as hell to get home and not find it here, to say nothing of having to pick the lock on my own apartment door."

"Don't be too grateful," he replied. "I had to see you anyway. We've had a change in plans, and you won't be going on the Canadian trip. How are your legs?"

"Hurting like hell. I couldn't take any pain killer because I had to fly. I was afraid I might fall asleep and end up in the Atlantic."

"Do you think you'll be all right tomorrow?"

"I hope so. Why?"

"We sent someone else to Canada with Mario," Kendricks said. "With Bobby Kennedy off his tail we could now get him in and out of the country. Anyway, the Cubana pilot was beginning to get nervous. We've got a longer trip for you. You're going to Europe tomorrow. I want you to fly the Comanche into La Guardia, leave it there, and take a cab to Idlewild. You're ticketed on TWA flight 900 into Madrid at 7:30 P.M."

"Great! Madrid sounds better than Peterboro."

"When you get to Spain, check into the Ritz Hotel, where reservations have been made for you." He took a large envelope from his pocket. "Here's your new passport, credit cards, and driver's license, which should be all you'll need, except for this." He unbuttoned his shirt, removed Mario's money belt, and handed it to me. "The 320 thousand dollars is still intact," he said. "And speaking of money, from now on your paychecks will be held for you by the branch manager of the Suburban Trust Company in Bethesda, Maryland.

"One of our people will contact you to show you around Madrid after you've caught a little sleep. Then phone the commercial attaché at the embassy, which is about fifteen blocks from your hotel up on the Serrano. Identify yourself and make an appointment to see him immediately. When you're alone with him, use the phrase 'It seems extremely dry this year in Madrid.' If he's our man, he'll answer with, 'It's true. The rain does stay mainly in the plains.' "

"Isn't that a bit corny?"

"Perhaps, but any other code reply could be natural. With this one there'll be no mistake. After what you've gone through in the past week you know what we're up against. I still find it hard to believe that Castro's boys could coordinate and pull off the operations they have."

"My God! I haven't told you what happened to me on the way back. Have you heard from Rodriguez today?"

"I haven't had any reports from Miami. I've been waiting here for you most of the afternoon."

When I had filled him in, Kendricks began pacing up and down the living room. "The Casa Verde—that I believe," he mused. "The Fontainebleau, I believe. What I can't believe is that your bomb was planted by Castro's boys." He pounded his fist into his hand.

"There may be another explanation. Did you use the ILS for your approach in either Bimini or Miami?"

"No. But I didn't have to."

"Then it could have been installed earlier."

"Yes, because it wouldn't explode unless the pressure switch malfunctioned. . . ."

"Unless the switch had malfunctioned? When was the last time you used an instrument approach?"

"Now that you mention it, Ed, I haven't at all—not since I've been flying the Comanche."

"Then it could have been done anytime."

"I suppose so."

"That must be it. I'll bet the explosive was installed to be in reserve for future use. It probably could be activated with one simple adjustment whenever the need arose." Then, almost to himself, Kendricks muttered, "Shaw and his group are damn fools. They're always playing with fire."

"Shaw? Who's he?"

"Clay Shaw. He's a contract consultant with the Agency and

is associated with a number of companies the section uses as cover. Shaw heads the trade center in New Orleans, which is a perfect cover for the work his organization does for the Company in South America."

"But why would they booby-trap the Comanche?"

"I'm not sure they did, and until I've done some checking I'm not prepared to talk about it. Now about the trip. Through an associate of Shaw's named Jack,* Mario has arranged for you to buy some Schmeisser and Thompson machine guns in Athens. Many of our purchases for the Bay of Pigs operation were arranged through him. The weapons are being brokered through a Canadian firm, but the source is in Greece, and that's where you will have to go to make the buy."

"Why Greece?" I asked.

"Reasonable question. Because the arms they have are new—packed in their original crates, complete with spare parts," Kendricks replied. "The Germans left the Schmeissers behind when they evacuated Piraeus in 1944. The Thompsons were split off from our MAAG program by some Greek general who wanted a few thousand American dollars for his Swiss account."

"Some deal. We have to buy back our own stuff?"

"Don't knock it, Robert. It's cheaper than buying new equipment in the States."

"I suppose it is, but it still galls me," I replied.

"Dave Ferrie helped to arrange the arms buy with Jack and now works for Clay Shaw. He'll meet you in Athens. After you've made the buy and checked the merchandise, Ferrie will deliver the cash in Switzerland and complete the transfer of the weapons to Mario, first through Liverpool and then . . . shall we say Guatemala? Now I'm going to get my tail out of here and let you get some sleep. I guess I don't have to remind you that you better be watching your ass every second." With a "Ciao," he walked out the door.

I washed up and walked across the street to the shopping center. In the Woodshed Bar I ordered a hamburger platter,

*"Jack" was ultimately revealed to be Jack Ruby, the Dallas nightclub operator who killed Lee Harvey Oswald.

putting away a couple of extra-dry Gordon's martinis before it arrived. Within an hour I was back in the apartment packing my bags for the trip to Madrid.

The next morning the pain in my legs had diminished to a dull throb, and I took several aspirin instead of my codeine pills. After a leisurely breakfast I headed for the airport, although I still had plenty of time. My flight for Madrid didn't leave until 7:30 P.M. and, once I'd tied the Comanche down at La Guardia, it would take me less than thirty-five minutes to make the change of airports in the light afternoon traffic.

I left Friendship at one o'clock; it took me about an hour to fly into La Guardia. By three o'clock I had taxied the bird to the Old Marine Terminal, removed my luggage, checked in, and given instructions for refueling. I did a quick scan of the area for possible pursuers and then took a cab to the TWA terminal at Idlewild.

The plane wouldn't leave for several hours, but I wanted to check through customs and immigration early. I needed plenty of time to study the crowds for potential enemies. After an hour and forty-five minutes in a corner of the temporary international bar, I was satisfied that no one had the slightest interest in me. With martinis as a soporific, I fell asleep on the spacious jet almost as soon as I was settled in my seat.

As my plane took off from Idlewild, Mario Kohly was returning to Washington's National Airport after his final meeting with the arms broker in Canada. He was met at the airport by his Washington attorney, Marshall Diggs, and Senator Owen Brewster. They both seemed elated as they told Kohly that a meeting had been arranged with the president's military advisor, General Maxwell Taylor. In the cab, the senator related the chain of events leading up to the meeting.

"It appears," he said, turning to Mario, "that the brothers are stymied in trying to free the Bay of Pigs prisoners. The president has finally realized that you have absolute control of the underground and now wonders if you could also unite the Cuban splinter groups here in the United States."

Kohly nodded and looked out the window at the Jefferson

Memorial as they crossed the Fourteenth Street bridge into the city.

"I will meet with the general, of course," he said. "However, I will make no promises. When I could get no help for the prisoners from the United States, I made contact with ex-president Goulart of Brazil, who is a close friend of Castro's, but not so close that he won't cooperate with me if there is enough money involved. You see, Senator, I have my own plan. If I can raise twenty-five million dollars, I will give it to Goulart. He will give Castro fifteen million dollars, keeping ten million for himself, if Castro will agree to move all the prisoners to a remote Cuban port. Goulart will then send a Brazilian ship to deliver coffee, and the few guards assigned to the prisoners will allow them to escape to the Brazilian ship. Once the men are safely in an American port, preferably Miami, Goulart will break off with Castro and recognize my de facto government in exile. You understand, of course, that only when all this is accomplished will the twenty-five million be released to Goulart and Castro. This plan will allow the 2506 Brigade to return to the United States as heroes who have escaped from Castro's prisons. And, incidentally, it will align Brazil with the United States."

"It sounds like a wild scheme, Mario, but you know the players better than I do. Taylor just might buy it. Particularly if you can unite the Cubans here in the United States and provide the cooperation of your underground as well."

"We shall see," said Mario. "By the way, have you heard any more reaction to the hard sites being built in Cuba?"

"Nothing," the senator replied, "and I wouldn't dare bring it up."

"It should be an interesting meeting tomorrow," mused Mario.

The cab turned left into H Street, and as they looked across Lafayette Park the lights of the White House were burning brightly.

Chapter Six

The Ritz in Madrid is one of the most beautiful and exclusive hotels in the world. When the head porter parted the heavy brocade draperies in my room, I looked out the full-length French windows and found that I had a balcony overlooking a garden courtyard with a magnificent marble fountain.

My watch said that it was already after two, which meant that all of the shops in town would be closed until five. Our embassy also closed between one and five, so I had plenty of time before I could call for my appointment with the commercial attaché. I decided to honor Kendricks's suggestion and take a nap.

The phone woke me at 4:30 and a husky female voice asked if I were Robert Porter. Her voice startled me for a moment; it hadn't occurred to me that my contact might be a woman. When I said yes, she continued: "You don't know me, but my name is Susan Kreisberg. I'm an American student studying under a Fulbright scholarship at the University of Madrid. I was contacted by a mutual friend who told me you might need an interpreter. He also asked me to tell you that Madrid is very dry at this time of the year."

Relieved, but feeling a little silly, I replied, "Yes, I understand the rain stays mainly in the plains."

She giggled. "He told me you thought that was one of the corniest lines you'd ever heard. Welcome to Madrid."

"Thanks." Then, intrigued, I said, "Let me ask you something. If you're a student, how old are you?"

She said, "Old enough to take care of myself. Why don't we meet in the lounge for cocktails? It's just off the lobby. I have red hair and I'm five ten and a half with my shoes on. You won't be able to miss me."

"Give me half an hour to shower and shave." Then I remembered.

"Hold on. I have to call the embassy when it reopens."

"Don't bother," she said. "The commercial attaché won't be there until first thing in the morning. Tonight I've been instructed to show you Madrid and make sure you stay out of trouble. I understand you've had your share lately."

Thirty minutes later I stepped out of the elevator and spotted a tousled head of strawberry blond hair. As I crossed the room, my contact rose and turned with a smile, extended a white gloved hand, and greeted me with, "Mr. Porter, I presume."

By the time we had finished our second martini, I had learned that she was studying music and languages on her scholarship and was intent on earning a master's degree. She was only twenty-two and, in her senior year at Wellesley, had allowed herself, mostly as a lark, to be recruited by the CIA as a student observer in Europe. She was, I was dismayed to learn, an avid admirer of Jack Kennedy. Her father was a well-known psychiatrist in the Washington area.

At Susan's suggestion, we dined at the Casa Botin. Afterward, while we were sipping our coffees, she looked at me thoughtfully, then asked abruptly: "Why don't we go home? We'd better stop at my apartment. It's over near the university. I'll need some things."

"Fine," I said, only mildly startled by her directness, and asked for the check.

Susan excused herself. "I'm going to powder my nose. I'll meet you downstairs in the bar."

Most of the drinkers downstairs appeared to be Americans. When I ordered a brandy grasshopper, the bartender grinned and said, "American officer club style?"

Surprised, I replied, "Sí. But with four shots of cognac."

He replied in perfect English, "But, of course. I was chief bartender for the American officers' mess for the past four years."

I said, "In that case, make it two; I'm expecting a friend."

"Ah, yes," he said, "the beautiful redhead you were dining with."

I gave him a searching look. "As a matter of fact, yes. You don't seem to miss much. Do you know her?"

"Sí, señor. She comes here quite often. Usually with young officers from the American air base outside Madrid."

"Oh," I replied.

"You are not one yourself, señor?"

"No, just an ordinary tourist." I was beginning to feel a little uneasy—and a bit jealous—when I spotted Susan coming down the stairs.

She sat down beside me, looked up dreamily, and asked, "Miss me?"

Before I could reply, she giggled and spoke to the bartender. "Bueno, Alfredo. I see you're fixing Señor Porter a drink."

"Sí, señorita, and one for you. We were just discussing the points of interest in Madrid."

"I'm sure you were. And, perhaps, all the men I've been here with?"

"Señorita," he waved his hands, starting to protest.

But she smiled sweetly and continued: "Don't worry, Alfredo. The gentleman is my fiancé."

"Señorita, I didn't know. Congratulations. And to you, Sir. Please call me Alfredo. And the drinks are on me."

"Thank you, Alfredo."

As he moved down the bar, Susan said, "Alfredo bears watching. He's the only bartender in Madrid who can afford to drive a Pegaso. It's the only handmade, completely custom Spanish sports car and one of the most expensive in the world. They start here in Spain at twenty thousand dollars plus."

"What you are telling me is, he doesn't make his money tending bar."

"Unfortunately, a lot of talk goes on here that shouldn't, particularly among Americans. Alfredo soaks it up and stores it until someone pays him to squeeze it back out."

"I'll watch myself," I said, and pulled our bar stools together so that our legs touched. Susan slipped her hand into mine and said, "We had better drink up. You should be at the embassy no later than 10:30 tomorrow morning, and we still have to swing by my place."

She drove me to the air base the next afternoon. The commercial attaché had arranged for me to leave for Athens on a MATS flight at 3:30. When I arrived at the U.S. air base in Athens at 7:30, I found an unobtrusive black 1961 Chevrolet with Greek license plates waiting for me. It was driven by a young American sporting an ill-fitting suit and crew cut. He said his name was "Mike" and that he was to drive me to a rendez-vous with Dave Ferrie in Piraeus, about twelve miles east.

In front of a waterfront rooftop cafe called the Vassilena, Mike opened the car door for me and said, "My instructions are to be at your disposal, Sir. So, if you don't mind, I'll park the car on a side street and make it a point to be seated a few tables from you. Now, if you will please go straight through to the stairs behind the shop, you will find there is a lovely rooftop view of the harbor."

I picked a secluded table and ordered gin on the rocks. The place was crowded, mostly with Greek patrons. Mike came in and took a table near the door. He sipped a bottle of "Fix" beer and appeared calm, although it was well beyond the scheduled meeting time. As I signaled the waiter for another drink, a tall, good-looking man, wearing sun glasses and a straw hat, appeared in the doorway. He was about my height with light brown hair, and as he removed his hat and glasses and scanned the terrace I saw the bald spot at the back of his head. It was Dave, all right.

He spotted Mike, crossed the room, and sat down next to

him. After a few words together, they both got up and walked toward my table.

Mike said, "Sir, this is Dave Ferrie." Dave gave no sign of recognition, so I didn't either.

"I hope you'll excuse me for being late," Ferrie said. Before I could reply, he added, "You don't mind if I call you Bob, do you?"

I said, "Of course not. The way Mike's been ignoring me I was beginning to need a friend."

He chuckled and turned to the driver. "Would you mind bringing the car around while I pay the tab?"

"Right," Mike said, and disappeared down the stairs.

When he had gone Ferrie said, "Excuse the formality, but our young friend wasn't told that we know each other. Good to see you again. I'll be flying you back to Madrid as soon as we've finished our business here."

"You mean tonight? Jeez, I hope it isn't another flight like our last one!"

Ferrie acted as if he hadn't heard. "The warehouse is only a few blocks away, down on the docks." He lowered his voice. "You have the money, of course?"

I nodded. "Of course, but I'll have to see the merchandise first."

"Certainly." Then he leaned closer and added, "Incidentally, you'll only need two hundred and forty big ones. Jack struck a better deal than we had expected, so the rest of the money can be used for other gear."

Within two blocks we had left the brightness of the city and were driving between the darkened warehouses that lined the Piraeus waterfront. Mike pulled the car to a stop in front of one with a newly painted sign that read "Permidex S.A." Below it was a much older sign with an arrow indicating that the other side of the building housed "Centro Mondiale Commerciale S.A."

We got out and Mike unlocked the warehouse door, locking it again behind us. Then he switched on a battery of lights. The place was filled with tier upon tier of crates reaching to the ceiling and marked "machine parts" and "machine tools." Most of them were new and stenciled in English with the names of firms from all over the world. Many were U.S. companies, such as Cincinnati Machine Tool, South Bend, and Caterpillar.

Mike took a clipboard from a hook beneath the light switches, examined some papers, and asked us to follow him. He led us to a stack of long boxes resting on pallets. Mounting an electric fork lift, he lowered the top box to the floor. It bore the name 'Philips Globenfabriken,' which I recognized as a large Dutch multinational firm.

With a crowbar, Mike pried off the top of the box. Inside were other boxes about four feet in length, eight inches deep, and twelve inches high. He pulled one out and opened it. Inside, embedded in Cosmoline, was a German Schmeisser submachine gun in pristine condition along with a complete set of spare parts, including an extra barrel and cleaning equipment.

"There are two thousand of them here," Dave remarked. "We're also to get two hundred and fifty Thompsons."

Mike again boarded the fork lift and proceeded down the line to another stack of crates marked Westinghouse Electric. The crate he opened contained boxes of brand new Thompson submachine guns, also with spare parts.

"O.K., Mike," Dave said. "Put everything back together." Then, turning to me, he added, "They'll be transshipped to Liverpool, then on to Guatemala. Now if you'll just initial these papers and give me the cash, we'll have the stuff on shipboard within three days."

It took us about forty-five minutes to count out the two hundred and forty thousand dollars. I distributed the eighty thousand around the belt and put it back on. Quite a bit of change, I thought.

It was 7:30 in Washington, D.C. Manuel Rodriguez had just arrived from Miami. In the dining room of the Blackstone Hotel on Seventeenth Street, Mario Kohly was bringing him up-to-date on his all-day session with several members of the administration, including the president's military advisor.

"Well, compadre," he said, "it appears that our troubles may be over. I have been assured that the president has agreed to support my de facto government in exile if we can unite a majority of the Cuban exile groups here in the United States as we did the underground forces at home."

"I don't believe it," Rodriguez replied. "As an American would say, I can't believe we've gone from chicken shit to chicken salad."

"It's hard for me to believe, too, chico, but I have the assurance of General Taylor himself. I proposed a new counterfeiting operation as well, so we can use all the cash we raise here and abroad to equip another strike force and supply our men in the Escambrey."

"I'm sorry, padre, I still don't trust them. And what about the missiles . . . did they say anything about the missiles?"

"I tried to bring it up once or twice, but they refused to discuss the matter."

"I don't like that at all."

"Well, to use another American expression, amigo, it's the only game in town. Now listen carefully: I want you to go back to Miami. These official documents, which I have signed, are your authorization to set up delegates to a united congress. You know who the leaders are. We will join them all under the banner of the United Organizations for the Liberation of Cuba."

"O.K., padre. But what do I say when they ask me about the prisoners from 2506 Brigade?"

"Tell them I've made a proposal to the administration to get the boys out. Now, while you're in Miami, I'll go to New York to try to unite the factions there. We have only thirty days to accomplish this task."

"Madre de Dios! How?"

"With the help of our sacred mother," Mario said, and signaled the waiter for his check.

Dave Ferrie, flying a T-33 jet trainer put at our disposal by the air force, dropped me off at the Madrid airport at 12:40 A.M. I caught up with Susan at the Casa Botin, and by the time we got back to the Ritz most of the night was gone. I was still dead-tired when the phone jolted me awake at 8:30. It was on a nightstand on Susan's side of the bed, and I charged around the bed and caught it on the fifth ring. The hotel operator informed me that it was a Zurich call for Mr. Porter.

Dave Ferrie's sleepy voice came at me through the antiquated instrument. "Hi, stranger; I guess you know where I am."

"And I guess you know what time it is."

"I'm at the Permidex office," he continued, "and they just received a telex for you. The Company wants you to return to the States via Paris immediately. We've already made a booking for you."

"Is there anything else I have to do about the merchandise?" I asked.

"No. I'll handle it from this end. Tonight you'll be laying over in Paris at the Plaza Athénée, on Avenue Montaigne, where you'll be contacted and given further instructions, same code word and reply as Madrid."

I glanced at Susan. Her eyes were wide open and she was watching me intently. "O.K. Let me get this straight. I'm to head Stateside via Paris. Now, how do I get there?"

"Take Air France flight 510 out of Madrid at noon. It gets into Paris about one o'clock Paris time. As I said, your reservations have been made. Good luck. I'll see you at home one of these days." The phone went dead.

We spent the morning making love, packing our things, checking out of the Ritz, and depositing Susan's gear at her apartment. By then we were running out of time and I got on a public phone to Air France to confirm my reservation. They said that flight 510 was running about two hours late, so Susan and I decided to have an early lunch at Horcher's on the Serrano.

We were both half-smashed when Susan deposited me at the immigration and customs hut at Madrid airport. She cried when I kissed her goodbye, and I didn't dare turn around as I trotted up the stair ramp to board the Air France Caravelle.

I was in my room at the Plaza Athénée and unpacked by three o'clock. I took a quick shower and stretched out for a nap, leaving word with the desk to wake me at six o'clock. It seemed that I had scarcely closed my eyes when the phone rang. I rose, shaved, and changed into fresh, lightweight clothes. It was now 7 P.M. and since I didn't really expect my contact to reach me until early the following morning I decided to go down to the English bar, have a few cocktails, and then take a stroll. Later I could have dinner at one of the sidewalk cafes along the Champs Elysées that I had so long wanted to visit.

I told the concierge where I would be and then went to the barroom, which was done in fake English Tudor. As my eyes adjusted to the dim light, I saw that only one person, other than the bartender and me, was in the room. He was a heavy-set man of indeterminate nationality or age, sitting at a cocktail table near the entrance.

I ordered an extra-dry Gordon's martini on the rocks and as I contemplated it, was startled by a voice behind me, asking in a midwest American accent, "How was New York when you left it?"

It was the man who had been sitting at the table. "Well, it was still there when I left several days ago," I replied cautiously.

"You wouldn't perchance know what the climate's been like in Spain, would you?" he asked, sitting down beside me.

"It seems extremely dry this year in Madrid," I said and swallowed hard, waiting for his reply.

He took a long sip from his highball. "Yes, the rain does stay mainly in the plains . . . I suppose."

I said nothing. My evening of sightseeing had just evaporated.

"My name's Hampshire," he said lethargically, extending a puffy hand. He was so different from what I had expected that I began to wonder if his reply to the code might have been an accident.

"How about joining me at my table?" he asked. As I followed him to the table, I studied him, wondering if he might be ill. But once we were away from the scrutiny of the bartender, his eyes twinkled a bit and he said, "My wife and I have just come back from an extended tour of the Soviet Union."

"Really," I said, perturbed. "Where did you go?"

"All over, but one of our stops was in Minsk." The notion that any American could travel through Russia in 1961 put me off again, and I had almost concluded that our verbal code exchange had indeed been a coincidence when Hampshire continued: "You must come upstairs and meet my wife. She's a good friend of Dr. Kreisberg's."

The mention of Susan's father couldn't be a coincidence. "Really?" I said. "I'd love to meet her."

"Fine," he said, rising. Then he addressed the bartender. "Alfred, put this on my tab."

Alfred, who was tending to a French couple who had just entered, saluted politely and said, "Yes, Sir."

I watched Hampshire lay a five new franc note on the table and followed him into the lower lobby. When we were alone in the elevator, he asked, "What's your room number?"

"522."

"Fine. I'll call you there in a few minutes." He punched the buttons for the second and fifth floors. As the car came to a stop at the second floor, he smiled and stepped out. I watched him disappear down the hall.

The phone was ringing as I opened my door. It was Hampshire. "Meet me in 410 as soon as possible," he ordered.

Startled, I pulled the phone away from my ear, looked at it, then replied, "Be right there." I literally hadn't had time to get my key out of the lock. The exit stairs were a few doors away, so I walked down the flight rather than wait for the elevator. When I knocked on the door of 410, Hampshire opened it and invited me into the suite.

In the bright light of the foyer I observed that Hampshire was older than I had thought—at a guess, close to sixty-five. His wife appeared to be about ten to fifteen years younger and was magnificently dressed. They smelled of money.

Without introducing his wife, Hampshire announced, "I have a package for you to deliver back in the States."

I watched as he took an envelope full of papers from her, continuing, "Just tell Kendricks that this is the information he wanted from Harvey." Then he made me repeat the name: "Harvey." It was not for some time that I was to learn that "Harvey" was a code name for one Lee Harvey Oswald.

I took the papers and asked, "Do you also have my itinerary?"

"You're booked out on a BEA flight to London in the morning, with a connecting TWA flight into Idlewild."

Chapter Seven

Fourteen hours after leaving Paris, I was answering the airport page at the temporary TWA terminal at Idlewild. It was Kendricks calling. He told me to take the airport bus around the complex to the executive terminal, where he and the Comanche were waiting. I wondered why he had bothered to meet me, but was pleased to avoid the cab ride to La Guardia, where I had left the Comanche a few days before.

When I joined Ed he said hello and then busied himself with filing an instrument clearance for the flight back to Friendship. The weather was getting murky and he wanted to beat a line of thunderstorms moving in from the west.

There was lightning in the western sky when we rolled up to the south terminal at Friendship a little over an hour and ten minutes later. We had to rush to get everything unloaded and the bird tied down before the rain started.

We were dodging the first drops on our walk to the terminal when Ed picked up the conversation almost where he had left it the last time I saw him. "I guessed right about the explosive in the Comanche," he said. "It was installed by Shaw's people and rigged into the glide slope so it couldn't go off until a mechanic made one last adjustment to complete the circuit. I've learned that Shaw knows about the call you got from Rodriguez in Savannah. He's been told that you found nothing on the airplane. So, as far as Shaw knows, the Comanche is still rigged."

"Damn," I said. "I'd almost rather it had been Castro than one of our own people."

"Me, too, but there's one consolation. We're now checking every piece of equipment going in and out of Miami and New Orleans, which is Shaw's territory. While you were gone, we found two of our southern-based cars with homing devices on them. The irony is that he's using gear on us that we gave him to check on his own people."

"It sounds like you have a wild-eyed bunch of right-wingers on your hands."

"Listen, Robert, some of those bastards are to the right of Genghis Khan. If Shaw had his way, the brothers Kennedy would be drawn and quartered."

"They're bugging us with our stuff in our own vehicles?" That amused me immensely. "In effect, we're spying on each other?"

"Everyone in this business spies on each other. Christ, we have almost as many FBI men on our payroll as J. Edgar Hoover."

We climbed into a new Ford Galaxy Ed had parked on the lot. On the way to Baltimore he asked, "By the way, where are the papers you picked up in Paris?"

"Good thing you asked. I'd forgotten all about them. I was told to tell you they came from 'Harvey.' They're in my briefcase. I've got them sandwiched among some magazines I picked up at the airport in London."

"Good enough. We'll get to them when we get to your place."

As we plunged into the Baltimore Harbor Tunnel another thought occurred to me. "What was the big rush about getting me back to the States?"

"Mario is back in Washington. He has what he needs to manufacture the plates for the new currency and he's ready to turn the project over to you."

"Turn it over to me? Damn it, Ed, what's going on?"

"It's very simple. Mario made a direct request that you

handle this phase of his operation. He's got everything you'll need. He's also relying on you to handle the communication purchases and other details. In fact, at the moment you're the only one of our crew he trusts. Besides, I suspect that your legs aren't in the best of shape and you probably should stay put somewhere for a while."

"They could be worse," I replied.

"Well, I think you need some rest. Besides, this will keep you out of the limelight and away from the attention of that vindictive SOB, the attorney general."

"My, how you talk about the heir apparent to the throne."

"That's nothing compared to some of the adjectives the boss has used lately. If our president and his brother sit on the missile information to serve their own political ends, it's my opinion that he won't live through his first term."

"Things are heating up?"

"You better believe it. With characters like Shaw around, anything can happen. The Company's in the middle of a full-scale war with McNamara at the DOD, and the president's trying to put pressure on Senator Chavez to curtail our unvouchered funds. To make matters worse, he also wants to instigate a complete investigation of our activities. Something's got to give and I know it won't be the Director."

"You know, Ed, I guess I'm convinced. I'd be more comfortable working in Baltimore. I'm not a political animal at heart."

"Then you should be pleased to know that Mario has apparently been given tacit approval by Maxwell Taylor to carry out this counterfeiting operation, so it shouldn't get sabotaged like the last one. But officially, of course, we won't know anything about it."

"That's reassuring. Where's this operation based?"

"About a mile and a half from your Baltimore apartment, in a section called Rosedale."

"You mean just over the hill?"

"That's right," he replied, smiling. "Tomorrow we're to meet Mario and the technical people over there."

Kendricks swung the car from the Harbor Tunnel Throughway into the Pulaski Highway exit, and within a few minutes we were turning left on Moravia Road to the Cedonia apartment complex at the top of the hill. He pulled into the parking slot next to the front door.

He helped me deposit my luggage at my doorstep and then left, after reminding me that he would pick me up at ten in the morning.

I had just finished my breakfast when there was a resounding bang on the door. It was Kendricks.

"Mario should be arriving in Rosedale any minute," he said.

We piled into Ed's car and within ten minutes had arrived at 6324 Hazelwood Avenue, an expansive bungalow set apart from a small group of houses and at least one hundred feet from a winding country road. A long gravel driveway led to a parking lot at the rear.

En route we had crossed over the beginnings of a large road construction project that I assumed to be the extension of the Baltimore Harbor Tunnel. At the rate the surrounding farmland was being developed, it would soon be so heavily populated that covert operations here would become impossible.

Ed apparently had the same thought; as he pulled the Galaxy into the drive he said, "When we started this operation it was in the middle of nowhere."

"We're actually not that far from the city, are we?"

"About ten miles."

When we got out of the car in the lot behind the bungalow, I was surprised at its isolation. Although the houses on either side were fairly close, the trees and shrubbery were so dense you couldn't see them. Before we could knock at the door to the breezeway, it was opened by a women of about thirty with long blond hair.

Ed said, "Cynthia, I'd like you to meet Bob Porter."

"Hi," she said. "Come on in. I'm just making fresh coffee. Mario hasn't arrived yet. He called and said he was going to be a little late. He's picking up Commander Pons, who used to be the Cuban naval attaché in Washington."

I thought the place looked like any other contemporary ranch house until Cynthia closed and locked the door behind us and said, "Let's go down to the lab."

We followed her through the kitchen and down the backstairs. Passing through a heavy door that appeared to be fireproof, we entered a layout almost as impressive as Cabell's establishment in Washington.

A man about my age jumped up as we entered. Ed introduced him as Ross Allen. "Ross will be working with your group," he said.

During the next half hour they gave me a guided tour through a facility that would make most of the better commercial laboratories look ill-equipped. There was a complete precision model shop, an environmental test laboratory with humidity, temperature, and acoustical test chambers, and an assemblage of other instrumentation that was overwhelming. The main laboratory contained everything from Cambridge galvanometers to several of the most modern 545 Tektronix oscilloscopes, complete with all the available plug-in units. There was also a complete photographic darkroom.

"We wanted you well equipped," Kendricks said. "For your information, this whole facility in an emergency is independently powered. Also, if you noticed the telephone and power pole at the front of the drive as you came in, they carry independent loops isolating the local power company from any possible carrier current taps. In addition, all the phone lines have been looped and checked for taps and, in the event of a power failure, sitting in that large two-car garage is a twenty-five kilowatt, gasoline-powered generator."

"It's incredible," I said.

Cynthia spoke up. "We'll have to make room for the printing press in one of the upstairs rooms." Then, turning to Ross, she asked, "What type of equipment are you planning to use?"

Ross said, "I've ordered an A. B. Dick machine from the local distributor. It should be delivered within a few days."

"This house is a perfect cover," I said.

"Your funding will be taken care of by commercial subcontracts," Kendricks said. "You will supply the necessary out-of-pocket cash."

"Which reminds me," I said, "I still have a chunk of it."

"That's what I mean."

It was well past noon, and Cynthia asked, "Does anyone want some lunch? I made some sandwiches earlier. There's plenty of room in the kitchen; it's our conference area. And I would like to eat before the kids get back from Sunday school."

"Kids?" I asked, surprised.

"Yes," she replied. "I have a son who's seven and a daughter who's five. Don't worry. They've been living with this operation for two years already."

"Cynthia is an ex-nuclear engineer from Martin," Kendricks interjected. "She and her husband put together the lab facilities here."

No one offered an explanation as to where her husband was and, fortunately, something told me not to ask. I learned later that she was in the midst of separation proceedings.

I declined the sandwiches, remarking, "We just finished breakfast, but I could use some coffee."

As we took seats around the table, a car pulled in and parked. At a nod from Ed, I got up and looked out the window. It was the Buick convertible I had driven in Florida, still carrying Dade County plates. In a moment, Mario, Commander Pons, and Bill Grosh, Mario's chauffeur and bodyguard, appeared at the door. After several minutes of hugging and clapping each other on the back, Ed brought the group to order.

"We're going to make this Mario's secondary headquarters. You're well equipped and well staffed, and the operational plan is as follows: Ostensibly, you'll be working on commercial developments, the primary one being a video tape recorder. That's the cover, but you'll actually be working on one. Are there any questions on that point?"

Cynthia asked, "What you're saying is, in effect, we'll be working on two projects simultaneously. One covert and one overt."

"Affirmative. Perhaps more. Granted, it makes it tough, but with the way the administration's been acting we don't want the Kennedy whistle blown on us again."

"Who's going to know about this operation?"

"We've got several key senators like Brewster from Maine and Chavez from New Mexico, and a few reliable congressmen.

Mario can give you their names. You'll have to go to Washington, Bob, to explain the whole operation to some people, but Mario will carry the main ball. In a word, you'll be carrying the load here alone from this point forward. You have your telephone code number if you need us. It's imperative that you keep as low a profile as possible."

Cynthia said, "What about the Company project my husband was working on?"

"I'm afraid it will have to stay in the works, at least temporarily."

"What's that one about?" I asked.

"It's an anti-jamming device for the Agency crew on Nebraska Avenue, which is under a contract with the Comcor Corporation. As you know, Bob, they're funded by the Agency."

"O.K.," I replied. "Now, do I understand that except for emergencies I'm to contact no one at the Agency, and especially Section C?"

"Right. I'll contact you. However, when your projects require it, we will provide you with a Comanche 250, which should make life a lot easier. You won't need it for at least six months."

Then Ed turned to Ross. "You are in charge of our other project. Bob will fund you for the purchase of surplus equipment for re-outfitting Mario's underground army in the hills. They're lacking adequate communications equipment and other warning gear to keep out of reach of the Castroites. You can coordinate this with Mario and Bob."

Ed turned to me and said, "There's one other thing about logistics. Ross will be living here in the house, and I think it'd be wise for you to move in as well. We don't want your activity to create too much of a stir in the neighborhood. Also, I want you to maintain your present code name and ID."

With that, Kendricks said that he had to get to Washington. I didn't see him again for fourteen months. I was knee-deep in running my own show until the fateful day in October 1962 when the Kennedys brought the country to the brink of nuclear war.

Chapter Eight

Tuesday, October 16, 1962, had been just another dreary work day until Chuck Cabell called and asked that I meet with him and Kendricks at 9 o'clock that evening at my Baltimore apartment. The pace at which we had worked for the past year had strained relations between all the members of the team to the limit. As instructed by Kendricks, I had been living in the house and rarely was able to break away to spend a night at my apartment. We had produced two sets of plates for low denomination pesos and were at work on the large denomination. Cabell had been right about the timetable; the job would take another eleven months.

Work was also proceeding on a linear scan, high-resolution magnetic recorder. The results were so positive that we had been getting serious attention from the entertainment industry and the National Security Agency. It appeared that our techniques were yielding results superior to theirs. Cynthia's husband appeared occasionally to work on the "Comcor" system, which we kept isolated from the other projects, but he and Cynthia had not patched things up and she and Ross had a thing going. Part of the living room had been partitioned off to house the printing press.

Cabell's call was a welcome relief from the drudgery, and the urgency in his voice prompted a flood of speculation. The only unusual occurrence that could even remotely relate to us was a news report that on Saturday a Castro patrol boat had been sunk off the Cuban coast by an exile raiding vessel. And on Wednesday, an exile group known as Alpha 66 had raided the port of Isabella de Sagua.

When I pulled into the parking slot at my apartment building the yellow convertible was already parked two cars away. I hurried up the stairs and, for the first time in more than a year, was face to face with Ed Kendricks and Charles Cabell. We shook hands and the general invited me to sit beside him on the divan. He moved the ashtray and magazines off the coffee table, zipped open his briefcase, and pulled out an audio tape recorder, a magnifying glass, and a large set of 11 x 14 photos.

Pointing to the top one, he said, "This photograph of a new ballistic missile launch site being prepared in San Cristóbal, Cuba, was taken a couple days ago. On the morning of the 14th, to be precise. Yesterday we took one of another site at Guanajay, which is almost finished."

"My God," I said, "more of them. But they don't look like the one installed last year in the Camaguey."

"That's because the Camaguey site is the master control center. These new installations are temporary satellites of that master installation. They're controlled by a computer in the Camaguey just as our systems are from Omaha."

"Jesus Christ!" I exploded, stunned.

"I'm afraid he can't help," Cabell retorted. "The installation that you surveyed last year was ready for firing then. That installation is complete with nuclear warheads and everything but the kitchen sink. These new ones are backup sites, and from what Kohly's underground tells us we're sure they have a hell of a lot of permanent sites installed. We're still trying to find out just how many. At any rate, the Soviet arms buildup in Cuba over the past year has been massive. It's beginning to look like they're setting up a major strike force."

"Why did the president wait this long? I assumed something had already been done. I haven't heard a thing in the last year."

"You've been stuck in that basement too long, Robert. If nothing else, the president and his brother are smart politicians. They knew they'd be in trouble this year. Have you read the latest Gallup polls? Right now it appears that the Republicans are going to take a majority in both the House and Senate. If that happens, the Kennedy clan will be powerless to control a large enough block for their intended succession."

"Succession?" I asked.

Kendricks interrupted. "Of course. Bobby takes over after Jack abdicates the throne, as it were. Then young Ted."

"Back to business," Cabell said firmly. "The Camaguey control site you found is now guarded by at least eight independent SAM missile installations and a MIG-21 fighter force. It is also surrounded and guarded by a large ground force installation. In our opinion, it would be almost impossible to knock it out with bombers. On the island there are known to be at least sixteen more SAM-2 sites, not including the eight I just mentioned. Over and above these units are five surface-to-surface missile installations that could be used against any attempted operations by our Navy.

"These bases," he said, pointing to a clump of buildings, "are specifically designed to knock out heavy ships. As for the ballistic stuff, San Cristóbal, near the northwest coast, has four temporary MRBM [medium range ballistic missile] sites under construction, and the Guanajay, closest to the States, has two temporary IRBM [intermediate range ballistic missile] sites being built, backed up with another MIG defense force and a bomber strike force of IL-28's. About ten miles west of where you went in during the Bay of Pigs invasion, there are two more MRBM sites underway at Sagua la Grande. That's a total of six. Five miles east and a few miles inland, at Remedios, a third solitary IRBM installation is being prepared.

"It's totally baffling that all these temporary installations should be openly under construction when the Soviets already have all the hidden hard sites reported by the underground. The

Ruskies must be so confident that they can knock us out or intimidate us that they haven't even bothered to camouflage these new installations."

"Something's screwy, that's for sure," said Kendricks.

"I take it we've resumed the U-2 flights?" I asked.

"That's affirmative. In fact, the president ordered in low range Air Force FR-101's and Navy F-84 recon aircraft, now that the situation has gotten out of control."

"What's going to happen now?"

"If you want my honest opinion, I think the son of a bitch in the White House may wait long enough for the Russians to risk taking a crack at us," Kendricks said.

"Christ! Isn't there anything the section can do?" I asked.

Cabell responded, "Yes. We want Mario to send in a team to attempt to knock out the computer center and we need you to convince him. If we can nail that, the Russians will have to back off."

"What does the cabinet think?" I asked.

"The bastard hasn't had the guts to tell the cabinet," Cabell said angrily. "He's got his own private little group working on the problem. He calls it the Executive Committee or, as Bobby refers to it, the Ex Com. And if I know some of the types that have been called to serve on it, including our illustrious director, they'll want to either invade or bomb the livin' shit out of them. Actually there's no reason for the Russians to back down. The little traitor waited too long."

Kendricks said, "We want Mario's underground to try to take that control center tonight."

"That's going to be tough," I said. "The pictures Pepe took showed that their control apparatus was buried in bunkers that must be fifteen to twenty feet underground."

"That's true, Robert, but the only protection is a cyclone-type charged fence around the perimeter. Hopefully, this means they don't have many guards. If they can get inside the compound, Mario's boys can drop explosive charges down the ventilator shafts. We have mapped their locations from the pictures taken by Pepe. In addition, they'll set a heavy mine charge to destroy the underground communications cable that connects the computer to the microwave relay transmitter. If time permits, they'll also try to knock out the transmitter. Simultaneously, another group will attack the radio communications building. If we can manage to detonate all the charges within a few minutes, they won't know what hit them until it's all over."

"I suppose that's what the guns I bought last year were to be used for?"

"Partially. Which brings us to why you're here. The general will brief you on a new assignment."

Cabell said, "Things are moving rapidly. I know you haven't seen much of Ed so he may not have told you, but I've been relieved of my post. The president instructed the new director to replace me several months ago. My status with the Company is the same as Clay Shaw's, which means I'm only a consultant."

I was not only shaken, but baffled; what was Cabell doing here? Then I realized I should have known better. As far as Kendricks was concerned, only the title had been removed. In spite of orders, Cabell was still deputy director.

He continued. "Let's get to the business at hand. Mario's men have discovered that Jack spent several weeks in Cuba in both April and July of this year."

"Jack?" I interrupted. "He's the one who arranged the arms buy I made in Athens, isn't he?"

"That's right," Cabell said. "He gets into Cuba via Mexico City. We knew he'd been playing both ends against the middle, but we looked the other way until Red China started trading cocaine for sugar. It appears that Jack may have seen a golden opportunity to make a buck. While he was running in guns for Kohly's underground, he may have been running out narcotics for himself.

"We suspect he had it arranged so that refugees brought into the U.S. by his group paid part of their fare by bringing along several ounces of the hard stuff. If we're right, the SOB has no risk at all. He operates extensively out of both Dallas and Miami."

"That's the territory under the control of Kohly's United Organizations, isn't it?"

"For most of the Cubans, yes. However, some of the Cuban extremists and our own right-wingers—the Minutemen types—now run with Shaw in New Orleans."

"I must say, things have changed in the last fourteen months," I said.

"You said it," Cabell replied. "Now, about Jack's activities in Dallas. What I'm getting at is our suspicion that Jack is running a wide open narcotics business under the protection of the Company and, if he is, he knows we can't stop it without blowing our cover. To make matters worse, Dave Ferrie, who's supposed to be under our direct control, is now operating closely with Shaw's crew."

"Does Shaw know what's going on?"

He thought for a moment, then said, "Hell, I don't really think Shaw knows about the narcotics. Interestingly enough, most of Shaw's Dallas and New Orleans personnel were recruited from the Minutemen, which, one would think, should preclude any narcotics activity. That's the other reason we're both here; we want to make sure Kohly isn't involved. You're the closest to him."

"Yes," I said, feeling uneasy. "Who else could be implicated?"

Kendricks interjected: "It could be Shaw's right arm and Ferrie's superior, a man in his forties called Guy Banister, a contract employee about whom I know very little. He's an ex-FBI man reported to be an active member of the Minutemen and head of the Anti-Communist League of the Caribbean. We suspect that group may be part of a Miami-based organization called the Anti-Communist Brigade. Banister also founded an organization called the Friends of Democratic Cuba on January 9 last year. The FDC was originally an arm of an organization known as the Cuban Revolutionary Front, which organized the Bay of Pigs invasion, and later became known as the Cuban Revolutionary Council."

"I remember that Mario opposed the Front because he considered it to be composed of former Commies," I said.

"That's true," Cabell agreed, "and what worries me is that a lot of people we used to count on are getting out of control under the new regime. We don't know whom we can trust. We even set up a direct contact inside Banister's organization, but we now suspect that he also has gone to the far right."

"Who controls Jack . . . in Dallas?" I asked.

"Until now we had assumed that Banister was coordinating Jack's activities. Today, we're not sure."

"I didn't know any of this, Sir," I said, "but I'll try to find out whether Mario does."

"I'd appreciate it, Bob. Up until now there was no need to involve you, but it could become a serious situation. We know Shaw's group is getting out of hand and we want to make sure Kohly isn't getting away from us, too."

"That I understand. Banister must have quite a crew working for him," I said.

Kendricks spoke up. "To be precise, several dozen—although only a few are in the inner circle. He uses Dave Ferrie now as a personal aide and pilot. There is also a young man named Hugh Ward, who is used both as a hatchet man and research man. And a pilot by the name of Maurice Gatlin, Sr., who is supposed to be another of our inside men. Perhaps the most dangerous of all is a Cuban hit man named Carlos Rigel."

"Did Shaw get Banister through the Company in Washington?"

"No, he was introduced originally through a lawyer in New Orleans by the name of Guy Johnson, a former officer in the Office of Naval Intelligence and now Shaw's personal attorney. What really has me worried is something more sinister. Gatlin claims he spotted another of our fringe operators with Dave Ferrie and Banister several times last week. He's a man who recently finished an assignment for us inside the U.S.S.R., actually the 'Harvey' whose package you picked up in Paris."

Kendricks said, "I still think it was Bill Gemelo that Gatlin spotted. He looks enough like Harvey to be his twin."

"Could be," Cabell agreed.

"Who's Gemelo?" I asked.

"He's another of Banister's boys who often operates for Jack in Dallas. He usually works with a partner named Jim Hart. They are also active in the Free Cuba Movement, and our suspicion is that they were lent to Jack by Banister to help with the narcotics operation."

"That's interesting. And under Shaw's nose?"

"Apparently," Cabell said. "Well, at any rate, when President Kennedy reveals that the missiles are in Cuba, all hell will break loose. Every radical element from the John Birch Society to the Ku Klux Klan will be after his ass."

"Literally as well as figuratively," Kendricks chortled.

"What do you think could happen?" I asked.

Cabell held his hands together, pursed his lips, and said, "I think someone might try to assassinate the president."

"Good God!" I remarked.

"*Thank* God!" said Kendricks.

Cabell's face registered no emotion at either comment. He was silent for a few seconds, then continued. "We must, of course, know what's going on if for no other reason than to protect our image. So we should gather as much information on any potential plot as possible, particularly if any of our people are involved."

"What if we find out too late?" Kendricks asked.

Cabell looked at him steadily. "That's a chance I think we have to take if we are to maintain an effective organization. But we're going to try to cover all the bases. Shaw's already training several paramilitary teams, possibly with some of our own and Kohly's men, for God knows what. We've got to know what Kohly knows about what's going on down there."

"Can you give me another rundown on those people so I know who and what I'll be looking for?"

"Sure," Cabell replied. "Commit them to memory. Then I'll give you your tentative assignment. Give him the data, Ed."

Ed reached into a briefcase sitting beside his chair and pulled out a number of folders. "To recapitulate, here's a rundown on Shaw's inside group. First is Shaw himself, who sometimes uses the aliases Clyde Bertrum and Alton Bernard. He is currently, and has been for some time, president of the New Orleans International Trade Mart. He is also on the Board of CMC and the Permidex Corporation, CIA-funded companies with which you are familiar. His official relationship with the Agency is as a consultant. Second in command in both the

Dallas and New Orleans areas is Guy Banister. Up until 1955, Banister was in charge of the FBI field office in Chicago. He then went to New Orleans to become deputy superintendent of police, a position he held for several years.

"After leaving that post, he became violently anti-Castro and started his own highly specialized detective agency. He located his offices at 544 Camp Street, which also houses the Free Cuba Movement, which is part of the United Organizations. It's possible that this group is part of Kohly's new outfit —the Cuban Christian Democratic Movement or CDM for short. We need to find out. In addition, Banister publishes an anti-communist rag called *The Louisiana Intelligence Digest*. As stated before, he first met Clay Shaw through a mutual friend, Guy Johnson, who was formerly with the Office of Naval Intelligence. Johnson's still in the naval reserve and is also Shaw's attorney.

"Banister's top aide is Dave Ferrie, who in the past occasionally worked for Banister as an investigator and transporter. You met him on your flight to Cuba and in Athens. I don't know if you know it, but Dave had some unfortunate publicity that labeled him a homosexual and he was dismissed as a flight officer for Eastern. Ferrie now appears to be the most important and versatile man under Banister and Shaw's command. We are told that he has set up a paramilitary training facility at Lake Pontchartrain, Louisiana. It also may be for Kohly."

It was coming awfully fast and I was struggling to fix the names and roles in my memory.

"In addition, he has trained several of his compatriots to fly and has personally run several missions into Cuba, similar to the one you went on with him.

"Under Shaw's direction, Ferrie and Banister are also known to have compiled the largest collection of anti- and pro-communist intelligence dossiers in Louisiana. It has to be a massive file, considering all the Cubans located in that area. In fact, being an old FBI man, Banister modelled his system after theirs, and the information file consists of both friends and enemies. If our sources are correct, the 10-23 classification deals with Cuban matters, the 23-5 category deals with the Cuban

Democratic Revolutionary Front, and the 10-209 classification is simply the Cuban file. Category 23-14, we are told, is Shaw's personal file."

"I'd love to see that," I said, and then added, "I gather that you want me to find out what Mario's role is in the operations in New Orleans."

"Frankly, yes," Kendricks said, "that's the idea. Shaw, if he controls Kohly's forces, may go wild now that Chuck has been officially removed as deputy director. After all, just consider what he did to our vehicles and aircraft while Chuck was still in command. You see Kohly frequently here in Baltimore, and may be able to learn something."

I nodded and he continued.

"Now, let's get back to Banister's people. There is Hugh Ward, whom we've already discussed and who is one of Ferrie's more adept pilot trainees. About Carlos Rigel we know very little, except that he does odd jobs for Banister and Shaw and is probably a professional assassin. Then, of course, there is Jack. Jack's working partners in the Shaw group are Hart, Gemelo, and Charles Hunter, about whom we don't know much."

"They all operate out of Dallas?" I asked.

"Either there or Miami."

Cabell spoke up. "Don't brush over Gemelo too fast. And more importantly, Gemelo's double, Harvey."

"Let me go over this again," I interrupted. "Harvey was the one who gave the envelope to Mr. Hampshire that I collected in Paris?"

Cabell replied, "The same."

"Now, tell me more about Gemelo and Harvey. You say they could be twins?"

"Yes, and to date, although I don't know it for a fact, I suspect that neither one knows the other exists. But they both seem to be operating under the Shaw/Banister umbrella. We know Harvey is now in Fort Worth, living with his brother, and that Gemelo is under Jack, probably in Miami. We also suspect that Banister and Harvey had some contact before Harvey left for Russia, but we have no hard evidence to support such a conclusion. Ferrie was supposed to have taught him as a CAP cadet a few years back, but we can't prove it."

Kendricks said, "Another problem. We're making large-sum payments to Shaw, direct, and he disburses the funds as he sees fit. That's still the arrangement, even though Chuck is no longer deputy director."

Ignoring that comment, Cabell said, "Well, for whatever it's worth, Harvey's history is an interesting one. He's kind of a sleeper—smarter than he looks—which is always helpful in our business. While in the Marine Corps, after being trained as both a radar operator and cryptographer, he was assigned to our base in Atsugi, Japan. While working there he learned Russian. Atsugi, as you probably know, is the base that launches most of the covert U-2 overflies of China and the U.S.S.R. From there they go into Turkey."

"Just like Gary Powers," I interjected.

Kendricks said, "Anyway, that's where he was trained. He did a covert stint in the Philippines with his MAAG group and, in September of fifty-nine, at our request, he applied for and, within three days, got a hardship discharge. For obvious reasons, when we sent him to Russia posing as a defector, it was changed to a dishonorable discharge. From the marines, he went home to New Orleans. After spending a few days with his mother, he was disbursed two thousand dollars from our local New Orleans office located across from 544 Camp Street, in the federal office building. He had a top secret clearance, as well as a crypto clearance, and was on a sensitive mission."

"What do you mean by sensitive?" I asked.

"Harvey's assignment was to get into Russia, claim to revoke his citizenship, and defect to the other side with all our top secret codes, radar data, frequencies, and whatever else he had memorized. He was to be used for an internal security operation in Russia. Hence, the establishment of the anti-American, pro-Commie identification. His job was to make contact with a girl in Moscow who's the niece of a KGB colonel and get her out of Russia so her uncle could defect. Although the uncle was married, the girl was his only blood relation."

Cabell picked up the narrative. "It was a complex mission.

He took a ship to England and then was passed on to Helsinki by land. The boys in London felt he should make the trip overland instead of by plane. They figured it would make his defection look more authentic. Using ground transport, it took him almost two weeks to get to Moscow. When he arrived there, acting on his instructions, he charged into the American Embassy and denounced his American citizenship. Next, again as instructed, he contacted certain Russian officials and gave them detailed information on our radar, intelligence frequencies, and codes. It had been prearranged, of course, to discontinue sensitive transmissions as soon as he arrived in Moscow, and to change every frequency and code he passed to the Russians within a day or two after he appeared at our Moscow embassy. This gave the Russians time to verify the accuracy of what he told them, but also kept them from learning anything really important.

"The operation worked perfectly in the opening stages, but Harvey was then isolated in Minsk for two years. Following normal procedure, we arranged, on several occasions, to have American tourists bring out data that Harvey had gathered, and actually got some fairly valuable information. The envelope you picked up from Hampshire in Paris warned us that Harvey felt he was under suspicion and had to get out. He did manage, however, to marry and bring the KGB colonel's niece with him. It wasn't easy. He had to slash his wrists and act like a maniac to get the girl and their baby out."

"Baby?" I said.

"Harvey had married the girl to give her status that would help him get her out of the country. Apparently he also fell in love with her. We pulled them out on a prearranged plan where he would ask our Embassy to loan him some money and issue him a passport. Our man at the Embassy provided him with over four hundred dollars to pay for their transport. So far, simple.

"On the night of his arrival back in the U.S. one of our people debriefed Harvey and immediately reported into headquarters in D.C. He was told to send Harvey directly down south to await further contact. He finally hooked up with Jack in

Dallas, and we think the FBI hired Harvey to speak for them, as well.

"Also, Harvey's wife has been a gold mine of information. We're waiting now for her uncle to come over. At any rate, as you can see, we've got an army of people on the payroll down there, one way or another, and we want to double-check what the hell is going on. Comprende?"

"O.K.," I said. "Anybody else?"

"No. Ed will keep you updated on the New Orleans situation. Officially, I can't do anything to help, but I may be able to give you some advice. Good luck to you both." With that, the general gathered up his papers, said goodbye, and left for Washington.

When Kendricks and I were alone, he looked at me quizzically and asked, "Well, how 'bout that?"

"I'm limp," I replied.

After Kendricks left I reached Mario by phone and learned that he already had a group poised and ready for a strike at the control center. Despite his disenchantment with the administration, he had agreed to order his team in the next night—the 17th—not to help the U.S. but to save his countrymen from a potential holocaust if the U.S. decided to attack Cuba with a nuclear strike force.

The next day and a half were hectic, and by late Thursday morning, the 18th, I was becoming concerned because I hadn't heard anything from Ed about Mario's Cuban strike. I was pretty uptight at noon when Cynthia, on the lab intercom, told me to pick up the phone. It was Kendricks.

"Can you meet me at the Colony Seven on the Baltimore-Washington Parkway within two hours?" he asked urgently.

I said I could, but that I might be a few minutes late because I was in the middle of some things. He said he'd wait.

As it turned out, I was actually early and, as I pulled the Jag up the motel's front drive, Ed was just entering the coffee shop. He spotted me and waved. I locked the car and followed him in.

At two in the afternoon the restaurant was almost deserted,

with the exception of one or two lingering customers. Ed picked an isolated table next to the window, ordered two cups of coffee, and said, "The Director has rebriefed the president on the status of the satellite missile sites the general showed you Tuesday."

I nodded.

"Mario's group failed. They did a lot of damage but didn't manage the coup d'état."

"Oh, Christ!"

"Of the twelve men who made the attempt, only one survived, and he was tortured to death in Havana last night."

"Poor bastard," I mumbled. "Now what?"

"At the moment, we're helpless. The Ruskies know we failed to knock out their control center, but they'll assume we will try again. Now, the question is . . . will they risk going to war? At any rate, as of tomorrow, our armed forces will be on national alert. God knows what the president's committee is going to recommend."

"I assume the Director's all for launching an invasion?"

"Something like that. Or, at least, nothing short of a saturation bombing mission."

"That would be futile," I said.

"That's right. The Russians have nothing to lose . . . they're dug in too deeply and a successful invasion would mean they'd lose their toehold in the western hemisphere. At any rate, they're still at it in the White House. The next few days will tell the tale."

"Is there anything you want me to do?"

"Yes. Mario may elect to send in another team. If so, he'll need some specialized gear."

"I understand. I just hope he won't need me to go with it."

"I would seriously doubt it. I'll keep you briefed. And remember, Mario desperately needs those pesos now. It's his last chance to knock out the Castro regime."

"O.K., Ed, I'll push as fast as I can. But you know how meticulous the work has to be. One goof and we blow the whole operation."

Within minutes we were heading in opposite directions on

the Baltimore-Washington Parkway.

On October 29, we again met at the Colony Seven after another request that I get there as soon as possible. When I pulled up the drive Ed was sitting at the same table we had occupied almost two weeks before. I was feeling pleased over the news reports that the missile crisis had been settled without an all-out confrontation and that the missiles were on their way back to Russia. I sat down opposite Ed and signaled the waitress for a cup of coffee. My lighthearted mood changed rapidly as he started talking, his voice low but filled with rage.

"Those rotten sons of bitches have done it again. Mario has just gotten a report via the underground that the Russians dismantled the temporary sites and moved the missles back to hidden hard sites in the interior. They're still there, ready to go. Kennedy didn't allow one goddamn outbound freighter to be boarded so that we could be sure the missiles were on board. The Navy is having a fit. Mario swears he has absolute proof that the control site is still operational and that not one damn missile has left the country."

"No wonder they didn't bother to camouflage San Cristóbal and Guanajay. They were meant to be discovered. If what you are saying is true, the implications are insidious. It's easy to see why Khrushchev backed off."

"What's insidious," said Ed, "is that Khrushchev sent Kennedy two letters on the 26th, but the president only made the second one public."

I looked at him skeptically. "Are you implying that the missiles are still in Cuba and Kennedy knows it and agreed to it?"

"That's our belief. Kohly's boys have us convinced that they're still there. We think that Khrushchev made a deal not to rock the boat on our missiles in Turkey if Kennedy agreed to allow theirs to stay in Cuba. Khrushchev knew Kennedy had let the missiles stay in Cuba for over a year, without protest or telling the American people. He's been able to use that knowledge as a perfect political ploy to keep them there. Kennedy's career would be over if his deception were revealed."

"I'm absolutely stunned."

"So am I. And madder than hell. Mario's trying to get another appointment with Bobby to show him that he knows the missiles are still there and that he can prove it."

"He's a glutton for punishment."

The waitress brought my coffee. When she had left, I asked, "What the hell does this mean?"

"I'll tell you exactly what it means. The Democrats will stay in office, the missiles will stay in Cuba, with an executive guarantee that Cuba will remain a communist-bloc country. Kennedy has promised that we will never invade Cuba or help the Cuban exiles do it. The simple truth is that his past duplicity gives him no choice. He can't afford to invade Cuba and free it from Castro because our citizens would then discover that the missiles are still there and that the Kennedys deceived them. The Kennedy dynasty would be ended. By thwarting the exiles and conspiring with the Kremlin, the brothers have saved their political necks.

"What's worrying me now is the possible second-order consequences. God knows what Shaw and that bunch of hotheaded Cubans and right-wing extremists in New Orleans will do if they get many more blows like this one. The president and his brother have been thwarting them at every turn, and I'm afraid that at some point they'll lose their heads and retaliate.

"To make matters worse, Kohly's on the blacklist again for refusing to cooperate with the White House to free the Bay of Pigs prisoners. Kennedy wouldn't go along with Mario's plan to get the prisoners released for twenty-five million dollars, and he turned thumbs down on recognizing a de facto Cuban government. He said he was going to send an attorney, James B. Donovan, to Cuba to get the prisoners released for nothing.

"Mario's having fits and Shaw will be, too, when he finds out about it, so for God's sake see what you can learn about Mario's involvement in New Orleans."

I nodded and said, "I'll speak to Mario. I haven't seen him in quite a while and I need him to check the plates."

"I'll have him get in touch with you the first of the week."

Kendricks paused, seeming to debate whether to say more, and then concluded, "Now, one last thing. We are going to make another attempt to assassinate Castro, this time with Mafia help."

He smiled grimly as we left the place. I couldn't speak for his drive south to D.C., but I had a sick feeling in the pit of my stomach when I arrived back at Hazelwood Avenue.

Things were going well with the projects although we had run up against technical difficulties with the high-speed recorder and some problems with final details of the new fifty peso note.

I met with Kohly and his Cuban exile leaders in New York the first week in February, and we decided that because of the massive printing job that would have to be done it would be better to farm it out to a commercial establishment. Subsequently, Mario, for security reasons of his own, had arranged for a printer outside of the Agency.

To make matters worse, I hadn't been able to get Kohly alone long enough to get any answers to the questions raised by Kendricks. Consequently, when Ed called to request another meeting at the Colony Seven, I was at a loss to know what to tell him about Mario. He was impatiently pacing up and down beside the yellow Buick in the motel parking lot when I pulled the Jag in beside him.

We both got into the Buick and Ed lit a cigar, but he didn't ask about Kohly. Instead, he said, "I thought you should be informed that the situation in New Orleans appears to be under control, at least for the present. Shaw has been informed that the missiles are still in Cuba. As expected, his reaction was pretty violent, but I don't think he'll do anything rash as long as he still has hopes for the counterfeiting project. Obviously, that raises your work on Hazelwood Avenue to priority number one."

"I'll be able to deliver the plates no later than the last of September or the first of October," I promised. "Also, although we have encountered some problems, it looks like the high-speed magnetic recorder may have fantastic possibilities."

"That's great," he said. "But don't let it distract you from the currency project. We're still trying to wipe out Castro by more direct means, but what you're doing is our real ace in the hole."

I felt almost contented on my trip back to Baltimore. Much as I hated being in that cellar, I knew we were nearing the end of a successful project. If our luck held, it could blow the Cuban economy off the face of the map.

Chapter Nine

The old air conditioner in the office at 544 Camp Street rattled and shuddered in a futile effort to cope with the heat and humidity of the New Orleans summer. It was June 20, 1963, and Guy Banister had just finished a telephone call to Clay Shaw.

Banister had reported the grim news from Mario Kohly's underground, confirming an official report of early May that more than 17,500 Russians were still in Cuba. What hadn't been reported in the press was that most of them were there to man missile sites. On top of that, word had come from Washington of Kennedy's agreement to a nuclear nonaggression pact with the Soviet Union, and of his decision not to extend the Cuban refugee exchange program beyond the June 30 expiration date.

Coming as it did on the heels of a year-long succession of frustrations at the hands of the Kennedy brothers, the news infuriated the rabidly anti-communist Banister and brought a similar reaction from Clay Shaw. Shaw asked Banister to bring Dave Ferrie to his house for a strategy session at five o'clock that afternoon.

When they arrived at Shaw's house on Dauphine Street, Banister pushed the bell beside a red door set into a high, white brick wall. As he and Ferrie waited, Banister said, "Clay lives in a glorified carriage house. If you're lucky he may give you a guided tour."

Shaw greeted them and they entered a large courtyard where the heat of the day receded within the protection of the thick, vine-covered masonry walls. He led them toward the building at the far end of the courtyard. Dave observed that the lower floor of the carriage house had been expensively remodeled. Large panels of glass had replaced the original wooden doors, and through them he could see that the entire ground floor was given over to a huge living room and a compact gourmet kitchen. In the courtyard outside stood a large glass dining table surrounded by wrought iron chairs. From the glimpse Dave had of the other furnishings, he could see that Shaw had superb taste.

Their host took their order for drinks, and when he went inside to get them Banister leaned over and whispered, "He's got two of the wildest bedrooms you've ever seen. One's for sleeping and the other's for parties."

When Shaw reappeared and handed them their glasses, he asked Dave if he would care to look around.

"Definitely," Ferrie replied. They stepped into the living room and he found himself surrounded by gracious French antiques, some of them grouped around a large, low coffee table. Scattered over the highly polished floor were several antique oriental rugs. On one wall a huge gold-leaf mirror hung over a priceless antique French provincial desk.

Dave said in awe, "It's beautiful."

His words were punctuated by the clamor of the door chimes. Shaw excused himself and returned in a few moments with two additional guests.

One, short and stocky with a round face, was introduced as Jack Ruby, from Dallas. The other, who Shaw said came from Miami, was a rather thin, good-looking man named Bill Gemelo.

Shaw brought drinks for the late arrivals and they all took

seats. Clay looked intently at the expectant group. "Gentlemen," he said, "with the exception of Dave Ferrie, you all know each other. Jack, Dave also works for Guy. He's third in command here in New Orleans."

Ruby nodded, and Shaw continued.

"I don't need to tell any of you the extent to which the president and his brother have been playing footsie with the Commies. For a year and a half they let the Russians build up their missile bases in Cuba without telling the American people they were there. They sabotaged one counterfeiting operation and God knows how many assassination attempts, by alerting Castro to our plans. They caused a disaster at the Bay of Pigs by withdrawing the naval air support. Now they're allowing the Russians to maintain a huge force in Cuba to man missiles the American people believe were removed. But that's not all. We have now learned that they are going to stop trading Cuban refugees for medical supplies and plan to sign a nuclear nonproliferation pact with the Soviet Union. Unless Kohly's counterfeiting operation works, the Russians, through Castro, are going to have a permanent, missile-equipped military base right in our front yard."

Shaw continued. "I'm still hopeful that Kohly can destroy the Cuban economy with his counterfeit money, in which case we'll have a second chance. But if that goes down the drain like everything else has, I want to be prepared with an alternative. Guy, we've talked about it before, so you know what that option is."

"Sure," Banister replied flippantly. "If we can't get Castro because of the president, we'll get the president first so we can get at Castro."

There was a moment of silence. Then Ruby recoiled visibly and the other men blanched.

Noting their reactions, Shaw continued in his typical, coldly controlled manner. "I can understand why you find the suggestion startling. The assassination of a president may seem a monstrous act, but not if the alternative is an America under communist rule. Please understand, I don't propose to undertake it if there is any alternative, but we must be prepared if we are left with no other choice."

The others still sat in stunned silence, except for Banister, who watched Shaw expectantly, an eager smile on his face. The smile became a derisive grin when Shaw turned to Ruby and said, "Jack, you've got a lot of work to do because you're going to be in charge of this operation."

Ruby cringed in his chair, his face white. "Me?" he stammered, almost choking. "Me, assassinate the president? I . . . I . . . I can't do it."

"You not only can, but you will," Shaw said, his tone cold and uncompromising. "Unless, of course, you'd like to go up for twenty years on a narcotics charge."

Ruby gasped and squirmed uncomfortably. "Narcotics charge? What the hell are you talking about?"

"Come off it, Jack," Shaw said impatiently. "I know all about your little drug operation and your tie to the syndicate through Louis McWillie. I know you've been running guns into Cuba using Company money—and running Chinese narcotics out. You play ball with us or you're going to get slapped with a charge, and if the Feds don't nail you, your Mafia friends probably will."

Ruby was silent for a moment, then asked, "What if Kohly's counterfeiting plan works?"

"Then we won't need your services and it won't make any difference, will it? But in case Kohly fails . . ."

Ruby looked straight at Banister. "What do you want me to do?"

"Let me give you some ideas. Number one, to insure success we should have at least three teams ready. Whether we use them all will depend on the location. And we don't want amateurs. They should be skilled operators—professional hit men—so nothing gets screwed up."

Dave spoke for the first time. "Where do you propose this job be done?"

"Well, it's obvious the mountain won't come to Mohammed, so we will have to go to the mountain," Banister replied.

"You mean Washington?" Ruby asked.

"Unless you can figure a way to get Kennedy to come to New Orleans or Texas, I suggest you think in those terms."

"Of course," Shaw interjected, "it's always possible that Kennedy may come this way on a political trip. He's almost certain to go to Texas because he needs to carry the state in the Congressional elections next year. In that case the mountain might come to Mohammed. I'll have some friends on the Hill check to see if the White House has anything planned."

With that, Shaw dismissed the group, suggesting that they meet again in a month. As they moved toward the door, he asked Banister to remain.

Banister fixed a fresh bourbon and water and collapsed into one of the lounge chairs. Clay Shaw sat down opposite him on the large divan, and said, "Well, that went pretty well. Ruby caved in just as I thought he would, and now that he's committed I think our worries are over. After all, he and his syndicate friends have everything to gain and nothing to lose. They want to get back into operation in Cuba. But we need a foolproof plan, and seeing Gemelo again gave me an idea."

"What do you mean?"

"His striking resemblance to Lee Harvey Oswald. Maybe we can use it."

"How?" Banister asked.

"Well, like Ruby, Gemelo knows he's in trouble if we want to put him there. He's been picking up Jack's drugs in Miami. Ruby arranges to get refugees out of Cuba, and they bring the stuff in for him as part of their fare. What if we had Gemelo pose as Oswald and put him on one of the assassination teams. If we worked it right, Oswald could be the patsy and everyone else would be home free."

"It might work, although Oswald may be too smart to be used as a decoy. Did you know he's back in town?"

"No, I didn't," Shaw said, frowning. "What's he doing here?"

"Ruby sent him over from Dallas, probably because he knows Oswald is tied in with the FBI and didn't want him around. Lee's working over at the Reilly Coffee outfit. I've kept tabs on him by paying him to distribute Fair Play for Cuba Committee pamphlets around town. I'm using him to ferret out left-wing types by getting them to join a New Orleans chapter of the FPCC that we set up under Oswald's Albert Hidel and Lee Osborne aliases."

"That makes it even better," Shaw said eagerly. "You've already got him set up as a Commie sympathizer, and the record shows that he defected once. What if we made it look like he planned to do it again—maybe set him up with false visas obtained from the Russian and Cuban embassies in Mexico City?"

"You mean have someone impersonate him down there? It might be tough. The Company photographs everyone entering those buildings, you know."

"Who cares? By the time they've checked the photos the president would be dead and so would Oswald. And the whole thing would be arranged so everyone would believe that Kennedy was the victim of a crazed Commie assassin!" Shaw paused, his face flushed with excitement. But in a moment he sobered and asked, "One question. Where's Oswald's Russian wife?"

"That could be a problem," Banister replied. "He's really hung up on her. He brought her down to join him early last month." Banister thought for a minute, sighed, and said, "Well, let me sleep on it. And remember, for an operation as complicated as this one, a lot of people would have to be involved. That could mean leaks."

"I'm sure you can handle that," Shaw replied. "Since you're Oswald's Company contact, setting him up should be a lead-pipe cinch. Good. Well, let's mull it over and discuss the plan again in the next few days. I'd like to have something settled before our next meeting with Ruby. Meanwhile, I think it would be wise to put all of your new men on some assignment in the boondocks. I've had the feeling lately that someone is reporting to the Director everything he can learn about our activities. We certainly don't want any word of this to get out."

"God, no! I'll take care of it immediately."

"Thanks. I'll wait to hear from you," Shaw said, and escorted Banister to the door.

Mario and I were on our way downtown to meet with the printer. I had checked into the Gotham when I arrived in New York the night before, and in the morning I walked the few blocks up Fifth Avenue to meet him at the Plaza. We caught a cab about 10:30 and as we headed downtown he brought me up-to-date on what was happening in Cuba. Although it was only June, the temperature had soared and I was soaked with perspiration when we pulled up in front of Churchill's Restaurant twenty minutes later.

I was surprised to see Manuel Rodriguez standing on the hot sidewalk outside the restaurant with a heavy-set, florid-faced man who wore a nondescript suit with only one distinguishing feature—an obvious bulge under the jacket.

Mario paid the driver while Manuel introduced me to William Harris. A sixth sense told me that somehow Harris didn't look like a printer, and the fact that he was carrying a gun made me doubly apprehensive. However, it was Kohly's show and in the face of his confidence in Harris I had nothing really substantive with which to challenge his judgment.

In the air-conditioned comfort of the Churchill I began to feel better, and after we had ordered a round of drinks I asked Harris if he had done work of this type before.

He replied that his firm printed large quantities of currency for several South American countries under legitimate contracts.

"That's reassuring," I said. "Could you be specific as to the countries?"

"Several," he replied evasively.

My comfort index dropped another notch when I asked if his equipment was designed to do multiple color gradations from a single plate. Instead of providing information on the type of equipment available, he simply said, "Why, sure." His answers to a number of other technical questions were equally unrevealing.

Then Harris changed the subject by asking me when the plates would be ready and, without thinking, I replied, "Within the next ninety days."

He seemed disappointed. "That long?"

For the first time Mario looked at him suspiciously, and Harris seemed to realize that he might have made a mistake. "No offense," he said hastily. "I was just curious about the timing because I have to work the job into our production schedule. This is our light season, and I'd like to get started as soon as possible."

I found him increasingly annoying and said rather testily, "I'm sure you realize that many lives are going to depend on the quality of this currency. We've got to do our best on the plates, and we've got to be certain that you'll do a quality job on the printing."

"Oh, sure, sure," he said apologetically. "Don't worry. We've had a lot of experience and we'll do everything right."

I tried again to ask him specifics about paper, ink, and printing techniques, but his answers were not responsive and I soon realized that it was pointless to press him further. Mario finally broke up the meeting by telling Harris that he would be back in touch. The three of us headed back uptown. I could hardly wait to get into the cab to voice my concern.

"He's the damndest printer I ever saw," I said. "I suppose you noticed that he was packing a weapon?"

Both Manuel and Mario looked startled and, almost in unison, said they hadn't noticed.

"Well, he was," I said. "And from the answers I got to my questions, I'd say he knows less about printing than Cynthia's eight-year-old son has learned watching the A. B. Dick machine on Hazelwood Avenue."

Mario looked perturbed for a moment but shook it off. "I admit he sounded strange," he said, "but I have confidence that he is all right. He was recommended by a very reliable person."

I said, "Nobody in our group, I hope?"

"As a matter of fact, no," Mario replied, "but someone just as good—a reputable attorney and friend of Cuba in Annapolis, Walter Schultz."

"Well," I said, "he may be a friend of Cuba, but I hope you know who his friends are in Cuba because I smell a rat."

Manuel spoke up. "I am concerned, too, compadre."

Mario shook his head. "I don't agree, but even if I did we're committed. Besides, I don't know anyone else who would do the job on speculation."

"You mean no money up front?" I asked.

"That's right. At first he said he wanted fifty thousand dollars in advance, but when I protested he finally agreed to accept some of the pesos he prints as collateral."

Although the arrangement was not credible, I felt powerless to change it. I asked Mario if he'd mind dropping me off at Fifty-fifth Street. I didn't relish the thought of walking back down the blistering sidewalks from the Plaza to the Gotham.

"I'd hoped you'd stay long enough to meet some more of our people here in New York," Mario protested.

"I will another time," I assured him, "but the less exposure I have now the better, and I have a hell of a lot to do back in Baltimore."

"O.K.," he acquiesced. "I'll be in Washington next week. Meanwhile, thanks for coming."

When the cab pulled to the corner in front of the Fifth Avenue Presbyterian Church, I got out. As the light changed, the Cubans continued up Fifth Avenue and I walked across Fifty-fifth Street into the refreshingly cool Gotham lobby.

The Terrace Bar was almost deserted, and instead of going directly to my room to check out I went to the bar and ordered a Campari on the rocks. I sat there staring at it and worrying about Mario's unlikely printer.

I made excellent time on the trip back to Baltimore. It was just six-thirty when I drove into the Hazelwood Avenue parking lot. Ross appeared at the breezeway door looking distraught. As we walked into the kitchen, he pointed to the phone and said, "Pick it up and tell me what you think."

I put the receiver to my ear and through the dial tone could hear the distinct click of an automatic switch being activated. Sophisticated as it might be, the tap was very noticeable because of the special isolation circuits on our own lines. I slipped the receiver down on the hook, looked at Ross, and asked, "Who do you think it is?"

"I don't know, but you'd better tell Kendricks immediately."

"You're right. I'll call when I get back to my apartment. No, better yet, I'll call from a booth."

"Damn!" said Ross. "Do you think the Kennedys are on to us?"

"After our meeting in New York today, I wouldn't be surprised. I told Mario I smelled a rat. I'd better call him when he gets back to Virginia."

Ross asked, "Where's he living?"

"At the River House. His lines are probably tapped, too. If he calls and I'm not here, suggest a face-to-face meeting." Then I asked, "Where's Cynthia?"

"She's working in the lab."

"Fine. Tell her I'll see her first thing in the morning. I'll stay at the apartment tonight."

"Got ya. Meanwhile, let's keep off the phone. If I need you I'll drive over."

Twenty minutes later, when I entered my own apartment, I picked up the phone and listened intently. There was a lot of background noise but I could still detect the double click of an activating switch. I replaced the receiver in the cradle, walked over to the shopping center, and called Kendricks from the Woodshed.

As the Baltimore summer wore on, a pattern of unrelenting heat, high humidity, and rainy weekends prevailed. By the end of July, everyone on the project was exhausted and short-tempered, and I decreed that we all take off for a long weekend. We were within thirty days of striking our first proofs. As complex as the plates were, I was delighted with their accuracy and confident that bills printed from them would be undetectable as counterfeit even by the most sophisticated electronic scanners.

After our phones had been tapped in June, we had switched lines twice but were never able to shake our mysterious eavesdroppers for more than a few days. The only agency we couldn't penetrate was the Treasury Department, so we concluded that the taps must have been placed by the Secret Service. Kendricks had supplied us with scramblers, but we didn't rely on them totally and any important calls were made from public telephones.

My concern about Mario's printer had not abated. He kept pushing for a firm delivery date, and I had finally been compelled to promise Mario that he could pick up the finished plates on September 30. It now appeared that we would be right on schedule.

Guy Banister was pleased with the progress that had been made in the past month. Shaw's contacts on the Hill had reported that the president, on September 24, would announce a trip to Texas to visit Governor Connally later in the year. If Clay decided to go ahead with the assassination plan, Ruby would be prepared with arrangements to carry it out in any one of three cities. The main emphasis would be concentrated in Dallas, with San Antonio and Houston as alternate sites.

Meanwhile, Banister had a group working on a plan to assassinate Kennedy in Washington on September 26. He and Shaw did not intend to implement it, but it gave them a chance for an organizational dry run and also would test whether there were any leaks in their organization. Banister had also been making progress on Clay's suggestion that they set up Oswald. The New Orleans branch of Kohly's CDM group, using the code name "Bravo Club," was training in paramilitary tactics at Lake Pontchartrain and had recruited Lee Harvey Oswald as a member just before the fourth of July. By the 19th, Oswald had left the Reilly Coffee Company and was working on full-time assignments.

Then Jack Ruby came up with an intriguing bit of information that Banister relayed to Clay Shaw and Dave Ferrie on July 26, at a meeting in Dave's apartment.

"I think we may have run into a piece of luck," Banister told the others. "I've had a report from Ruby that in March Oswald bought a 6.5 millimeter Mannlicher carbine through a Chicago mail-order house, using his Albert Hidel alias."

"Mannlicher?" Shaw asked. "What's that?"

"It's an Italian service rifle. The 6.5 mm model is an inferior early edition. Oswald got his complete with a four-power scope for just under twenty dollars. The 6.5 is not very accurate, especially when it's used with old ammo. However, there is a later version 7.35 Mannlicher, which is quite something else. With a properly sighted four-power scope, it is an excellent sniper's rifle. They haven't made military cartridges for it since World War II, but there are plenty of good cases available for reloading."

"Very interesting," Shaw said. "But what are you getting at?"

"Look, Oswald's already identified with the 6.5 Mannlicher. Why can't we equip our teams with the more accurate 7.35, use fragmentation bullets in them so the caliber can't be identified, and then plant a spent 6.5 slug or two that have been fired from Oswald's gun. That would tie the assassination weapon right to Oswald."

"Well, well, well," Shaw said softly. "What about the 7.35 rifles? Are they available?"

"I would say they'd have to be. Thousands of them were imported into this country after the war. Why don't you ask Kendricks to see if he can get some for you. Tell him you're outfitting a group of exiles to go after Bosch. Kohly claims he's as bad as Castro and that his government will be the first in South America to recognize Fidel Castro if Bosch isn't deposed."

"O.K., I'll do it tonight," Shaw agreed. "Now, how are Ruby's plans coming?"

"He's moving ahead," Banister replied. "We're at the point now where we can implement the plan whenever you give the word."

"How long will it take to set the wheels in motion?"

"Well, now that we know for sure that the president's going to swing through Texas, I can send teams into Dallas, Houston, or San Antonio. With thirty days' lead time we can arrange everything down to the last detail."

"All right," Shaw said. "Now let's hope that someone gets Castro or the counterfeiting plan works, so we don't have to do it. But I must say, I'm not very hopeful."

"Neither am I," Banister agreed. "Well, I'll move ahead on setting up Oswald, so that if you give the word we can swing into action. Meanwhile, request those Mannlichers. We're probably going to need them."

"I'll give Kendricks a call later this evening," Shaw said.

Lee Harvey Oswald must have felt that his move from Dallas to New Orleans was one of the luckiest breaks of his life. For the first time since he had been drawing his two hundred dollar stipend from the FBI he had something positive to report. Only yesterday he had hit real pay dirt: the location of a secret arms cache at Lake Pontchartrain. He had just finished relaying the information to the Dallas office, even though he suspected that the Bureau office in New Orleans might already know of its existence. At least it would show that he was on the ball. With his two undercover assignments, he and Marina should be able to start putting something aside for themselves and the baby.

Ross and I were checking a proof of one of the Cuban notes when Kendricks called.

"I've heard from Shaw in New Orleans," he said. "He wants us to supply him with some 7.35 mm Mannlicher rifles. He says he needs them for an exile group that's planning an attempt to get Bosch."

"If that's the case he's making a pretty good choice," I said. "The 7.35 is a highly accurate sniper's piece."

"As good as the '03 Springfield," Ed agreed, "and they shouldn't be hard to find in one of the surplus stores. I'd like you to check around and see if you can pick them up."

He signed off and I sat there for a moment, puzzling over Shaw's request—and Kendricks' apparent lack of concern about it, in view of his suspicions about the man. But then I thought, "What the hell, mine not to reason why," and I got out the Yellow Pages and began checking the surplus stores. I finally found the rifles at Sunny's surplus store in Towson, Maryland. I went out the next morning and picked up two Mannlichers, and later sent Ross to buy two more. I notified Kendricks that I had them and he sent someone out to pick them up. I gave the courier three of the rifles and kept one for myself.

Chapter Ten

During the late summer and early fall of 1963, Guy Banister carefully spun the web that would ultimately trap Lee Harvey Oswald as the lone assassin of President John F. Kennedy. If Oswald had any misgivings about the things he was asked to do he put them aside, pleased to be gainfully employed and able to do things for Marina. Bizarre as some of his assignments were, he cooperated without question.

The only sour note in an otherwise well-orchestrated plot was sounded in the early morning of August 1, when Banister reported to Clay Shaw that the FBI had confiscated Kohly's weapons cache at Lake Pontchartrain. Eleven Cuban exiles were arrested in the raid, and Shaw and Banister were concerned about who might have leaked the information to the Bureau. Could the informant possibly be anyone who knew about their other plans?

They finally concluded that the FBI must have been tipped off by one of the new men sent down by Kendricks from Washington, none of whom knew anything about the assassination plot. They had no way of knowing that Lee Oswald, while cooperating with them, had turned in the report to earn his monthly stipend from the FBI.

One of the most masterfully stage-managed episodes involved a public altercation between Oswald and Carlos Bringuier, head of a Cuban exile group known as the Student Revolutionary Directorate. Banister told Oswald he wanted him to infiltrate Bringuier's organization to gain information about it and suggested that he do so by offering his services as an ex-Marine. He didn't tell Oswald that once he had done so an incident would be arranged in which Bringuier would discover him distributing his pro-Castro literature on the street. The result was predictable; the hot-tempered Bringuier would turn on Oswald, feeling that he had been betrayed.

As instructed, Oswald approached Bringuier and told him he was an ex-Marine who wanted to work against Castro. During this conversation Oswald promised to bring the Cuban his Marine Corp guerrilla warfare manual the next day, which he did. Although Lee didn't realize that he was being set up, it was now certain that Bringuier would recognize him when he found Oswald handing out FPCC literature.

Several days after the second meeting with Bringuier, Oswald went to the office at 544 Camp Street to pick up some pamphlets and get further instructions. Banister told him that Shaw had arranged for him to distribute literature at the entrance to the Trade Mart, where he would get maximum exposure. He told Oswald that he and Shaw were both pleased with his work, that his efforts had resulted in the addition of many names to their list of left-wing enemies.

Banister, meanwhile, got a message to Bringuier that someone was planning to distribute pro-Castro literature at the Trade Mart. Within the first hour after Oswald took up his position, he had handed out more than one hundred and fifty pamphlets and was still going strong when three Cubans jumped him. One of them was Carlos Bringuier. The altercation ended with Bringuier, his companions, and Lee Harvey Oswald in the custody of the New Orleans police department.

All four men were charged with disorderly conduct and disturbing the peace. However, Bringuier and his companions were released almost immediately, while Oswald was still held. Lee tried to reach Banister and, failing that, asked to see a man from the FBI field office the following morning. He was released after paying a ten dollar fine for distributing literature without a permit.

As a device to attract attention to Oswald's connection with the pro-Castro Fair Play for Cuba Committee, the episode succeeded beyond Banister's expectations. Not only did the local newspapers carry the story of the scuffle, but Lee was interviewed by a local radio personality, William Stuckey, on a program called "Latin Listening Post" and was invited to debate Bringuier at a later time.

When Oswald reported to Banister after his release from jail and his radio appearance, Guy expressed pleasure at the success he had achieved. He assured Oswald that his new prominence would lure many additional left-wing types into the open. Although Oswald was vaguely troubled by the image he was building as a supporter of Castro, he told himself that it was for a useful purpose. He was further comforted when Banister gave him a cash bonus.

On August 21, Oswald reported to Stuckey at the radio station for the scheduled debate with Bringuier. He found that Stuckey had invited another guest, Edward Butler, who was introduced as the executive director of the Information Council of the Americas. Throughout the broadcast the other participants tried to brand Lee a communist defector. Oswald was shocked that they had information he thought was known only to the CIA, and he squirmed uncomfortably as they spent the entire fifteen-minute program quizzing him about his Russian experiences, implying that he was a traitor.

He left the studio greatly depressed by the unexpected turn of events but was somewhat relieved when Banister sympathized with him, gave him another bonus, and told him that the FPCC project was over.

His apprehension returned shortly thereafter when Dave Ferrie asked him what he had done with his Italian Mannlicher. For some reason, Dave's face had actually turned ashen when Lee told him that before moving to New Orleans he had buried it in the back yard of his Dallas apartment building. Dave regained his composure when Lee added that he had protected the carbine from the elements by wrapping it in oily rags and placing it in a waterproof bag.

When Oswald asked Dave why he was interested in the carbine, he was told that they were looking for that particular type of weapon for a special operation out of the country. Lee said he would be happy to get it the next time he was in Dallas.

Oddly, the sense of urgency had disappeared, for Dave replied, "No, we don't need it yet. We just want to have it available in case we do."

There was something strange about the conversation; Lee wondered whether he should report it to the Bureau. He decided he had better dig a little first, but he had the uneasy feeling that something was not right.

Richard Carson Filmore was madder than hell. It was Thursday, July 18, 1963, and he was scheduled to begin his annual vacation at five the next day. Instead, he was now faced with the prospect of an extended assignment in the sweltering heat of the Louisiana bayou country.

Filmore had served for several years as an infantry captain in the Korean War and had received several decorations for his exploits. After that conflict he had become an agent for the Central Intelligence Agency and was working for the Company when his plane crashed in Baltimore in 1957. He had done some work for the CIA in the Orient and then had returned to the States to work on special assignments for Kendricks. Since the Bay of Pigs he had also managed to become an inside man for the Agency in Kennedy's new Defense Intelligence Agency.

Despite his objections to forgoing a vacation for an assignment in what he considered to be the left armpit of the universe, Filmore's attitude changed when Kendricks explained the mission.

"In short," Kendricks summarized, "we suspect Shaw's organization of planning to assassinate the president. Your job is to find out how, why, where, and, if possible, to become part of the plot."

"Assassinate the president? That's kind of wild, isn't it? Don't those guys work for us?"

"Yes, to both questions," Kendricks replied. "But the way things have come apart in the last year, anything can happen. Several weeks ago I got a request directly from Clay Shaw for several 7.35 millimeter Mannlicher rifles. I had Bob Porter pick them up for him and wouldn't have given it another thought except for one thing. Dave Ferrie, one of Shaw's men, flew all the way from New Orleans to Washington in a Piper Tri-Pacer to pick them up."

"My God, he could have walked faster!"

"Almost. Normally, he would have used a Company plane, which would have been a hell of a lot faster, but if I'm right I think I know why he didn't."

"Why?"

"Because he would have had to use one of the commercial airports in the Baltimore-Washington area, and he didn't. Our courier delivered it to the Campbell Company strip just off Route 7, north of Baltimore."

"I'll be damned! But for a simple pickup like that, what difference would it make?"

"I don't know. It seems unnecessary, and that's why it bothers me. There has to be some reason they handled the pickup the way they did and I want you to try to find out what it is. Take a flight out tonight for New Orleans. Register in one of the better hotels under your DIA code name of Joseph Kramer. I recommend the Royal Orleans. No one would expect one of our men to be in a fancy joint like that."

Filmore smirked in agreement.

"There are several specific things I want you to look into. First, we want to know who is running a paramilitary operation at Lake Pontchartrain. I suspect one of Kohly's United Organizations is running that facility, but don't know for sure. However, if it is Kohly's operation, and if it is tied in any way into an assassination attempt, we've got one hell of a can of worms. It could mean that the Company and all Company-related support groups in the United Organizations would be cited for conspiracy if our illustrious leader gets bumped off."

"After the Bay of Pigs, that's all it would take to really get the outfit hung," Filmore said.

"Precisely," Kendricks replied. "Now, if you decide it's safe to chance it, try to penetrate the Shaw/Banister organization. Your best bet probably would be to establish an identity as a member of the Minuteman organization, since they're all tied up with that outfit. Both Banister and Ferrie are active members, and I assume Clay Shaw is too."

"If it looks possible, I'll sure give it a try."

"And one other thing. Keep your eyes open for a chap by the name of Lee Harvey Oswald, code name Harvey. He did an overseas assignment for us in Russia and is now in New Orleans working for Shaw. We have rumblings from inside the Bureau that he may be an FBI informer. If so, I'd like to know."

"Will do, Chief. How am I to get hold of you?"

"Use my phone code number. They'll patch you through to anyplace I happen to be if it's important enough. Otherwise, just leave a message. Now, get your ass in gear. There's an Eastern flight that leaves in less than two hours from National."

On September 16, 1963, to develop an outside witness who could subsequently tie Oswald directly to the assassination plot, Dave Ferrie arranged a party at his apartment for a New Orleans insurance salesman named Perry Raymond Russo. The plan was to encourage Russo to overindulge in alcohol and then expose him to a conversation in which Bill Gemelo, posing as Oswald, and Clay Shaw, using his Clyde Bertrum pseudonym, would discuss the assassination plot.

Shaw was skittish about the plan, but Ferrie assured him that Russo, under the influence, would not take seriously anything that was said, nor was he the type who would report it if he did. The important thing was to fix the conversation in his memory so that he would recall it when it gained significance because of subsequent events.

The episode went as planned. Ferrie and Gemelo kept Russo's glass filled, and by the time the other guests had departed Russo was in an alcoholic haze. For the next half-hour, without stirring from his chair, he listened to a carefully rehearsed conversation between Gemelo, Ferrie, and Clay Shaw, a shadowy figure he would later recall meeting under the name of Clyde Bertrum.

The conversation was replete with such phrases as "triangulation of fire," "assassination teams," and "how great it would be if the country were free of the traitor." It was carefully constructed to sound like idle speculation, and for five years Perry Raymond Russo would have no conscious recollection of it. But one day it would be brought into vivid focus under the influence of sodium pentothal.

As he entered the courtyard of his house after leaving the party, Clay Shaw heard the telephone ringing. Walking briskly across the garden, he slid open one of the large glass doors and grabbed the wall phone in the kitchen. It was Guy Banister.

"I'm glad I caught you," Banister said. "I was afraid you might not be back from the party. I wanted to let you know that I've discovered who it was that tipped off the FBI on the arms cache out at the Lake."

"I hope it wasn't one of our people," Shaw said.

"Well, yes and no. It seems I made a mistake on a man I brought in several weeks ago."

Banister paused and Shaw said, "Please continue."

"Well, this man came to the office and introduced himself as Joseph Kramer. He said he was a Minuteman, and claimed to be a friend of the Minuteman president, your friend DePugh. He also carried papers indicating a background that didn't stop, among them credentials showing that he was a former combat infantry captain, skilled in guerrilla tactics. His record also included extensive training in our new special forces."

"He sounds like a real winner," Shaw said. "What makes you suspect him?"

"Well, even at the time I must confess I thought he was too good to be true. In fact, I had him checked out through the Bureau and got confirmation that he was everything he said he was. That held up until today, when I received a confidential report from one of my friends in the Director's office that a covert operator down here—a man named Richard Filmore—

had filed a startling report. He said Filmore reported he was working under cover with a group of Cuban exiles on a plot to assassinate the president on September 26."

"What! Who the hell is Filmore? That name doesn't ring a bell."

"It didn't with me, either. But, on a hunch, to get a set of his fingerprints I had one of the bellhops over at the Royal Orleans, where Kramer is staying, take a water glass out of his bathroom after he went down for breakfast this morning. I just got a report back from my friend at the Bureau that Filmore is none other than Joseph Kramer."

"I'll be damned," Shaw said. "It's a good thing we set up the decoy operation for September 26 or we might not have smoked him out. Well, let's see what develops in the next few days. Meanwhile, keep cool and give some thought to what we're going to do about Filmore."

Richard C. Filmore, on September 16, 1963, was a worried man. After arriving in New Orleans, he had succeeded too well in gaining the confidence of Guy Banister. Kendricks had helped by arranging for the Department of Defense to supply a dossier on one Joe Kramer to the FBI, so that when Banister queried the Bureau they confirmed Kramer's authenticity. Coupled with his pretense that he was a Minuteman with connections to the president of that organization, it was enough to cause Banister to welcome him with open arms.

It had not taken him long to confirm Kendricks' suspicion that an assassination plot was afoot, but Filmore hadn't bargained for his own selection as the executioner of the "fall guy" on the assassination team. The operation was scheduled to occur in Washington on September 26th, and his was to be a major role in the elaborate getaway plan.

Filmore had to play along to avoid blowing his cover, but he got increasingly nervous after several unsuccessful attempts to communicate with Kendricks, who, he was told, was out of the country. Finally, frantic, he notified his parallel contact in the DIA. When he finally did get Kendricks he was reassured that something would be done. But, when nothing happened for several more days, he became convinced that he was on the expendable list. He was.

Filmore was not about to participate in an attempt to assassinate the president, but without help from the Company he didn't know how to avoid it. He knew that it would be fatal to contact the local FBI field office because Banister, with his connections, would know about it in minutes. He didn't know that the September 26 plot was simply a dry run, or that because of it his cover had already been blown and that Banister knew his true identity.

Filmore's last desperate official effort to warn of the impending plot and get himself off the hook was made on the morning of September 19, when he posted a personal, air mail, special delivery letter to FBI Director J. Edgar Hoover, explaining in detail the proposed plan of a group of Cuban exiles, along with American mercenaries, to assassinate the president in Washington on September 26. By September 20 paranoia had begun to seize him. Even his DIA contact had evoked no action.

His fear mounted that night when he had another meeting with the assassination team, which consisted of four other men —two Cubans and two Americans. Later, in the hotel bar, Filmore had several quick drinks to steady his nerves while he attempted to plan his escape. He had given up trying to get help from his official contacts in Washington, D.C.

As he sat there trying to figure out what to do, he was distracted by a disturbance in the lobby. Through the glass paneling of the cocktail lounge he saw a man being escorted from the lobby by two policemen. As he watched, he formed the seed of an idea that might save him and the president. By late that evening, the idea had grown to a full-scale plan, and he went to bed confident of what he had to do.

The following morning, Filmore arose at dawn and, by eight o'clock, had checked out of the hotel and caught a cab to the airport. By nine he was checked in on the first Delta flight to Dallas, waiting for his flight to depart and inspecting the crowd for possible pursuers. He failed to notice the swarthy Cuban who, from a distance, was tracking his every movement.

Once in Dallas, Filmore immediately went to a pay phone and

dialed a check-in number given the team the night before by Banister. The party on the other end was to provide the time and rendezvous point for the assassination team's flight to Washington on the morning of September 22. They were to have several days in Washington to set up, prior to the president's return to the city.

His instructions were delivered routinely, and when he hung up he felt totally safe. Now that he had checked in, he believed he had at least twenty-four hours to get out of the country and into Mexico. Picking up his bag, he proceeded from the phone booth to the American Airlines desk in the main concourse and purchased a ticket to El Paso. When the plane was called just prior to 10:30 he climbed aboard, still completely unaware of the Cuban close on his heels. In flight, he had two Bloody Marys and a light lunch and arrived in El Paso confident that within an hour he'd be safely across the Mexican border.

The Cuban seated across the aisle several rows behind Filmore had forgone the drinks, but he ate lunch voraciously. By the time the big plane reached the ramp at the El Paso Airport, Filmore had unbuckled his seat belt, pulled his bag from under the seat, grabbed his raincoat from the overhead rack, and proceeded rapidly up the aisle. Although other passengers immediately began crowding the aisle, the heavy-set Cuban managed to stay almost within reach of him.

Filmore finally noticed him as he was walking down the ramp towards the taxi stand and, for the first time since leaving New Orleans, sensed danger. The Cuban, seeing he'd been spotted, increased his pace to close the distance between them. Filmore ran to the first cab, leaped in, and said, "Get going, fast. Take me to the downtown bus station." As he slammed the door, he pushed the lock down. As the driver pulled hurriedly away, the Cuban was tugging futilely at the door.

Looking back through the rear window, Filmore could see the swarthy Cuban gesturing wildly to the driver of the next cab in line, pointing toward them, and then jumping in. Filmore promised the driver a ten dollar tip if he could lose the pursuing vehicle and then leaned back in his seat, trying to decide what to do.

His original idea had been to create a large enough incident on the Mexican side of the border to publicize and expose the assassination plot while outside the jurisdiction of the U.S. authorities. It was now obvious that Banister knew he was deserting, and he assumed they intended to kill him. But if that was the case he couldn't go into Mexico without encountering Banister's Mexican allies, who, by now, were probably sitting in Juarez waiting for him, in the event he crossed the border.

Out of desperation, he decided on an alternate plan that would give him a breather, preferably safe in the hands of local police authorities. If he could remain free of federal officials, he might be able to tell his story. Through the rear window he saw the other cab slowly gaining on them.

"If you can't lose that cab, take me to the largest bank in the city. And make it fast," he told the driver.

"Sí, señor," replied the unruffled Chicano driver. A moment later he veered off the highway into a series of alleys and side streets that he negotiated at breakneck speed. For a brief moment, Filmore thought they had lost his pursuer, but as they pulled onto a main street, he again spotted the Cuban's cab relentlessly following. The driver saw him, too, and screeched to a halt in front of the State National Bank of El Paso.

Filmore grabbed his bag and raincoat, threw a ten dollar bill on the front seat, and sprinted across the sidewalk to the bank's main entrance. A hundred feet behind, the pursuing cab pulled to the curb and the Cuban jumped out. Filmore quickly walked to a counter where he could watch the entrance, grabbed a deposit slip from the rack, and started writing. As he stood there, one of the bank guards stopped a few feet away, facing him. Filmore glanced quickly at the door and saw that the Cuban was about to enter. Reacting instantly, he pulled his automatic from the spring holster under his arm and, under the eyes of the startled guard, pointed the weapon at the ceiling and fired two shots in rapid succession.

As glass showered around them from a shattered fluorescent fixture, the guard stood transfixed, his mouth wide open. He didn't move as Filmore calmly put the gun back in its holster, picked up his bag, and walked to the entrance. He sat down on his suitcase and waited to see what would happen. The Cuban, anxious to avoid the chaos that would certainly follow, had disappeared around the corner of the bank. Meanwhile, the guards had regained their composure and rushed Filmore, disarming him quickly while the manager called the police. He submitted to them quietly.

On the morning of Sunday, September 22, Attorney General Robert Kennedy called the president at Hyannis to tell him about a confidential report he had received from the Defense Intelligence Agency outlining a plot against his life. Unlike the countless similar crank reports they had received, he said, this one apparently came from an agent who worked for the CIA.

The most unaccountable aspect of the report, Bobby told his brother, was the information that some time after the initial report was received the man who had reported it had walked into a federal bank in El Paso and deliberately gotten himself arrested by firing a pistol into the ceiling.

Why, the president asked, would the man have done anything so ridiculous?

The attorney general replied that the report stated the man had been afraid for his life and wanted to be in the custody of local authorities. He had insisted that he was an unwilling part of an organized conspiracy, which he was afraid to report to a federal agency. He had slipped up when he picked a federal reserve bank, because that immediately involved the FBI.

Robert Kennedy signed off after assuring the president that he would check the report out thoroughly, particularly in view of the president's approaching trip to Texas. He had scarcely replaced the telephone in its cradle when it began ringing. It was the office of Robert A. Morgenthau, United States Attorney for the southern district of New York. The caller reported that they had just confirmed that Mario Kohly would deliver the counterfeit peso plates to the "printer," Secret Service Agent William Martin, alias Harris, on Tuesday, October 1. Arrangements had been made for the transfer of the plates and the arrest of Kohly by Treasury agents in the lobby of the Waldorf Astoria Hotel. Bobby thanked the man and then made another phone call to instruct the Secret Service to make certain that not only Kohly but all the participants in the counterfeiting were arrested simultaneously.

Then he called the president, thankful that he could give him some good news for a change.

On September 30, Guy Banister sat at his desk absorbed in a report from Jack Ruby. Earlier in the week, he had instructed Jack to create a series of incidents in Dallas that would lay an unmistakable trail to Lee Harvey Oswald as the lone assassin of the president, if that action became necessary. Ruby's report described the successful completion of one of these incidents on Friday the 27th.

Banister had given Ruby the name of a wealthy, aristocratic Cuban exile, Señora Sylvia Odio, whose parents were both political prisoners of Castro. Señora Odio lived in Dallas and was known to be a member of the Cuban Revolutionary Junta (JURE), another of Kohly's United Organizations. Ruby instructed Jim Hart, Bill Gemelo, and Charles Hunter to visit Señora Odio, ostensibly to solicit funds on behalf of the Junta. Gemelo was to use the alias Leon Oswald; Hunter was called Leopoldo; and Hart used the name Angelo.

The deception worked perfectly. Señora Odio's sister answered the door and quickly disappeared inside the house. The trio pressured Señora Odio heavily on behalf of the exile groups, and she soon became very suspicious. As they were leaving, Hart commented that time was short and that, although they had just arrived from New Orleans, they had to leave again on a trip but would be back in touch shortly.

The next morning, to indelibly cement the trio's visit in her mind, Charles Hunter, using his alias of Leopoldo, telephoned Señora Odio and told her that Leon Oswald was an ex-Marine and a crack shot. He said that Leon complained that Cubans lacked courage because, by all rights, the president should be assassinated for letting the boys down at the Bay of Pigs.

Señora Odio became very upset when Hunter suggested

that Leon should be permitted to go ahead and carry out such a plan, which he could easily do. Sensing her nervousness, Hunter changed his tactics and remarked, "Of course, it would be just as easy for Leon to kill Fidel Castro. He can do anything . . . you know, like getting into the Cuban underground. He has all the right connections."

Señora Odio had shakily replied, "Please, Sir, don't contact me again. I'm really not interested in these matters or in a position to do anything to help you."

She would put all memory of the incident out of her mind until November 22, 1963, when the newspapers reported the arrest of a suspected presidential assassin, Lee Harvey Oswald.

Banister read the report with satisfaction. All of the pieces were falling into place. The day before, the *New Orleans States-Item* had carried a front page story of the official announcement that President Kennedy would make a swing through Texas sometime in November. Clay Shaw's information had been right. If the assassination became necessary, the mountain would come to Mohammed, and Mohammed would be ready.

Chapter Eleven

In the house on Hazelwood Avenue, October 1 was greeted with a mixture of relief and satisfaction. Everyone on the team was pleased with the counterfeit peso plates. All the minute flaws had been corrected and the registration was perfect. I was confident that the currency printed from the plates would be absolutely undetectable as counterfeit, even with sophisticated electronic scanners. All that now remained was to await the pickup man who was to deliver the plates to Kohly in New York.

Meanwhile, I couldn't shake my doubts about Kohly's "printer." In fact, I was so dubious about William Harris that while we waited, I suggested to Ross that we hide the proofs, the ink drawings, and other paraphernalia used to make the actual plates. Ross agreed and, while Cynthia looked on in dismay, we removed the refrigerator door, unscrewed fifty-four fasteners that held the plastic lining, stored the material, and screwed them back in again. Ross then hung the door back on the refrigerator.

Before closing it, Ross grabbed a cold beer and commented,

"No one will ever find that stuff in there."

Cynthia, who had been sitting patiently while we worked on the door, spoke up. "Why don't you guys knock off tonight and go out and celebrate. The job's done, and you've earned it."

It sounded like a good idea, but before Ross or I had a chance to say anything a car pulled into the rear lot. Mario's courier had arrived.

During the next few minutes, we gave detailed instructions to Mario's right-hand man, Bill Grosh, a seasoned mercenary, on how to handle the plates so they wouldn't get damaged in transit. Within twenty minutes of his arrival, he was headed north.

Ross and I spent the rest of the day in the basement cleaning up the chaos created during the last final push. I was interrupted about 5:15, when the telephone rang.

Cynthia picked it up in the kitchen, then called me to come and get it upstairs. She held her hand over the mouthpiece as she handed it to me, saying, "It's New York. I think there's a problem."

It was Kohly. "Bob, I'm with Harris, the printer. He wants to know if it would be possible for you to catch a plane to New York this evening and meet with us. He's evidently encountering some problems with colors."

It was all wrong, and a cold chill went up my spine. "Encountering problems with colors? Padre, how?"

"He said he needs advice on blending the colors that go on the front of the document."

"That's nonsense, Mario," I said. "He has the original sample we provided him. There shouldn't be a problem duplicating that. Anyway, there's no way I can come up. Maybe tomorrow, padre, but there's no conceivable way I could get to New York tonight."

"O.K., chico. He wanted me to ask. I'll tell him what you said."

"O.K., Mario. But watch your ass. I have a damn funny feeling about this whole thing. As I said before, I think your printer stinks."

"Right, chico," he said and hung up.

Ross, who had come up from the lab, was sitting at the

kitchen table, beer in hand. I told him about Mario's call and suggested that, rather than go out, we have dinner at home and stay near the phone.

Ross, sensing how worried I was, cheerfully agreed. "How would you like some spaghetti?" he asked. "I'll have a hamburger." It was a great concession, because Ross loved spaghetti but was allergic to tomatoes.

By nine o'clock, it had been dark for nearly two hours. I still hadn't heard anything more from Mario and was growing more concerned every minute. Around 9:30, the spaghetti was almost ready. Cynthia had fed the children and sent them to bed. The three of us were finishing cocktails, and Ross had just started to fry his hamburger when we were startled by a loud knock at the breezeway door.

I looked at Ross, who said, "I didn't hear a car come up the drive, did you?"

"Hell, no," I replied.

Cynthia went over, flipped on the spotlight covering the rear lot, and reported that there were no cars in sight.

The banging resumed, even louder, and I said, "It doesn't sound like a neighbor. Well, there's not a damn thing to do but answer it. With all the lights on, they know we're here."

When I opened the door two men were standing in the breezeway, one slightly to the rear of the other in the shadows.

The one in front identified himself saying, "We're with the Secret Service. We're looking for Mr. Robert Porter, a woman by the name of Cynthia, and a Ross Allen."

"Come in, gentlemen," I said politely. "I'm Robert Porter."

As the first man stepped into the kitchen, the second one appeared out of the shadows, carrying a Thompson submachine gun. I stared at it, and he dropped the muzzle slightly so that it wouldn't point directly at my stomach. Two more men stepped out of the darkness and followed him through the door. Obviously, the house was surrounded.

I closed the door, and the first man to enter produced his credentials and handed them to me. "I'm William Holt, U.S. Treasury Department, from the Secret Service office here in Baltimore.

Ross steadfastly cooked his hamburger, and when Holt looked at him he casually flipped it over as you would a pancake. Ross and I both grinned, and I asked, "Well, Mr. Holt, what can I do for you?"

He looked absolutely nonplussed by our attitude. "We have warrants to arrest all of you and orders to search these premises. I'd also like to ask you a few questions."

I said, "Go right ahead. You don't mind if I finish my dinner, do you?" and sat down.

He gave me a puzzled look, then he said, "You know damn well why we're here."

As I put a fork full of spaghetti in my mouth, I replied, "Why don't you get a beer out of the refrigerator and tell me about it."

He was losing his patience, and after glaring at me he turned to the two men standing behind him and snapped, "Well, don't just stand there, get the hell on with it."

They convulsed into motion, but I stopped them by saying, "Be careful searching this floor. There are two young children living here and we don't want them scared out of their wits."

Holt looked as if he didn't believe what was happening to him, but he backed me up. "Well, you heard him. Move!"

"Yes, Sir," they answered in unison, heading quickly out of the room.

"About the beer?" I remarked, turning to Holt.

He said, exasperated, "Damn it, Porter. I don't drink on duty," and sat down in the adjoining chair.

I turned around to Ross, who was still cooking and flipping his incinerated hamburger. "I think you'd better take it off, Ross."

"You're right, I don't think I'm really hungry." He turned off the flame. "I'll just have a beer." He looked at the Secret Service man for approval.

Holt nodded and Ross walked over to the refrigerator, opened the door, grabbed a beer, then slammed it shut. He opened the bottle and sat down at the table opposite Holt and myself.

Cynthia, with Holt's permission, went to her daughter's room to tell her not to worry about the men searching the house.

Holt turned to me in frustration and asked, "Can I see you privately . . . somewhere?"

"Sure. Let's go down to the electronics lab. You haven't checked there yet." I left my spaghetti and we descended to the basement, leaving Ross and Cynthia and the other agents upstairs.

As we walked through the library I said to Holt, "I think you'd better have this," and reached up to the top shelf of one of the bookcases to take down my Walther.

Out of the corner of my eye, I saw Holt make a move toward his gun and quickly exclaimed, "Don't worry." As I handed it to him I said, "Be careful, it's loaded."

He relaxed. "Sorry. You understand, we've got to be extremely careful. Sometimes those things go off!"

"I understand completely," I said. "What I can't understand is why in the hell this whole thing is happening. It's obvious that the government's right hand doesn't know what the hell the left one's doing."

Looking slightly embarrassed, he commented, "We're under direct orders to deliver you into the custody of the United States District Court in New York as of tomorrow."

At that I got upset for the first time and repeated, "New York?"

"Yes, Sir." Then he spoke quietly. "Off the record, we picked up your associate Kohly late this afternoon trying to pass your counterfeit plates to one of our agents."

I said, "Are you telling me that little shit Harris is really a Secret Service agent?"

"That's right," he replied. "By the name of William Martin. We have Kohly, we have you, and we have the plates. Now we want the original negatives and artwork. We know they're here, damn it, so you might as well give them up."

I hesitated and then, acting upon impulse, I said, "I believe all that material was delivered."

"To whom?" he shouted.

At that moment the phone started to ring, so I looked at Holt and asked, "You don't mind if I answer it, do you? It's obvious your agency is the one that had it tapped."

He looked at me blankly and said, "Go ahead. I'll listen

in on an extension."

"There's one on the next lab bench," I said, pointing.

He nodded and I walked into my office and picked up the phone.

It was Bill Grosh, sounding worried. "I haven't heard from the old man. I think something's wrong. I called a friend at the Waldorf when I got back to D.C., and he said someone matching Mario's description had been picked up by federal agents in the lobby."

I said, "I've heard the same thing. I understand they're looking for all of us. I would recommend that you give yourself up."

He said, "What the hell happened? What are you talking about?"

"I've been told that Mario is in custody and I assume it won't be long before we are, too. In which case, since we really haven't done anything illegal, I would recommend that you go to your attorney and place yourself in his custody until the authorities pick you up. That way you'll be thoroughly protected."

He sensed that something was wrong at my end and his voice became guarded. "Thanks," he said, "I'll take it under advisement," and hung up.

Holt and I returned to the kitchen, where Cynthia and Ross were calmly cleaning up the dinner dishes, and sat down at the kitchen table. Holt sent one of his agents to search the huge basement, and the man soon came back up the stairs.

"My God, Bill!" he said. "It'd take us a year to go through all that stuff, and then we'd probably never find what we're looking for."

I said, "I have to agree. If the stuff you are looking for was here, that is."

Holt turned to me and said, "Mr. Porter, I think you'd all better come downtown with us."

I decided to try a little cooperation. "Agent Holt, these two people really had nothing at all to do with this operation. I'm prepared to make a full statement. The woman must stay here with her children, and Mr. Allen is just an employee of mine working on electronics projects."

Grudgingly, he said, "All right. I'll accept that for now, but I'm going to leave an agent in the house. Meanwhile, you come downtown and make your statement."

Half an hour later I was in the Secret Service office in downtown Baltimore, being fingerprinted and photographed. After half an hour of conversation with Holt, it was clear that there was no longer any point in concealing the location of the additional plates, negatives, and artwork. Someone had informed the Secret Service about our operations, and we had been under surveillance for months. I told Holt I would surrender the material and, less than an hour and a half after we had left, we were back at the house taking apart the refrigerator door.

When the agents pulled out the cache, Holt said, "Well, I'll be damned. And you offered me a bottle of beer, knowing the stuff was right there."

I said, "Well, there's nothing like keeping hot currency on ice."

Even the agents laughed, and things became relaxed. Holt said, "Cynthia can stay here tonight with the children. We'll pick her up and take her downtown in the morning after they leave for school. We'll also take your word for Mr. Allen, but I'm afraid we're going to have to take you downtown tonight. Is there anything you want?"

Since it was now about two o'clock in the morning, I said, "Well, you did interrupt my dinner. . . . I'm still hungry."

So on the way back downtown we stopped at the White Coffee Pot at North and Charles, where we had sandwiches while we talked unofficially about the operation. I was sorry I hadn't had an opportunity to tell Kendricks what had happened, but I was sure that Ross would, so I wasn't too perturbed. I found myself, in the wee hours of the morning of October 2, a VIP prisoner in the Baltimore City Jail. For four hours I had a cell to myself.

At 8:30 the next morning Holt picked me up and drove me out to the Eastern Office of the First National Bank. It was located on Route 40 and was where I had stashed the old, out-of-date pesos in safety deposit boxes. By 9:30, we had stopped by Hazelwood Avenue to pick up Cynthia, and she and I were in the federal courthouse waiting to be arraigned. I was thankful that Ross had already called a good friend of mine, Fred E. Weisgal, who was, at the time, considered the best criminal attorney in Baltimore. Fred appeared at the Federal Marshall's office around ten o'clock, just prior to our hearing, and Cynthia and I were both grateful and relieved.

He said, "Don't worry. I have instructions to take care of everything." Within an hour we had both been arraigned and charged with the making of counterfeit plates, conspiracy to counterfeit, and a host of other miscellaneous charges that Morgenthau and the attorney general hoped to make stick. Fred arranged to have Cynthia released on her own recognizance and for a $25,000 bond to be posted for me. When we walked out of the Federal Building, we were besieged by reporters and photographers. Fred whispered in my ear, "Just act normally and say nothing."

I nodded.

We walked up Fayette Street to his office, and after he had disposed of the press he said, "I'll take care of all official statements. If you get cornered by the press, refer them to me."

"O.K. Any other instructions?"

"No," he replied. We turned into a building at the corner of Charles and took the elevator to his offices. He asked Cynthia to sit in the waiting room, explaining, "I've got something to discuss with Bob." Inside, he closed the door and said, "You'd better get in touch with Washington right away."

"Will do. First, let me ask you a question. In your honest opinion, what's the upshot of this going to be?"

"I would assume Morgenthau will want to try you in New York, and we'll stop him if we can. Maybe your friends in D.C. can have some pressure put on there. Now, Kohly is another matter. If what you say about the Kennedys and the missile crisis is true, Morgenthau probably has instructions to give him the chair."

"That's not a goddamn bit funny," I said.

"I didn't say it was funny," he replied. "Just understand that the next few months are going to be one hell of a rat race. The only sure chance you've got of staying out of jail and, for that matter, alive, is if the president contracts an incurable case of the plague."

"Thanks a lot," I said.

"Keep in touch," he urged and turned around to his dictating machine. In the outer office, I grabbed Cynthia's arm and we took off. Ross was waiting in the car just outside the entrance. After we had started up Charles Street, he said, "Thanks for getting me off the hook, ol' buddy."

"Don't mention it. They probably know you're as guilty as sin, but they can't prove it and I had to have someone out operating."

"Like I said, thanks a lot," he retorted. "Anyway, as you might have guessed, I got hold of Kendricks. He's alerted Kohly's people in Miami and New Orleans. Unfortunately, however, not until after they had read about his arrest in the morning papers."

"Yep. I imagine they're a lot of confused people. Well, I guess it's back to the video tape recorder."

"Why not?" Cynthia and Ross said in unison.

It was one A.M. on the same day when Guy Banister finally reached Clay. He had been trying for an hour, but Shaw had been to the theater and had stopped by Brennan's for a late supper. He was barely asleep when the phone rang.

"What's so important that you had to call me this late at night?" he said with irritation. "Couldn't it wait until morning?"

"Clay, when you hear what I've got to report, you tell me," Banister replied. "Kohly was arrested in New York this evening by the Secret Service and charged with conspiracy, counterfeiting, and everything else they could think of."

"Dear Jesus!" Shaw whispered.

"That's not the worst of it. Less than two hours ago, they busted the whole operation in Baltimore, confiscating everything that could be used as evidence."

"Damn those bastards," Clay said. "What do you think will happen?"

"I understand they'll all be arraigned tomorrow. I think

140

the administration will try and throw everything in the book at them."

"My God. All of Kohly's work . . . his organizations . . . Guy, what do you know about Johnson?"

"Johnson? You mean Vice-president Johnson?"

"Yes, of course. Lyndon Johnson."

"Nothing, really, Sir. Although I understand he's predictable, conservative, and won't go off half-cocked. And he sure as hell has no love for the communists."

Shaw was quiet for a moment, then said, "Thank God Kendricks and Kohly and the Secret Service don't know what we've been planning down here. Start the machinery ticking. We haven't got anything else left."

"Right, Sir," Banister said. As he hung up he glanced at the clock on the wall. It was exactly one hour and six minutes into October 2, 1963. In fifty-one days, Lyndon Baines Johnson would be the new president of the United States.

Chapter Twelve

Several days earlier, on September 24, Lee Harvey Oswald had endured another angry dispute with his wife. Marina apparently was not happy with her husband. Their arguments had become more frequent and violent over the past month, ever since his public altercation with Carlos Bringuier and the other Cubans. Lee, who seemed to be devoted to Marina, would endure her tirades as long as possible but ultimately he would begin shouting, too. It must have been a relief when Marina announced that she had decided to take little June and go back to Irving, Texas, a small town on the edge of Dallas. Her friend Ruth Paine had invited Marina and June to come and live with her.

Lee was probably saddened by the thought of separation but didn't object, feeling that if he and Marina were apart for a while it might help. At least he wouldn't have to invent any more explanations for his activities. But her absence also made it easy for him to say "yes" when Banister asked him to go on his first real mission, a trip to Mexico. He was to meet a man named Maurice Gatlin, Sr., in Monterrey, who would give him further instructions.

Now, while waiting for Ferrie to complete his checklist on the small twin-engine airplane, Lee clutched the briefcase Banister had given him and reviewed what he had been told to do. With the Tourist Card switch in Houston, and the phone call he had to make, he wouldn't arrive in Mexico until the following day.

Lee Oswald was unaware that his Mexican assignment was actually another complex scheme Banister had conceived to make it appear that Lee wanted to return to the Soviet Union. The elaborate plot required that Oswald switch identity cards with Carlos Rigel and then fly to Canada. Rigel, meanwhile, would remain in Mexico posing as Oswald. Once the plan had been completed, a convincing record would exist that Oswald spent most of a week in Mexico, visiting two embassies and attempting to secure visas to Havana and the Soviet Union.

Following Banister's instructions to the letter, Carlos Rigel watched Lee Oswald come through the main entrance of the Continental Trailways bus station in Houston, Texas. Ferrie had flown Lee into Houston from New Orleans late that afternoon. After dinner at the airport, he had caught a cab to the Trailways station.

The terminal clock said 9:45 P.M. In two hours and fifteen minutes, it would be September 25. Rigel observed that Oswald had followed instructions and was carrying the briefcase and luggage identical to that which Rigel had purchased that afternoon. As Carlos watched, Oswald looked around, then walked directly to the telephone booths and entered one that had an "out of order" sign taped over the coin slots. Oswald stripped off the sign, inserted a coin, dialed, and engaged in a brief conversation. Then he removed a folded envelope from under the telephone. Reaching into his pocket, Oswald pulled out a similar envelope and shoved it into the same space, then replaced the "out of order" sign.

"So far, so good," Rigel thought, as Oswald went into the men's room. Rigel walked hurriedly to the booth, snatched off the sign, retrieved the envelope, and opened it. It contained a standard FM-8 fifteen-day Mexican Tourist Card. It was numbered 24085, made out to Lee Harvey Oswald, commercial photographer. Smiling with satisfaction, Rigel found a seat in the terminal lobby and awaited the departure of the Continental Trailways bus to Laredo, Texas at 2:35 A.M.

Just after noon on September 25, Bill Gemelo—Lee Harvey Oswald the second—walked into the Selective Service Office in Austin, Texas. Posing as Oswald, he inquired about his draft status and said enough to focus attention on the real Lee Harvey Oswald's dishonorable discharge and trip to Russia. He was sure he had made enough of an impression so he would be remembered, and he was satisfied that the selective service personnel would identify him without hesitation as the authentic Oswald.

The plan was for Lee to meet Gatlin in Monterrey, exchange briefcases, and get his instructions. On September 26, Guy Banister reported to Clay Shaw that everything was going according to schedule. Oswald had met Gatlin, exchanged the briefcases, and was now en route to Canada.

On September 27, Carlos Rigel, who actually bore very little resemblance to either William Gemelo or the real Lee Oswald, climbed off a bus in Mexico City at 10 A.M. and walked the block to the Hotel del Commercio. After checking in and cleaning up, he took a bus across town to the Cuban Embassy, located at 160 Calle Francisco Marquess.

As he entered the consulate, his picture was snapped through a telephoto lens from a hidden position across the street. This surveillance was part of normal CIA routine and would be repeated when he entered the Russian Embassy the following day.

During the two embassy visits Carlos Rigel acted out his assignment with great skill, ensuring that the visit to Mexico City of a man named Lee Harvey Oswald would be engraved in the minds of those who met him. The visit to the Cuban embassy was a particular triumph because there he even managed an extended verbal confrontation with Mrs. Silvia Tirado de Turan, a Mexican employee in the visa office. When she told him that it was impossible to go to Cuba without first obtaining a visa to enter Russia, he pretended such indignation that Mrs. Turan finally called the consul, Señor Asque, who continued the heated argument with Rigel for several minutes.

Rigel was delighted to relate his success to Banister on the telephone. Guy told him that Oswald would be in Monterrey to exchange Tourist Cards once again following his Canadian delivery. The plan would allow both men to get back to the U.S. by October 3.

In Mexico City, on Monday, September 30, Carlos Rigel purchased thirty dollars and twenty cents' worth of international exchange orders to pay for the Mexican Transporte del Norte bus trip from Mexico City to Laredo, via Monterrey.

Following Banister's instructions, he had asked the Viages Travel Agency to reserve a seat for him on the 8:30 bus on October 2, under the name of H. O. Lee. He was also instructed to make another reservation in the name of Lee Harvey Oswald, on a Transporte Frontera leaving at 1 P.M. the same day for Nuevo Laredo, which he was not to use. Therefore, October 2 found Carlos in seat number 12 on the 8:30 bus, where he maintained a low profile, speaking to no one. Arrangements for the Tourist Card exchange in Monterrey were tight, because there was only a half-hour stopover. Banister had given instructions to make the exchange in the last toilet stall of the main men's room.

When the bus stopped in Monterrey, Rigel hurried off and made a beeline for the men's room. Inside the last stall he pulled off the toilet paper roll, rolled up the envelope with the Tourist Card and bus ticket and shoved it into the cardboard tube. He put the roll back in the holder and took up a post by the washbasin, pretending to comb his hair. Oswald finally hurried into the room and ducked into the last stall just as the bus was being called. He reappeared almost immediately, walked straight past Carlos, and disappeared through the swinging door. Carlos tucked the comb into his pocket, walked back to the end stall, entered, and retrieved the Tourist Card left by Oswald bearing the name of Alex Hidel.

Walking casually back into the lobby, he could see Oswald at the gate, ticket in hand, boarding the bus. When it had pulled out Carlos went over to a phone booth and placed a collect call to Banister in New Orleans. When Guy answered, Carlos reported that the mission had been accomplished. Banister told him to proceed to Dallas and report to Ruby within the next few days.

Oswald had called New Orleans on October 2, reported the successful completion of his trip to Canada, and received detailed instructions from Banister on the exchange of documents at the Monterrey bus terminal. He was also informed that plans had changed, and he should go directly to Dallas instead of returning to New Orleans. On arrival, he was to check in at the YMCA, where he would be contacted by a man named Roberto Navarro.

Lee was relieved when he had made the Tourist Card exchange without incident and was safely aboard the bus for Laredo. But even more exhilarating was the knowledge that he was going to Dallas rather than New Orleans. In a matter of hours, he would be back with Marina.

As the bus left the outskirts of Monterrey, Oswald looked down at his ticket envelope. He was caught up short when he saw that it was made out in the name of H. O. Lee. Quickly extracting the Tourist Card, he breathed a sigh of relief when he saw that it bore his correct name.

Pocketing both items, he settled back and began reading a paperback. After half an hour, observing the annoyance of his seatmate, he apologized and switched off the light, but he had already made an indelible impression on his disgruntled fellow passenger.

Oswald slept until they reached the border, where the immigration officials boarded and asked the passengers to present their Tourist Cards. The immigration officer passed down the aisle, checking Tourist Cards against a sheet attached to a clip board. When he got to Lee he studied his Tourist Card carefully, frowning as he compared it to his manifest sheet.

Finally, the official spoke directly to Lee. "Señor, would you please kindly step off the bus."

Oswald, still only half awake, started to object, and the immigration official said flatly, "Señor, either get off the bus or we will take you off the bus."

Oswald was near panic as he stepped into the street and stood waiting for the immigration man to finish checking the balance of the Tourist Cards. Finally the official left the bus and said, "Come with me, señor."

"What seems to be the trouble?" Lee asked.

"It's very simple, señor," was the reply. "Your Tourist Card does not match the manifest sheet. You're Mr. H. O. Lee, no? Or, are you Mr. Lee Oswald?"

"Oh," Lee said, "I'm sure I can explain."

"Explain it to my superior," said the official.

As Oswald followed him into the customs building he realized how the mistake had been made. The tourist agent who had made up the reservation had mistaken his first name as his last.

After a lengthy discussion, the immigration officials acknowledged the simple error and Lee was allowed to reboard the bus. He would have been more upset if he had known that the simple mistake had been deliberate. The Mexican officials would now readily remember him recrossing the border into the U.S. The records would show that Oswald had been in Mexico and had visited two embassies in an effort to defect to Cuba.

At 1:35 A.M., the Transporte del Norte bus crossed the international bridge into Texas. After a depressing hour in hot, barren, dusty Laredo, he boarded a Greyhound bus for Dallas, arriving there eleven and one-half hours later. It was now 2:30 P.M. on October 3.

At almost the same hour the first carload of Banister's men arrived in Dallas from New Orleans. For their headquarters, Ruby had rented a house at 3128 Harlandale Avenue in the Oak Cliff section of Dallas, just two miles from his own apartment. They had just seven weeks to plan, prepare, and execute the crime of the century.

Guy Banister had wasted no time in implementing the operation after getting the go-ahead, and if he entertained any doubts about its necessity they were dispelled by a subsequent call from Clay Shaw.

"Did you ever hear of Lou Berlanti?" Shaw had asked. "Berlanti from Miami?"

"Do you mean the international real estate tycoon and industrial developer?"

"That's the man."

"Sure. He was killed last month when his plane blew up over Lake Okeechobee. What about him?"

"Well. I heard a report today about that incident that could have a direct bearing on us."

"Oh? In what way?"

"Did you know that Berlanti was one of the largest backers of Kohly's United Organizations, and that he was carrying a large amount of currency and negotiable securities in the plane?"

"Hell, no! Was the money for Kohly?"

"Apparently, yes. My information is that Berlanti was on his way to Washington to deliver it to Kohly, although a specific request had been made to him by the White House not to provide Kohly with any funds."

"How much dough was involved?"

"I'm told he was carrying ten million in cash."

Banister whistled. "Wow! Ten million?"

"Ten million, plus another twenty million in Dominican bonds."

"My God, that really could have set Kohly's underground up to do something effective. What was Berlanti doing over Lake Okeechobee?"

"That I can't answer," Shaw said. "There's talk he was stopping at Tampa. That could have taken him over the lake."

"Well, it's damned unfortunate for Berlanti, and for Kohly, too. But what's it got to do with us?"

"Just this. The general impression is that Castroites were responsible for the crash, but I just discovered that the plane Berlanti was using was one of those we had rigged."

"You mean you think somebody activated an explosive charge that we had put in?"

"That's right."

"But Berlanti was on our side, and helping Kohly," Banister said dubiously. "Why in hell would anyone in our organization have done it? And if it wasn't one of our people, who else could have done it? All those aircraft charges had bypasses on them that supposedly only we knew about. You'd have to know what the hell you were doing even to find them."

"That's right," Shaw replied.

"Then what are you insinuating, Clay? What possible motive could anybody in our organization have? Or in the Company, for that matter? It doesn't make any sense. Now, Castro I can see . . ."

"Well, let's put it this way. If it wasn't Castro—and I'm still not sure it wasn't—who else wanted to see that delivery stopped? In fact, who tried to stop it in the first place?"

Banister was quiet for a moment, and when he spoke his manner expressed total disbelief. "Clay! Are you saying that the administration may have had something to do with it— may have gotten to one of our guys? I mean, that's really hard to believe! Given the need to do it, I can see the president or Bobby sanctioning the assassination of a foreign leader, but a prominent American citizen? Much as I detest both of them, and dangerous as they are, I think that's just a little too far out."

"You may be right," Shaw replied. "But if it was Castro, wouldn't he have had the plane hijacked to get the cash, assuming, of course, that he knew about it? That trip had to be a closely guarded secret. Berlanti and Kohly both knew that Castro agents are everywhere in the Miami area. Kohly and his people have had a couple of close ones that I'm sure he hasn't forgotten, so they certainly would have taken precautions. And even if they didn't, how would Castro agents know about the explosive on the plane?"

"There could have been a leak in Berlanti's own organization, couldn't there?" Banister asked.

"Of course, but again, how would they have known about the booby trap?" Shaw asked. "Now, let's look at my side of it. Kohly has been the main target of the Kennedys ever since he united the Cuban organizations and then wouldn't play ball the administration's way. Kendricks tells me that Colonel Hullet, General Taylor's assistant, made a specific appeal to Berlanti not to finance Kohly. Instead of complying, Berlanti published an open letter in the Spanish papers in Miami supporting Kohly's exiles, and then he took off in a plane loaded with dough for Kohly. Doesn't it tax your credibility to believe that the plane blew up from natural causes?"

"Well, maybe, but . . ."

"Wait a minute. That isn't all. Did you know that Kohly actually obtained the backing of the Church in Rome? Then, after a meeting with Cardinal Cushing in Boston, the president had one of his White House aides, McGeorge Bundy, write the cardinal, who's a longtime friend of the family. Bundy told the cardinal that Kohly didn't have the support of the exile groups and that therefore the president couldn't support him. You know, and the president knows, that's a lot of crap.

"Well, I'm not going to say any more," Shaw concluded. "But, just for the hell of it, check on the activities of our Miami people a day or two prior to that flight. I'd like to know if the White House got to one of them."

"If you say so," Banister agreed, reluctantly concluding that Shaw might be right.

Upon his arrival at the Dallas bus terminal on October 3, Lee Harvey Oswald went directly to the office of the Texas State Employment Commission, where he filed an unemployment claim and said he was looking for work. Then, feeling grubby from the long bus trip, he checked into the YMCA, as Banister had instructed. He used his serviceman's ID card to get a discount on the rate. After taking a hot bath, he shaved and flopped down on the bed to await his contact.

At about 5:30, there was a soft knock at the door, which woke him out of a fitful sleep.

When he opened the door, his young Cuban visitor introduced himself. "I'm Roberto Navarro. Jack sent me." When Oswald didn't respond, he repeated the name. "Jack Ruby."

"I'm sorry," Lee said, "I just woke up and I'm a little slow on the trigger. Come on in. It's good to be back in Dallas, but it's still awful hot for this time of year."

Navarro agreed, then said, "I have some cash and instructions for you. I'm to see that you get settled here so you can resume your cover activities as a member and organizer of the Fair Play for Cuba Committee."

Lee groaned. "I understand the need for a cover, but why the FPCC?"

"I'm sorry, I don't know. All I know is you'll be working for Ruby, who will get your orders from Banister in New Orleans."

"Comprende," Lee replied.

"Good. Now here are your first instructions. For the moment don't contact your wife. Tomorrow, go see the plant foreman at the Padgett Printing Company and apply for a job as a type-setter trainee. Then come back to the 'Y' for a meeting with Ruby. If you want anything, I'll be in the room next door."

"O.K., but I was hoping we could get that meeting over with tonight."

"No. That's not possible. Ruby's busy. However, I was told to give you twenty-five dollars." Navarro reached into his pocket, pulled out two tens and a five, and handed them to Oswald. "Take in a movie and have a good dinner. I'll see you tomorrow."

Before Oswald could ask any more questions, Navarro was gone. Lee put the twenty-five dollars in his pocket and went down to the cafeteria to grab a bite to eat before it closed. He was tempted to ignore his instructions and call Marina, but he didn't. Instead he went back to his room and read a book he had purchased at the bus station that afternoon.

That same evening, when Jack Ruby walked out of his office at the Carousel Club, he saw Wanda Killan, the cigarette girl, talking to her husband, who was sitting at the bar. It gave him an idea, and when she walked away he went to the bar. Hank Killan didn't see Ruby coming and would have been disturbed if he had. Jack had been known to get violent at times when husbands visited their wives at the club. Today, however, Ruby was in a friendly mood. He sat down on a stool and said, "Hank, good to see you again."

Startled, Hank returned the greeting, thankful that he hadn't caused Wanda any trouble. But he was surprised when Ruby inquired, "Say, I understand you know of some nice rooming houses around your area."

"As a matter of fact, I do," Hank replied.

"Good. I have a friend that just got into town. He's waiting for his family to arrive and would like to rent a place for six or seven weeks. As you know, I live over in the Oak Cliff area, but I'm full up. Could you recommend a place?"

Killan reflected for a minute and said, "Maybe I can. A friend I work with, John Carter, lives at a nice place in the 1000 block of Beckley, adjacent to the park. He mentioned just the other day that a room there was going to be available shortly. Why don't I check with him and call you."

"I'd appreciate it. And, incidentally, I'd also appreciate it if you didn't mention it to Wanda. Now, have a drink on the house." With that, Ruby turned and walked away.

Hank Killan was dumbfounded. Ruby buying him a drink and not throwing him out? Oh, well, he thought, there's always a first time, and if he could help Ruby it might also help Wanda. He watched the floor show until the intermission and then went to the phone and called John Carter.

The landlady answered and reported that Carter was out for the evening.

"That's too bad," Killan said. "Well, this is a friend of his. He mentioned to me the other day that you might have a room available . . . . He says it's a very pleasant place."

"How nice of him, but unfortunately I have nothing at the moment, although I expect a vacancy almost any day now."

"That may be soon enough. I'll call back or stop by in the next day or so."

"Could I tell John who called?" she asked.

"No, don't bother him with it. I'll see him at work tomorrow. Thanks again." Killan hung up.

When he got back to his seat at the bar, he saw that Ruby had made his rounds and was coming toward him. Hank raised his hand and motioned Ruby over. "I've got the number for you on Beckley. I tried to call my friend. He wasn't home, but the landlady said she expects a room to be available within the next few days."

"Good," Ruby responded, taking down the number. "I'll have my friend go over tomorrow. Thanks."

"Don't mention it," Killan said and watched Ruby walk toward his office.

Hazelwood Avenue, once a beehive of activity, had begun to seem like a morgue. It was Thursday, October 3, the day after the arraignment, and we were all despondent because all of our efforts had gone down the drain. We gathered in the kitchen for a council of war and, within an hour, had reached the consensus that we would continue on the tape recorder project and await some news of Mario. Ross said he thought he could take on an additional project if we could add to our team an expert in the tape transport field. We decided to form a partnership and bring in some outside investors in order to maintain the Hazelwood operation, which now was totally un-funded, leaving Cynthia and the rest of us high and dry. I made no further attempt to get hold of Kendricks. I had given him all the information I felt I was going to get from Mario. At this stage of the game, if he wanted us he'd contact us. Until then, it was best to keep a low profile.

Early in the morning of October 4, Lee Oswald had coffee in the 'Y' cafeteria and ran into Navarro in the hall as he walked back to his room. "I was just going down to look for you," Roberto said. "Jack Ruby's in the gym. He has some instructions for you and has found you a place to stay."

"Fine. Let's go."

The meeting with Ruby was short and sweet. He told Lee he could now go ahead and contact Marina. "Let her know you're back in Dallas. I've located a room for you through a friend of mine at 1026 North Beckley Avenue. It's run by a Mrs. A. C. Johnson, and will cost you eight dollars per week. Register under the name of O. H. Lee."

Oswald winced. Lee was the name that had gotten him into

trouble getting out of Mexico.

"This morning go out and apply for that job as a typesetter trainee at the Padgett Company. That will establish you with the Employment Commission. When you get settled in your new place, let me know. And, by the way, I'd dig up that rifle of yours over on Neely Street."

For a moment, Lee was startled, until he remembered his discussion with Dave Ferrie in New Orleans a few weeks before. "When do you need it?" he asked.

"Oh, any time in the next few weeks. There's no big hurry. I'll let you know where you can leave it until it's needed. In the meantime, I just would like to make sure it doesn't rust apart or anything like that. . . . For your sake."

"O.K.," Oswald replied, "I'll get it just as soon as I can."

Later that morning, after saying goodbye to Ruby and checking out of the YMCA, he applied for the job at the printing company. Lee knew he had made a favorable impression on the department foreman. But when the plant superintendent called the Jaggars/Childes/Stovall Company, where Lee had worked before moving to New Orleans, he got a negative response. Lee wasn't hired, which he assumed was supposed to happen.

After lunch he called Marina at Ruth Paine's and asked her if she would mind having Mrs. Paine come to Dallas to pick him up.

"Under the circumstances, I don't think I'd better," Marina said.

Disappointed, Lee asked, "Well, will you at least see me?"

"Yes," she replied, "but you'll have to get out here by yourself."

He hung up and swore to God he would learn to drive as soon as possible.

It took Oswald over two and a half hours but, to elicit sympathy from Marina and Ruth Paine, he hitchhiked out that afternoon. The ploy worked and he spent a surprisingly pleasant weekend playing with the children. On Monday, Ruth Paine drove him to the bus station in Irving. When he arrived in Dallas he took a cab to 1026 North Beckley, only to be told by Mrs. Johnson that she had no vacancies, but definitely expected one within a week.

Discouraged, he wandered around the neighborhood and at 621 Marsalis Avenue spotted a "room for rent" sign on a rather run-down house. He was ready to take anything and, after an abrupt and unpleasant interview with the landlady, Mrs. Mary Bledsoe, he rented the room and paid the seven-dollar weekly rent in advance. Only then did the sourfaced, acid-tongued woman announce a number of house rules that severely restricted him, but he figured that since it wouldn't be for long he could live with them.

After contacting Ruby by phone to let him know his location, he checked in at the Employment Commission Office to pick up referrals. For the rest of the week he spent most of his time in his room, reading.

On October 9, after spending close to an hour in the bathroom with a book, he was berated by his landlady, who demanded to know what he was doing in there and screamed about his lack of consideration for others living in the house. Lee lost his temper, made a few critical remarks about the quality of the accommodations, and went to his room and slammed the door behind him.

Two days later, on Friday, October 11, Roberto Navarro picked him up in a dilapidated Ford coupe of 1941 or 1942 vintage, perhaps even older. He was surprised, as they pulled rapidly away from the curb, that the ancient vehicle was in first-class mechanical condition.

"I've just checked out the rooming house on Neely Street," Navarro said. "There doesn't appear to be anybody there this morning so it might be a good time to get over there and dig your rifle out. I've got a couple of entrenching tools underneath the seat."

Surprised, Lee just nodded, while Roberto continued. "I have a blanket in the trunk that you can keep to wrap it in, and I'll drive you out to Irving this afternoon."

"Thanks."

"Do you have a safe place to store it?"

"Yes . . . I suppose so. We have a whole mess of belongings

in the garage."

When they arrived at the old Neely Street address, there was no one in sight. Roberto rang the bell, and when no one answered, they both went around to the enclosed rear yard and quickly accomplished their task. As Roberto threw the tools in the car and Oswald wrapped the rifle in the blanket, he remarked, "It's a good thing I buried it under the bushes. No one will notice that the ground has been disturbed."

Lee didn't tell Roberto that his .38 caliber Smith and Wesson revolver was still buried within a foot of where the rifle had lain. Something had told him to leave it there. They got in the car and Roberto dropped Lee off in front of the downtown library, saying that he would pick him up at his rooming house around 4:30 that afternoon to drive to Irving.

After leaving Oswald, Navarro drove directly to the Harlandale Avenue headquarters where the rest of the team was living. He took the rifle from the trunk, entered the house, and went down to the basement. After checking the rifle thoroughly to be sure it was in working order, he inserted a six-round clip, shoved a round into the chamber, and fired into a long, cotton-stuffed, wooden box. After waiting several minutes, he dug through the wadding and pulled out a hot, slightly misshapen bullet. Apparently satisfied with the result, he repeated the process four more times.

Navarro carefully placed the five bullets in a small box filled with cotton wadding, along with the empty cartridge cases. Then, after cleaning the rifle thoroughly, he wrapped it up once more in the blanket and placed it back in the trunk of the old Ford.

At 4:30 that afternoon, right on schedule, Roberto showed up in front of the rooming house. Lee heard the horn blow twice, urging him to hurry. As he hastened through the downstairs hallway, he ran into Mrs. Bledsoe and told her he would be back the following Monday.

"I don't want you staying here no more," she said vehemently. "I know someone's waiting for you, so you can leave your stuff till Monday, but you better find someplace else because I'm renting your room."

Taken aback, Lee snapped at her, "Thanks for nothing. It'll be a pleasure to get out of this crummy place. I'll see you Monday." He dashed out the door, not bothering to close it. He heard it slam as he got in the car next to Roberto.

By nightfall the 6.5 Mannlicher, which Roberto had thoughtfully cleaned for him, was hidden among the other Oswald effects in the Paine garage. Ultimately, it would become one of the most controversial weapons of all time.

After a relatively pleasant evening, Marina and Lee retired early. Ruth Paine, over dinner, had noted that he seemed terribly depressed. That was not surprising, what with Marina momentarily expecting a baby and Lee out of work. "I'll give Lee a driving lesson tomorrow," she mused, "and drive him into Dallas Monday morning so he can get his things." She had to go anyway, and she was curious about where he was living.

Jack Ruby sat at his desk in the Carousel, mulling over the available alternatives that had been discussed in his recent meeting with the Harlendale Avenue crew. They had been concerned mostly with potential sites and routes that the Presidential party might take on the forthcoming tour through Dallas. Unfortunately, it would probably be more than a month before they would have any hard information on the motorcade route and the locations the president would visit. The major conclusion he had reached during the meeting was not to use the volatile Cubans except to be lookouts and to create confusion during the getaway. Navarro seemed to be the only stable leader in the bunch.

Ruby picked up the phone and called Miami to leave a message for Jim Hart and Charles Hunter to come to Dallas the following weekend. In addition to Bill Gemelo and Carlos Rigel, he wanted other experienced pros on hand for possible use on the assassination teams. If only he knew that damn parade route or could even get a hint, it would probably reveal where the president would be speaking. With three teams there'd be no problem setting up a failure-proof ambush, but they needed time to work out and perfect the details.

Suddenly a potential solution occurred to him. Picking up the phone, he placed a station call to Banister's office in New Orleans. When Guy's voice came on the line Ruby said, picking his words carefully, "It's Jack, Guy. We can be sure of success down here if somehow you could do one thing for me."

"What's that?" Guy asked.

"We have a new Trade Mart here in Dallas. If the President could be persuaded to make a speech there, we could have everything organized for a failure-proof operation at least two weeks in advance, timed down to the second. We have sufficient people."

"What about afterwards?"

"Well, everything's located on freeways here. The Trade Mart's on the Stemmons Freeway and also within easy access of the Industrial Boulevard. Using a location near my place for transfer would require a maximum of five or six minutes. In fact, there's an exit right near Tenth and Ewing. It couldn't be better." Then he continued, "After that it's a straight shot to Red Bird Airport, where someone could be waiting with a plane."

"It sounds good," Guy said. "However, getting our friend to the Trade Mart wouldn't be easy. We aren't exactly 'in' at the White House."

"True. They probably have a dozen potential sites," Ruby agreed. "But the Trade Mart is a logical choice. It's brand new and the pride of the city. For our purposes, it would provide the necessary secure places. It's got more nooks, crannies, and catwalks than Carter has liver pills. It would be almost impossible for the security boys to completely cover it."

"It sounds good," Guy agreed, "but we don't even know that he's going to make a speech. He may just decide to swing through town and back to the airport. After all, he's only going to be in Texas for a day or so."

"We'll have to see what develops," Ruby replied. "But, just on the off chance, see what you can find out."

"Certainly. I'll be back to you shortly."

"What do you mean by shortly?"

"Dammit, Jack. Within a few days. Don't get your water hot." Then Guy asked, "By the way, how's our friend Lee

Oswald doing down there?"

"He's doing fine but not working yet. However, I'm planning a series of incidents for Gemelo shortly, so I have to get him out of the area temporarily. The ideal setup would be to get him a job somewhere near the potential site, if we only knew where it will be."

"We've also been thinking along those lines," Guy replied. "We could settle it now and arrange to conduct the operation at the airport."

"You mean Love Field?"

"That's your main airport, isn't it?"

"Yes, of course. . . . You have a point. The president has to take a plane in and out. I'll see what we can arrange. In fact, I'll get on it today. That could possibly be the best site of all. Don't even let them get into town."

'Yep. Besides, that's where the confusion will be the greatest. It would make matters easier."

"Right, Guy. I'll get back to you. But, just in case, see what you can do about the other. I'll continue checking the sources I have."

After hanging up, Ruby pondered for a few minutes, then called a friend at the airport and arranged to have Oswald hired as a cargo handler through the Texas Employment Board. Meanwhile, Banister called Clay Shaw.

"Clay, in your work as director of the New Orleans Trade Center, have you met anybody associated with the new Trade Mart in Dallas?"

"Not really. I know they've just built one, but I haven't seen it yet. Why do you ask?"

"I just talked to Jack Ruby. He would like to firm up his operational site, but we're afraid it'll be weeks before we have anything definite on Kennedy's trip. However, if we can pin down a specific place where he's going to be at an appropriate hour, we'll have more time to set up a foolproof situation."

"It certainly would help, but you're asking the impossible. It would take a lot of persuading from some high city or state official to influence the selection." Shaw paused, and then said excitedly, "Wait a minute. I have an idea. I'll call you back shortly."

Echoing Ruby's impatience in the earlier call, Banister asked, "What do you mean by shortly?"

"When I get the information," Shaw said dryly.

"Thank you, Clay. I'll talk to you later."

Shaw switched lines on the phone and dialed a special number in Washington. When Kendricks' phone was picked up, he said, "Scramble this. It's Shaw in New Orleans. Let me speak to Ed."

"Sorry, Sir. The party you want is not in. Is it important?"

"No. Just leave a message to have him call me at the earliest possible moment."

"Yes, Sir."

On Monday morning, October 14, Ruth Paine drove Lee Oswald back into Dallas. Killing two birds with one stone, she had arranged a visit with her attorney regarding her impending divorce. She had tried to take Lee to his rooming house, but he declined, saying he had an appointment in town.

When he left Mrs. Paine, Oswald went to Bledsoe's rooming house and picked up the bag he had left there on Friday, then walked on to 1026 North Beckley. This time Mrs. Johnson had a pleasant furnished room available for eight dollars a week. He took it and, remembering Ruby's instructions, registered as O. H. Lee. He paid a week's rent in advance, put his bag in the room, and asked to use the phone. Then, thinking better of it, he said it could wait, excused himself, and left.

Ten minutes later he called the local FBI office from a pay station a few blocks away. He notified the case officer of his new address and said he would be going to the library to get a new card so that they could use the library for their future drops.

That same afternoon, Ruth Paine and Marina had their spirits raised when a good friend and neighbor of Ruth's, Linnie Mae Randle, gave her a lead on a potential job for Lee. Linnie's younger brother, Wesley Frazier, worked at the Texas School Book Depository in Dallas and had mentioned that there was a job opening there. Ruth told Marina, who excitedly asked her to call the depository to check. Ruth reached Roy Truly, the depository superintendent, and he informed her that there was indeed an opening. He said he would be glad to interview Lee in person early the following day. That evening, when Lee called Marina, Ruth gave him the news. He said he'd go over the following morning.

His second call was to Jack Ruby to make similar arrangements for a library drop. Ruby, however, was not at either of his numbers, so Oswald, refusing to leave his name, said he would call later.

It wasn't until the morning of Wednesday the 16th that Clay Shaw finally received a return call from Ed Kendricks on the scrambler. When Ed asked Shaw what he wanted, Clay asked if he knew anyone high in the city administration of Dallas.

Kendricks was silent for a moment, then asked why.

Clay, who hadn't anticipated the question, was taken aback. Thinking quickly, he replied, "We are doing some additional checking on Ruby's narcotics activities and wanted somebody we could trust, outside the department, to make a local police inquiry."

When Kendricks didn't reply, he continued. "Also, as director of the New Orleans Trade Center, I'd like to make some inquiries about the new Dallas Trade Mart."

He knew he hadn't been very convincing when Kendricks replied, "I think we can find someone. I'll check it out."

"Thanks," Clay said. "There's no real hurry." And, as an afterthought, "By the way, how's Chuck Cabell taking the exile these days?"

There was another long pause before Kendricks said, very formally, "He's doing quite well in his retirement, thank you. I'll tell him you inquired."

Shaw said, "Goodbye," and hung up.

Kendricks was puzzled and disturbed. Shaw obviously could get to anybody at the Dallas Trade Mart on a reciprocal basis. Moreover, he had to know that Cabell's brother was mayor of Dallas. The whole thing smelled, and Kendricks decided he had better place a call to the general. For the first time in months, he got through without a hitch.

"I was just about to sit down to lunch," Cabell said. "What can I do for you?"

"I just got a strange request from Clay Shaw in New Orleans."

"Oh? What's he been up to lately? Do you still suspect he's plotting something against the brothers?"

"That's right, Sir," he said in a serious tone. "Now more than ever." He related the contents of his conversation with Shaw, and there was a pause while Cabell digested the information. "Well, tell him you talked to me. . . . No, hold it. On second thought, don't tell him you talked to me. Tell him you couldn't reach me. We mustn't become involved."

"Yes, that's the posture I thought we should take," Kendricks replied, ending the conversation.

Kendricks immediately placed a call to Clay Shaw. When he came on the line, Ed said, "Clay, I'm glad I caught you before you went to lunch."

Clay remarked, "We're an hour behind you."

"Damn, that's right. I keep forgetting. Anyway, I tried to get hold of Chuck. He's out of the country."

"That's a shame," Clay said. "By the way, after we hung up I remembered that Cabell's brother is mayor of Dallas."

"That's right, but I'm sorry, I don't think it advisable to go through him."

"That's all right," Clay said. "We'll find someone else."

"I'm sure you will," Kendricks said. 'Clay, I'm sorry I couldn't help; but keep in touch."

Clay was tormented as he recalled his two conversations with Kendricks. He had been obvious and stupid, and he hoped he hadn't aroused Kendricks' suspicions. In case they did decide to pull off their coup at the Trade Mart, it hadn't been smart to alert Kendricks to his interest in the place.

Lee Oswald was no doubt overjoyed about his interview. He had a job that would give him ample opportunity to do the thing he loved most . . . read. . . . It was only $1.25 per hour but with his extracurricular activities and pay, he could well afford it. Once he got his daily work schedule out of the way, there had to be a hundred places where he could sit down for an hour or two at a stretch and not be missed. His interview with Mr. Truly had gone very well, and he would report for work the next morning. He knew Marina and Ruth would both be happy that he had a steady job, and he would no longer have trouble explaining to Marina where his money came from. He hoped that Ruby wouldn't be too upset, but if he was Lee would remind him that he hadn't been given any paying assignments since he had arrived in Dallas.

The pace was quickening for Jack Ruby. It was already Wednesday, October 16, and, in addition to his regular activities, the assassination plot was moving into high gear. Jim Hart and Charles Hunter were to arrive the following evening and would check into the YMCA. By the beginning of the following week their plan of action should be fairly well crystallized, complete with alternatives. With the incidents he had planned, the pace of events would accelerate to a fever pitch. The only thing that could interfere with Ruby's plans at this point would be violence at a right-wing demonstration General Edwin Walker was leading against Adlai Stevenson, who would be visiting Dallas on October 24. If things got too rough it could cause the Secret Service to eliminate Dallas as one of the president's stops.

During the balance of the week, Lee Oswald got into the routine at the School Book Depository and cultivated Ruth Paine's neighbor, Wesley Frazier, who could provide transportation to Irving on weekends. On the night of Thursday the 17th, Lee again tried to phone Ruby and this time caught him.

Ruby said that he finally had a small mission for him to perform for which he would be paid. He was to attend a meeting to be conducted by General Edwin Walker. As Ruby explained it, this was to prepare him for a verbal confrontation at a meeting of the American Civil Liberties Union to be held at

Southern Methodist University on the 25th. He was to make himself as conspicuous as possible.

When Lee asked why, Ruby informed him for the first time that he was to have a key role in a major operation to be held within the next thirty days. When Lee tried to inquire further, Ruby said, "We can't discuss this one on the phone. I'll meet you next week and go over some of the details. Be watching the library drop for a message and, of course, some cash."

"Yes, Sir," Oswald replied, then realized he was speaking into a dead telephone. He had been checking the library every other day, with no action from either Ruby or the FBI. From now on, he would do it daily.

That weekend, while Ruby, Hart, Hunter, and Gemelo were setting up the assassination plan, Lee Oswald was having a full weekend. On Friday the 18th, Marina and Ruth had prepared a surprise cake for his birthday. And, on Sunday, two days later, Marina gave birth to their second daughter, Rachel, at Parkland Hospital. Because Lee couldn't drive, Ruth had to take Marina to the hospital, and he didn't get a chance to see her or the baby until the evening of Monday the 21st, after work.

On Wednesday night, the 23rd, he attended General Walker's meeting as Ruby had ordered. Jack had picked him up just down the block from his Beckley Avenue rooming house. After he climbed into the car, Jack had handed him a small briefcase which he said contained a small recorder with a built-in mike on one side. He had instructed him on how to use it and told him to sit in the front row and record Walker's speech.

When Lee had asked why, Jack had said stiffly, "Look, kid, I'm handing you fifty dollars in cash right now to do this job, O.K.?" Then, softening his tone, "If you must know, we want to see if Walker's going to make an inflammatory statement about Adlai Stevenson's visit to Dallas tomorrow. Is that all right?"

Lee had answered defensively, "Just asked. And thanks for the money. We had a baby last Sunday."

"Well, how about that. Congratulations."

"Thank you, Sir. And, oh, I almost forgot to tell you. I started a new job at the Texas School Book Depository last week."

With difficulty, Ruby had controlled his anger. He had already arranged to have Oswald hired as a cargo handler at Love Field. Now that had been fucked up. However, he had said only, "Good to hear it. I'll pick you up after the meeting. Call me at the Club Vegas when it's over and I'll come right away. I still have to brief you on your assignment for the Civil Liberties thing on Friday."

"Will do, Sir," Lee had said.

Ruby drove to the Club Vegas and called Banister and told him of the conversation. "I can't ask Lee to change jobs again, or he may get suspicious," Ruby said, "so I guess the airport site is out."

"Son of a bitch," Banister said angrily. "Well, at least you've been checking other alternatives. Now, how about the Walker thing? Shaw and I are concerned about the Stevenson visit."

"I think we can keep it under control," Ruby replied. "However, you can never be sure. Demonstrations can easily get out of hand and snowball."

"That's what's worrying me," Banister exclaimed. "But don't get the wrong idea. Clay and I think you're doing a hell of a job there in Dallas and I want you to know that your rewards will be substantial."

Ruby's voice brightened considerably. "I'll hold up this end."

"I'm sure you will. . . . When the situation clarifies and the site is selected, I'll be available to coordinate the action. We can't afford any slip-ups. . . ."

"You're absolutely right, Guy."

Ruby was in a jubilant mood when he left the club and went to the YMCA to pick up Jim Hart and Charles Hunter and put them on their buses. As he was returning from the bus station, he turned left on Main and headed toward Dealey Plaza and the triple underpass. When he stopped for the light at Houston, an idea exploded in his brain and, as the light changed, he started up slowly.

Looking to the right, he saw the Hertz sign flashing the hour on top of the School Book Depository overlooking Dealey Plaza.

As he speeded up to get on the freeway, he realized that Oswald now worked there. Then, as he passed the entrance sign to the Stemmons Freeway, the whole thing became clear. What a damn fool he'd been. It didn't matter what parade route was chosen for the president or even where he spoke. To travel between the airport and virtually any location downtown, the presidential motorcade would have to pass at least once through Dealey Plaza.

"There's absolutely no way," he thought out loud, "and I mean no way, they can get onto any of the freeways, coming in or out of town, without going through that triple railroad underpass. My God!" He was so excited that he almost hit a car that had slowed down in front of him. And what incredible luck about Oswald. Jesus, poor Oswald. When he got that job at the Depository, he didn't know how perfect a setup he'd trapped himself into. Thank God he didn't get that job at the airport. The getaway from here would be far less complex. It should be duck soup to use Red Bird Field.

Lee Oswald had managed to get a seat in the front row of the auditorium and, by holding the briefcase in his lap, was able to trigger the starting switch as Edwin Walker began speaking. He was mildly amused to recall that the last time he pulled a trigger on the general had been on April 1, only then he had been looking at him through the scope on his Mannlicher rifle. His assignment had been to fire some stray shots to frighten the general into thinking the Commies were after him, and loosen up some more Texas oil money for the right-wing cause.

He didn't know how long the speech lasted, but Walker was certainly boring. Not only that, he thought to himself, the man was both fascist and anti-Semitic. When it was over, he called Ruby to ask him to pick him up.

During the trip back to his Beckley Avenue rooming house, Ruby seemed so distant that Oswald was hesitant to ask what his role was supposed to be in the November mission. Then, as he opened the car door to get out a half-block from home, he asked Ruby if he had forgotten.

Still preoccupied with the new plan, Ruby put him off. "I'm

sorry, Lee. As a matter of fact I had. But don't worry. I'll be in touch with you after the A. C. L. U. meeting on the 25th. Right now, I've got to get back to my office and listen to this tape. I want to see if Walker's planning to create any trouble when Stevenson comes to Dallas. If he is, I've got to notify some of my friends down at the police department. What was your impression?"

"I'd say Walker's planning something. The mood of the crowd was bad. Although he didn't say anything about Stevenson, he referred to 'the people in power.' When you play it, you'll see."

"Damned intriguing," Ruby commented. "Well, thanks for your help. And incidentally, I've been told to tell you you'll receive a thousand dollars after the mission."

Startled, Lee repeated the figure.

"That's right, one thousand little iron men."

Lee was still having trouble with the number. "What the hell are you planning to do? Assassinate the president?"

Ruby just laughed.

Chapter Thirteen

On the evening of Friday, September 25, Lee Oswald was scheduled to appear at the A. C. L. U. meeting at Southern Methodist University. He was worried about it, because of the political tension generated by the demonstrations that had occurred during Adlai Stevenson's visit to Dallas the day before. General Walker had done his job well, and the hatred exuded by the demonstrating mobs had resulted in several arrests.

Lee was also upset because of Jack Ruby's insistence, following Lee's appearance at Walker's meeting, that he write a letter to Arnold Johnson, of the American Communist Party, reporting on the event. Ruby's explanation of the purpose of the letter was not very convincing, but Lee had finally agreed to do it, mostly because Jack was becoming visibly upset by his resistance.

When Lee arrived in Irving before going to the meeting, Ruth Paine's husband, Michael, was there. The two men attended the meeting together.

Following Ruby's instructions, Lee made himself conspicuous by standing up and challenging the speaker's assertion that the

John Birch Society was not anti-Semitic. Lee argued loudly that he had attended Edwin Walker's meeting earlier in the week and had heard the avowed Bircher make anti-Semitic statements—and anti-Catholic ones as well.

After the meeting, he got into a heated discussion with a group that included Frank Krystinik, a co-worker of Michael Paine's at the Bell Helicopter plant. Lee propounded Marxist views and was accused of being a Red; he spent the rest of the evening denying that he was a communist.

On Saturday morning he phoned Ruby to report what had transpired. Ruby complimented him and again asked about the letter to Arnold Johnson. Lee said he would write it during the weekend in Irving.

"Fine," Ruby said. He then asked Lee to rent a post office box, so they could communicate by mail. Lee agreed to do so, and Ruby concluded the conversation by promising that Oswald would receive a bonus the next time they met.

On Sunday Lee wrote the letter to Johnson; he mailed it when he returned to Dallas on Monday. He was looking forward to the promised bonus and the thousand dollars he was to receive for the assignment in November, and he was eager to keep Ruby happy.

On Wednesday the 30th, after phoning Marina and inquiring about Rachel, their new baby, Lee found a message from Ruby at the library drop, setting up a meeting on the following day. After several unsuccessful attempts to reach Ruby by phone, Lee finally got through to him after work on Thursday afternoon. Ruby confirmed their meeting for that evening, reminded Oswald to get a post office box, and suggested that they meet at 8 P.M. outside the terminal annex next to the main post office, where Ruby would pick him up in his car.

Ruby picked Lee up as scheduled and described to the frightened but silent young man a carefully laundered version of the assassination plan. When he dropped Lee off at his boarding house after the meeting, Oswald sat in his room for hours trying to analyze his situation. He had mixed reactions to Ruby's description of the November plot against the president. It had disturbed but not shocked him because he had almost been expecting something like it. It was frightening, but he figured that, other than making his Mannlicher carbine available and arranging the firing position at the Depository, he would not be directly involved in the assassination. The wad of bills Ruby had handed him as a bonus, and the promise of another thousand dollars to come, tended to offset his fears.

Lee kept to himself at the Depository on Friday. He could hardly wait for the day to end, because he was looking forward to seeing Marina and the new baby that evening in Irving. But the more his thoughts dwelled on his conversation with Ruby the more disturbed he became that he had let himself be trapped into a role in Banister's plot. He was sure that Ruby was an FBI informer, like himself, but Jack seemed to be a willing, even eager, participant. Lee wanted to report what he knew to the Bureau but didn't dare approach them because Ruby might find out about it. He decided he would have to find a way to get the FBI to call him.

An incident on Saturday, November 2, could have exploded the whole plot. Jim Hart, who had returned to Miami from Dallas to make a weekly narcotics collection from the refugee pickup, started a drinking bout early in the afternoon at a little Cuban bar in the southern part of the city. Bill Gemelo was not to meet him until 3:30, so he had a long wait. He had five boilermakers under his belt when several of the Cubans started needling him about the administration's attitude toward the Cuban problem.

By the time Gemelo arrived, Hart was being cheered and toasted by everyone at the bar. In his drunkenness, to prove his friendship he was boasting about the plan to assassinate Kennedy when he visited Texas. Gemelo broke into a cold sweat when he heard what was going on. He told the crowd that his compadre was a little loco and talking foolishness. When the Cubans began to get nasty, he threw a twenty on the bar and shouted that the drinks were on him. During the stampede for the bar, he dragged Hart out to his car.

Drunk though he was, Hart was terrified when Gemelo said,

"I'm only going to say this once, and you better listen. I should have you shot, and I would if you weren't so drunk that no one will believe you. But God help you if you open your mouth again. You'll be a dead man."

Gemelo was not aware that a Cuban at the rear of the barroom had been listening intently to the drunk's story. After visiting the same bar the following Saturday, the 9th, the man was reminded of Hart's boast about the assassination plot and decided to report it to the Miami police. They relayed it to the Secret Service, who wrote it off as another crank report.

On November 8, on Guy Banister's instructions, Dave Ferrie flew Bill Gemelo to Dallas in a borrowed Aztec. Gemelo's arrival in Dallas would signal the start of the final series of events designed to convince the world that Lee Harvey Oswald was the lone assassin of John F. Kennedy. Inside the plane's baggage compartment were Gemelo's luggage and two 7.35 millimeter Mannlicher rifles. The stocks of both weapons had been cut down so that they looked like sport models.

Jack Ruby met the Aztec at Red Bird Airport, along with one of the girls from the Carousel. As Ferrie taxied the plane to the gate, Gemelo nodded toward the girl and said, "That's Rose Chermi, the girl Hart's got the hots for. She's some kind of animal. . . . It's a goddamn shame she's a junkie. Ruby saw to that. She'd do anything for him."

They unloaded the rifles and Gemelo's luggage, and then Ferrie taxied the plane toward the runway. Ruby introduced Rose Chermi as "Marina." The men stowed the luggage in the trunk of Ruby's car, then walked with Rose toward a battered two-tone '56 Ford while Ruby explained the plan.

"The girl has borrowed a friend's children for the day. You'll know her only as Marina Oswald. That way you won't goof on names. The baby is about eight weeks old, and the other girl is three—about the same age as Oswald's kids. Call her June and refer to the baby as Rachel. I want you and your new family to make yourselves as conspicuous as possible in Irving. You'll be using a borrowed car and there's no owner's registration in it, so if you get into trouble, call me."

As they were walking toward the other car, carrying the box with the rifles, Ruby remarked, "I must say she's made up pretty well. Anyone seeing the pair of you will be sure you are Lee and Marina Oswald."

"You ought to know, Jack," Gemelo replied.

"Now," Ruby said, "after you're done, drive to Harlandale Avenue and call me at the Carousel. I want to tell you about another plan for tomorrow afternoon." He paused, and asked, "You did bring the telescopic sights?"

"Of course. And, as you requested, one isn't mounted."

"That's perfect. There are several gun and sporting goods stores in Irving. Find one and have the spare scope mounted. Tell them you'll pick it up later in the day, and be sure you tell them your name is Lee Oswald."

"O.K., got ya."

"Do you know how to get to Irving?"

"No, as a matter of fact, I don't have the faintest idea."

"O.K., it's simple. When you leave the airport entrance, make a left on Hampton. Go up to the first major intersection, which is Ledbetter Drive. Make another left and go approximately two miles until you hit the traffic circle. Then go north on Walker Boulevard, which will take you smack into the heart of Irving. That way you'll avoid all the Dallas traffic."

"Fine. Anything else?" Gemelo asked.

Looking at his watch, Ruby said, "It's now noon. Grab a bite of lunch and I'll expect to hear from you between three and four o'clock. The fastest way back is to come down Walker and then go east when you hit Illinois Avenue. It crosses Harlandale just about a block north of where you want to be. We'll take it from there."

When Gemelo looked into the two-tone Ford he saw a small girl sitting in the rear next to a baby in a bassinet.

"Marina," Jack said, "introduce Lee to the children."

"Rachel, June, meet Daddy." The three-year old giggled and the baby started to cry. Ruby reached in through the open back window, tousled the little girl's head, and said, "See you later."

"Well, family, I guess we'd better make tracks," Gemelo said.

Rose looked at him sharply. "Don't be a smart ass," she said, and the baby started screaming.

The wailing irritated Gemelo. "Please, Rachel!" he said, but the three-year-old started giggling again and the baby's screaming grew louder.

Rose, alias Marina, reached around and took the baby from the bassinet, cradled it in her arms, and started to rock it. When this failed to quiet her, she placed the baby on her shoulder, patted its back, and produced a resounding burp. The baby stopped crying and Gemelo, shaking his head, put the car in gear and drove down the airport drive. At Hampton, he turned left to Ledbetter as instructed.

When they reached Irving the baby was cooing contentedly in Rose's arms and she was prompting Gemelo to remember that the child was born on October 23.

"If you say so," he said, wrinkling his nose. "Do you need to change her before we get there?"

"Probably, but I'll wait and do it in the back seat while you're in the gun shop."

A large sign on the side of the building advertised "Gunsmith, Parts, Repairs, Etc." But as they drove by, it appeared to be occupied by a furniture store called simply The Furniture Mart. "We'll hit that on the way back," Gemelo said. "That will give me a chance to be seen with you and the children."

"All right," she agreed. "But how about lunch?"

"Later, baby," Gemelo replied.

Another block and a half brought them to a vacant parking spot, beyond and out of sight of the entrance of the Irving Sports Shop. Gemelo took the keys out of the ignition and left Rose in the back seat changing the baby. He opened the trunk and took one of the Mannlichers and a separately wrapped scope from the box. After sliding out the bolt, he walked back to the shop, where he made himself conspicuous by assuming a furtive manner. The man behind the counter cautiously asked what he could do for him.

Gemelo handed over the rifle and asked if he could get the scope mounted that day.

The clerk looked first at the gun, then at him, and said, "No,

Sir, I'm sorry. I'm pretty well boxed in. The boss is away and I'm short-handed."

"Damn, that's a shame," Gemelo said. "I wanted to use it Sunday."

Seeing his disappointment, the clerk relented. "I'll tell you what I can do. I'll work on it this evening and, if I don't get done, I'll finish it tomorrow morning. That way you can pick it up sometime tomorrow afternoon. Would that be O.K.?"

"It'd be great," Gemelo said.

The clerk took the scope and the rifle, placed them together on a rack behind the counter, and produced a tag with a wire attached to it.

"May I have your name?" he asked.

"Oswald. Irving, Texas," Gemelo replied.

"Thank you, Sir," the clerk said, filling in the tag and attaching it to the rifle. "See you tomorrow."

When Gemelo returned to the car, the three-year-old was in the back seat tearing up a coloring book and the baby was asleep in the bassinet.

At the Furniture Mart, he parked directly across the street. "This is our chance to be seen together," he said.

"All right," Rose replied. They crossed the street, Gemelo taking the hand of the three-year-old and Rose carrying the baby, and when they reached the store he said, "Stay here and look in the windows. I'll go in first and inquire about a gun part, then come and get you. That'll make a production out of it."

"All right," she said again. Taking the little girl's hand, she began inspecting the window displays.

Gemelo entered the store and was approached by a clerk, Mrs. Edith Wentworth. She asked if she could help him.

"Yes," he replied, "I'm trying to get a firing pin installed in my .38 Smith and Wesson revolver."

Mrs. Wentworth smiled ruefully and said, "I'm sorry, Sir, but the gunsmith that used to occupy part of these premises has been gone for quite some time now. This is strictly a furniture store. We really should have that sign removed."

"Oh," he replied looking around, "that's too bad. Well, since we're here, we might as well look at the furniture. We're moving to larger quarters soon and will need some things."

Gemelo motioned to Rose through the windows. As she and the children entered the baby started to cry, and another clerk approached her to see if she could help. They were the only people in the store, and the two women obviously were eager to make a good impression on a potential customer. They gushed over the darling children and asked several personal questions, which Rose blithely answered. After browsing for about half an hour, Gemelo said they would return in a week or two to purchase some things.

As they crossed the street to the car, Mrs. Wentworth told her friend, Gertrude Hunter, that she hoped they would return. "It would be a tremendous sale for me, if they took all the things they seemed to like."

Gemelo headed south on Walker Boulevard, stopping for hamburgers near the edge of town. They turned east on Illinois and within half an hour reached the Harlandale Avenue headquarters. It was only 3:20, but Ruby was already there.

When they had given Ruby a complete rundown and Rose and the children had left in the Ford, Ruby gave Gemelo a hundred dollars.

That night Jim Hart and Charles Hunter reappeared at the house on Harlandale, and the following day, along with Gemelo, Rigel, and Navarro, set about surveying the site and putting together the assassination teams. They were enthusiastic about Ruby's choice of Dealey Plaza for the operation. It provided several alternate escape routes and a number of places from which they could fire. In addition, they had their perfect patsy. Lee Harvey Oswald, with his known communist background and job at the School Book Depository, was a sitting duck.

Among them, they worked out the strategy for coordinating the crossfire and chose their partners. Gemelo had finally agreed to go along with the plan to use Oswald to set up the position at the Depository, although he didn't like it. However, since Oswald's rifle and spent cartridges were to be left behind it didn't require a clean-up man. He could just dump the weapon and go.

Banister would be the lookout and coordinator, and each

team would carry a miniature transceiver. In addition, they decided not to carry sidearms except in the vehicles. Final approval was needed from Ruby, but after several hours of planning they decided things were pretty well set. They ate TV dinners while actually watching TV, and after a few hours went to bed.

Late the next morning, Saturday the 9th, Gemelo put on a suit and tie as Ruby had suggested. Shortly after noon, after picking him up and briefing him on what to do, Ruby dropped him a block from Downtown Lincoln-Mercury.

At the same moment, Oswald was sitting quietly at a typewriter in the Paine home, drafting a letter to the Soviet Embassy. He had begun to sense a pattern in recent events that suggested Banister and Ruby might plan to use him in more sinister and threatening ways than the relatively minor role he had been assigned in the upcoming operation. Lee couldn't quite put a finger on it, but he felt a strong need to protect himself. He didn't dare communicate directly with the FBI because Ruby would know about it within an hour. Nor could he report to his CIA case officer, since Banister was one of the conspirators. Yet, somehow, he must disengage himself from the plot Banister and Ruby were putting together.

It occurred to him that if he wrote a letter to the Soviet Embassy, it would be intercepted on arrival by the overt side of the CIA in Washington. That should get him on the "to be watched" list during the forthcoming presidential visit. The local FBI office would be notified, and Ruby would have no other choice than to pull him off the operation and still pay him. He'd also leave a draft of the letter around for Ruth Paine to find. She might call the police. Yet, through all his planning he had mixed emotions. He sure needed that thousand bucks!

Gemelo entered the front entrance of Downtown Lincoln-Mercury and started browsing through the models on the floor. He eyed appreciatively the big Continental convertibles and sedans but bypassed them to walk over and sit down in a large wood-paneled Mercury station wagon. He had a lengthy discussion on the merits of the vehicle with a salesman, Albert Guy Bogard, and, after introducing himself as Lee Oswald, asked if it would be possible to take a demonstration ride. Bogard replied, "Not in this particular model. But I can let you drive a sedan that is quite similar. That'll give you the feel of how she handles."

For the next half-hour, Gemelo and Bogard test-drove the Mercury on the Stemmons Freeway. When they returned Gemelo said, "She's certainly a fabulous machine. However, it will be a few weeks before I have enough cash to make a down payment."

"Well, Mr. Oswald," Bogard replied, "I don't think you have to wait. I'm sure we can arrange something now. Why don't you talk to our assistant sales manager, Mr. Pizzo? He's over there talking to Mr. Wilson, one of our other salesmen."

Laboriously, Frank Pizzo explained to Gemelo the intricacies of financing an automobile. He went into the details of how much cash would be necessary for a down payment, time payments, finance charges, and the information that would be required for financing.

While Gemelo and Pizzo were talking, Bogard asked another salesman, Oran Brown, to take a close look at "Oswald" and to handle the sale if the customer returned while Bogard was not on the floor. He promised Brown that he would split the commission. Bogard went to the men's room and then rejoined Frank Pizzo and an irate "Lee Oswald." He hadn't heard the customer's caustic remark to Pizzo that even with a down payment the ridiculous need for credit references made it impossible for him to make a deal. "Maybe I'll have to go back to Russia to buy a car," Gemelo had said.

When he joined them it was obvious to Bogard that they hadn't made a deal. As they walked away, he handed Gemelo his business card, and assured him that something could be worked out once he actually had the down payment in hand.

Gemelo walked back to Ruby's car and reported on the incident as they drove back to Harlandale Avenue. Ruby was jubilant. "I'll report this to Banister tonight. He'll be delighted. And tomorrow should be another good day."

"How's that?"

"We're going back to that gun shop in Irving to pick up the Mannlicher. Tomorrow you're going to play sharpshooter on a rifle range."

"As a matter of fact, that's not a bad idea. I've never really fired one of the damn things."

That afternoon Gemelo retrieved the Mannlicher with the scope mounted. When he asked about cartridges, the clerk said that they didn't stock them in that caliber, but offered to order some.

"No," Gemelo said, "that won't be necessary."

Later, when asked about the ammunition supply, Ruby replied, "There's several hundred rounds in the trunk. All reloaded by an expert. Military ammo completely untraceable. Made in 1939, reloaded less than a month ago with fragmentation bullets, fresh as a daisy."

"How about Oswald's 6.5 mm, which I'll be using the day of the operation?"

"New ammo, out of the same box Navarro fired the test rounds from."

"I'll be looking forward to tomorrow."

At six o'clock in the evening on Sunday the 10th, Gemelo borrowed Roberto Navarro's ancient Ford and drove out to the Sports Drome Rifle Range near Grand Prairie, a few miles south of Irving.

At that moment, Lee Harvey Oswald was playing with his daughter, June, unaware that he was being impersonated a scant three and a half miles away. He was satisfied that Ruth Paine had read his letter. In fact, to give herself an excuse she had gone to the trouble of rearranging the living room furniture. He'd have to mail it in the next few days.

After parking the car, Gemelo took the Mannlicher from the trunk and entered the range. He approached a group of men and asked them if anyone could help him sight in a rifle. They pointed to a man who was standing by a shooter's scope looking as if he was about to pack up and leave. Gemelo walked over and introduced himself as Lee Oswald.

The man said he was Howard Price and asked what Gemelo wanted.

"I know it's rather late, but I'd like to get some practice in. However, I need some help in sighting in this scope."

"Well, it's getting close to seven o'clock, but I guess I can take a few minutes."

"I sure appreciate it. If you could check the patterns as I fire, it certainly would be helpful."

Getting down on the firing bench, Gemelo positioned himself and fired several test rounds while Price indicated where they were hitting. When he was finally satisfied with the results, he asked Price if he would mind double-checking the rifle for him by firing a few rounds himself.

Price hesitated, then said, "Well, I really don't feel like shooting it, but let me take a look through the scope and see how it is compared to the one I have."

As Price peered through, Gemelo asked, "Did you ever see a clearer one?"

"Never have," Price agreed. "It's a first-class scope. About four power, I'd say."

"Yes, as a matter of fact it is," Gemelo replied, "and I sure appreciate the help."

"Don't mention it," said Price, as he packed up and left.

Gemelo spent half an hour firing another twenty-five rounds, and then he retrieved his spent cartridges and paid for his targets. He carefully placed the Mannlicher back in the Ford trunk and drove off.

Roberto Navarro, who was waiting for him when he arrived back at Harlandale, asked, "How did it go?"

"It went just great. There's got to be at least a half dozen people who will remember me as Lee Harvey Oswald."

"Muy bueno! Ruby called and wants us to meet him over at the Carousel around ten o'clock, so why don't you change? We'll make the boss buy us a few drinks while we look at the girls, eh?"

"Right, Roberto," smiled Gemelo. He went upstairs, cleaned off the grime from the rifle range, and forty-five minutes later

Navarro drove the antiquated Ford into the lot at the Carousel.

When they entered the club, Ruby was already seated at a small table. It was far enough to the rear so that the music wasn't overwhelming, but it still had a good view of the stage. When Ruby saw them, he waved them over.

Ruby told them he thought Oswald was becoming suspicious and said they would have to be very careful with him until the operation was over. Gemelo, becoming uneasy, suggested that, as Oswald's double, he really shouldn't be in the club.

"I'm not so sure this kind of exposure is wise," he said. "Oswald's really not the type of guy to be seen in a place like this."

Ruby exploded loudly, "What the hell's wrong with a place like this?"

"Not a goddamn thing, Jack," Gemelo said quickly. "That's not what I meant. Oswald just isn't known to frequent night clubs. Everyone knows he's hung up on that young, good-looking wife of his."

"So . . . she just had a baby. It'll be a while yet."

"Well, that's a point, compadre," laughed Roberto. The tension evaporated.

Ruby explained in detail what he had told Oswald about the operation, including Lee's assignment at the Book Depository.

"How much time will I have with that 6.5 millimeter job?" Gemelo asked. "You know, don't you, that it's still got to be sighted in?"

"I've already considered that. Next weekend, you're going to the range again, this time with Roberto, while Rose Chermi and I drive out to Irving and pick up Oswald's rifle. We'll come back to the range and honk the horn when we get there. Rose will pass the rifle to you over the fence. When you're done sighting it in, pass it back. And try to make sure that somebody sees you. You can mark all the position settings with a sharp pin. If for some reason it gets knocked out of calibration, you'll have no problem putting it back to where it was. Then repeat the process with the two 7.35's."

"That makes sense," Gemelo said. "Then we can always compensate for windage based on the actual conditions."

"Right. Well, that takes care of that," Ruby said, rubbing his hands together. He turned to Navarro. "Roberto, you'll be driving the pickup car. Park your car near my place, maybe even at the zoo; we can decide the exact spot at the last minute. I've arranged to bring in a Nash station wagon from Louisiana. Like the black Ford, it should be totally inconspicuous. You're to park it in a strategic location near the railroad tracks, backed up behind the stockade fence. The fence starts at the edge of the pergolas, next to the School Book Depository, and extends around to the triple railroad underpass. It's right at the crest of a grassy slope. Banister will be driving an Olds sedan with a large trunk. He will park beside you, and you can use it for stashing your team's rifle and shells. Also, if for some reason you can't get away, it will be a place to hide until we can get to you. In the event that the man with me in the Criminal Courts Building, or Bill in the Depository, miss with their shots, your partner, Jim Hart, will have to deliver the coup de grace. We'll simulate it in a dress rehearsal sometime this weekend."

"Excluding Oswald, of course," exclaimed Gemelo.

Ruby gave him an impatient look and turned back to Navarro. "Roberto, in addition to driving, you'll be clean-up man for your team, which we'll call number three. I went through this with Jim Hart and Carlos Rigel last week."

Gemelo expressed surprise. "Carlos Rigel? What about Charles Hunter?"

"Banister wants him on the West Coast," Ruby replied. "Now, let's go over this once more. Bill, you will act alone as team number one, since we've agreed you don't need a clean-up man. I'll be on top of the Criminal Courts Building with Rigel and will function as clean-up man for team number two. Team number three, Roberto and Jim, will be behind the stockade fence.

"Guy Banister will act as coordinator. Each team will carry a miniature two-way radio so they can stay in constant communication with you. You will have ample warning in the event of an emergency or an abort. Banister will have a Secret Service identification card, so he'll have no problem carrying a radio.

Any questions?" Ruby asked.

"No, not now," said Navarro. But Gemelo, whose eyes had been darting nervously around the room, looked concerned. "The club's getting busy and we don't want to be overheard."

Roberto grinned. "Let's watch the girls for a while and have a few drinks. We've got a busy schedule tomorrow."

Ruby nodded and signaled the waitress.

After a few minutes, a couple came in and sat down at the next table. Ruby rose as a club photographer came by, her camera poised and a frozen smile on her face. He waved her away. "I'll see you later," he said. "Have fun." On his way to the office he told the waitress that the table was on the house.

On Wednesday the 12th, Lee Harvey Oswald mailed his letter to the Soviet Embassy. Following routine procedure, the Agency intercepted it at the main Washington Post Office on Thursday the 14th, screened, copied, and resealed it and sent it on its way. It was delivered the next day at the Soviet Embassy on Sixteenth Street and was processed by a Russian clerk. It was dismissed as another of the crank letters, most of them vituperative, that the Embassy received every day.

The CIA copy got more expeditious treatment. It was read at Langley on the 14th and, after a preliminary screening, a duplicate was routinely sent downtown to the Federal Bureau of Investigation on the same day. The CIA, ironically, moved too quickly. Oswald's name had not yet been computer-matched for any possible cross-links to the Company or, more important, to Section C. The system ground on efficiently and inexorably. On the day the Soviet Embassy received the original, the FBI copy was screened, and the Dallas office was notified by telex that one of their informers might be planning to defect.

On Saturday the 16th, on orders of the Dallas FBI bureau chief, Oswald was interrogated for four hours. He disclosed what little he knew of the proposed assassination plot against the president but his interrogator had trouble keeping him on that subject. He kept returning angrily to his annoyance that Marina was being intimidated by one of the local agents. He voiced his suspicion that the agent's interest was more personal than official.

The interrogator was so put off by Oswald's concern about Marina that he instinctively rejected everything else Lee had said. His report on Oswald's interrogation was typed on Monday the 18th and forwarded by mail to the Bureau in Washington. On Tuesday the 19th, a routine teletype was sent advising that the report was on its way. It would arrive too late. In three days the president would be in Texas.

On the day that their "patsy" was being interrogated in Dallas, Guy Banister and Hugh Ward left New Orleans for Texas in an old 1956 Oldsmobile sedan. Maurice Gatlin was left in charge of the office. Banister's luggage contained an assortment of identification cards and four small special frequency handy talkies, indistinguishable from the type used by the Secret Service. All this equipment would be needed by the assassination teams.

On Sunday the 17th, Gemelo played out the final act in the plot to nail Oswald to the wall. Navarro drove him to his final appearance at the Sports Drome Rifle Range. Howard Price, the chap who had helped him the week before, was at the range. Gemelo took position number eight, adjacent to the five-foot wall that surrounded the range, and for fifteen minutes shot the same 7.35 Mannlicher that he had used the week before. Satisfied that his scope sighting hadn't changed, he marked the settings with a sharp metal stylus.

Carlos Rigel was due almost any time with the other 7.35 mm, and Ruby or Rose Chermi would pass Oswald's 6.5 mm rifle over the fence at seven.

Promptly at 7:00 P.M. Gemelo placed his 7.35 millimeter carbine on the cleaning rack, walked to the fence, and leaned against it. He heard a tap on the other side and reached up to grab the weapon. Rose Chermi passed it over, and he had Oswald's 6.5 mm rifle in his hand. He was pleased that the incident had been observed by at least three people.

For the next half-hour Gemelo had a ball. He had brought two boxes of shells for the 6.5 mm weapon and used them all.

He made himself conspicuous by firing on two adjacent targets as well as his own, to the annoyance of other customers. One actually complained to the manager, who said he'd look into it but didn't. At 7:30, Carlos Rigel appeared carrying the second 7.35 mm and took a turn sighting in. Then, at 7:45, after carefully marking the sights on the 6.5 mm, Gemelo and Rigel picked up all three weapons and left. They knew they had made an unforgettable impression.

Ruby and Rose were parked next to Roberto in the Sports Drome lot, waiting to take the 6.5 mm back to the Paine garage. Gemelo handed it to Ruby and climbed into the old Ford. Roberto, with a wild spin of tires on gravel, gunned down the road.

Six days later, Howard Price of Grand Prairie, Texas, and a number of others would positively identify Lee Harvey Oswald as a visitor to the rifle range.

On their way back to the Harlandale headquarters, Roberto told Gemelo that Ruby had scheduled the final orientation meeting for Thursday. Banister would conduct the session. The dress rehearsal held the previous Saturday had gone without a hitch.

When they arrived at the house on Harlandale, Jim Hart was preparing to leave for Miami to pick up a shipment of narcotics. Ruby was due any minute with the needed cash, and when he finally arrived Jim had a pleasant surprise. With Ruby was Rose Chermi, complete with suitcase and overnight bag. She announced that she was to accompany him for three or four days.

Before they left, Ruby reminded them, "Now remember, you must be back by the morning of the twenty-first. That means you're going to really have to move. Remember, don't cut the time too short. We've already had to make a few minor adjustments, but I'll have all the details firmed up before I go to Houston on Thursday."

Two hours after the others had left, Ruby sounded less confident as he discussed the mission with Guy Banister. "We've run into a possible snag," he said nervously, "but maybe it's something we can compensate for."

"What the hell's that?" asked Guy.

"Well, I've heard rumbling that the Trade Mart has been selected for the president's speech. That means the motorcade is going to pass through Dealey Plaza either out Main Street or the Stemmons Freeway."

"So . . . what's the problem?"

"It's a tough one. If the motorcade doesn't take the Stemmons Freeway via Elm, we won't be able to develop any crossfire from the stockade fence where the Nash and Olds will be parked. That only leaves us with a rear target for teams one and two."

"What you're trying to say is that Hart won't have a clear shot if the motorcade goes directly down Main Street?"

"That's right," Ruby agreed. "The third team would be forced to shoot across two multiple-lane highways. With a rapidly moving target at that distance, I would give a thousand to one odds against the chance of a clean hit. By the time our man got his target sighted the car would be out of range. The target's got to be going away or coming toward you to guarantee a hit."

"That means we'd have to depend strictly upon the teams in the Criminal Courts and Depository buildings."

"Precisely."

"I don't think that's good enough," Banister exclaimed.

"Exactly my sentiments, but I don't know what we can do about it," Ruby said. "We also have another problem. We've been planning that Oswald would have a fatal accident after the operation, but I'm afraid that may seem too improbable. People might start to figure somebody's been setting the stage for something, particularly with all the artificial situations we've set up."

"You could be right," Banister said thoughtfully. "What's the alternative?"

"Well, I finally took the liberty of consulting an old friend of mine on the Dallas police force."

Banister's face turned suddenly white, and Ruby continued hastily.

"Now, now, Guy, don't get upset. He's completely reliable.

He's an officer who patrols the Oak Cliff section of town where we have our headquarters, and he's a solid conservative. He was in the club last Friday with another friend, Barry Weisman, who's a staunch right-winger and fellow Minuteman. They were talking about an advertisement that Weisman's going to run in the morning paper the day Kennedy arrives."

"Advertisement?"

"Yes. Evidently, he's raised money from some of his conservative friends to put a full-page ad in the *Dallas Morning News* slamming the president. Anyway, seeing him gave me an idea. I've known this cop for years and know I can count on him. I just told him that I'd like somebody to have an accident while being arrested. I did say it's my understanding that the fellow was wanted for a major crime and that if he knocked him off he'd be a national hero."

"Well, the whole thing makes me nervous, but if you're sure of him it will solve a big problem for us."

"I thought you'd see it my way. He'll meet Oswald at the theater, recognize him, place him under arrest, and while he's being taken in Lee will get shot trying to escape. But the cop doesn't know all that yet. He won't be told who his target is until Gemelo meets him after the assassination to give him the word. If something misfires, we'll just call it off. My officer friend will never have to know who we wanted or why we wanted him."

"And if the assassination's successful?" Banister asked.

"Simple. The officer will meet Gemelo . . . let's say at the corner of Patton and Tenth around 1:00 P.M. He'll be given Oswald's description and location. Gemelo will also tell him that he believes Oswald to be the president's assassin. Our police officer gets to be a hero for disposing of him, and we don't have Lee to worry about."

"You're sure we can trust him?"

"Are you kidding?" Ruby asked. "Once he's done it, he's as involved as the rest of us and won't dare say a word. Besides, it's his chance of a lifetime. It's hard to be a hero patrolling a beat in Oak Cliff."

"Well, I hope you know what you're doing. But I have to

agree that if the guy's all right it's the perfect solution, particularly if he doesn't know who he's to hit until the last
minute."

"It's the only solution, Guy. But, as I said, on top of that
he'll get a medal and be a national hero. He couldn't pass
it up."

"Yeh, how about that? Jack, sometimes I think you're a
genius."

"Nope, just know my people," Ruby beamed.

"Well, the last orientation meeting will be on Thursday. It
should be fascinating. Oswald's supposed to go out to Irving
Thursday night and bring his rifle back Friday morning. Did
you get it back in the garage without anyone seeing you?"

"It went without a hitch. On top of that, I put little Rose
Chermi in the car with Jim Hart to get her out of sight until
the big day. Since she doubled for Marina, I don't want anyone to see her and make the connection. They've been on their
way to Miami for several hours now."

Guy laughed, "I bet they didn't get beyond the first motel."

"That's their problem. All they have to do is pick up a couple
packages and be back by Thursday morning."

"I'm not so sure it was a good idea to send that junkie
with him."

"Don't knock it, Guy. As long as she's hooked she's thoroughly reliable. You could even say dependent."

Banister looked at him with loathing and said, "I hope so."

Banister had been prophetic about one thing. Hart drove
only 140 miles into Louisiana before stopping at the first
decent-looking motel he could find.

Allowing Rose a small fix, they took a shower together and
had a session in bed. At 8:30 A.M. on Monday the 18th, they
were on their way again.

Bill Gemelo, meanwhile, arrived at Miami International Airport just after midnight and was in bed in his apartment by
1:30. Before he went to sleep, he wondered how Jim was making out with Rose. Good-looking as she was, he couldn't see
swinging with an addict. He had enough problems delivering

the stuff without having to shack up with one of the end products.

On Tuesday the 19th, Roberto drove a dirty gray 1959 Nash Rambler station wagon into the parking lot behind the stockade fence overlooking the grassy knoll and Dealey Plaza. In the back of the wagon was a Dallas Power and Light sawhorse barricade. It was about five o'clock in the evening and the lot was active. Guy Banister was already parked in position in the 1956 Olds when Roberto backed the Nash into a slot beside him. They now had both cars in position, yet the Nash would be parked for only a day and a half, and when the lot was full it would be inconspicuous. Roberto would have ample opportunity to warm it up on Friday morning, prior to their getaway.

Dallas traffic at 5 P.M. is heavy with homebound workers, so Banister was not concerned that their action would be noticed. When Roberto had parked and gotten out, Banister slid from behind the sedan's wheel and walked around to unlock the trunk. When Roberto joined him he said, "Here's your 7.35. Put it in the back of the wagon with the seat pulled down over it." After transferring the carbine, Banister handed Roberto a box of cartridges, which he tucked into the tire well.

Banister's confidence that they would not be observed was misplaced. Francis Hernandez, Josephine Salinis, and Henrietta Farcas, on their way home from work at the McKell Sportswear Company at 501 Elm Street, saw them transfer the weapon but assumed that they were hunters. They changed their minds after the guns roared in Dealey Plaza thirty-four and a half hours later.

The rain had stopped but the narrow road between Baton Rouge and Opelousas was still wet and slick. To make matters worse, the construction on this stretch of Route 190 would not permit a steady pace. The speedometer on the little Ford ranged between thirty-five and seventy miles per hour. Suddenly, Gemelo and Hart heard a moan from the rear seat. While Gemelo concentrated on the road, Hart looked in back and then clambered into the rear seat where Rose Chermi lay writhing on the floor. Hart pulled her up beside him on the seat, then asked Gemelo for the flashlight from the glove compartment. Focusing the light on Rose's face, he pried open one of her eyelids and swore loudly. "Jesus Christ," he shouted, "the dumb broad overdosed herself. She's out like a light."

After spending most of the afternoon in Miami on Tuesday, the three of them had started back towards Texas. They were to make a delivery en route at Baton Rouge and time had been getting short. If they couldn't make it to Dallas by the afternoon of the 21st they were to proceed the shorter distance to Houston to catch the plane that Ruby was using on his trip to case the motorcade there.

When they had stopped to eat in Baton Rouge, Rose had excused herself to go to the ladies' room. It had been obvious to Hart and Gemelo that she needed a fix. The car had been hot, humid, and miserable because of the rain that had been with them, on and off, ever since they had left New Orleans. After they had left Baton Rouge, Rose had climbed into the back seat and Hart had gotten in beside Gemelo.

It was already after 11:00 P.M. on the 19th and Gemelo had been determined to drive as far as he could that night. They had been ten miles outside of Eunice with Baton Rouge some miles behind when Hart had discovered Rose in her comatose state. Now he was asking Gemelo, "What the hell do you think we ought to do with her? My God, we can't let her die on us . . . ."

Gemelo, disgusted, said, "Get hold of yourself. We're better off if she does. We sure as hell can't take her to a hospital, can we? How much do you think she knows?"

Hart hesitated. "It's obvious she knows all about Oswald. On our trip down she asked me what the impersonation bit was all about."

"Oh, Jesus!" Gemelo exclaimed. "What did you tell her?"

"Nothing, damn it! But, she claimed she knew something big was on."

"Don't give me any crap. What did you tell her?"

"Nothing, really. I just agreed with her that it appeared Ruby wanted this Oswald character set up for something."

"Did you say for what?" When Hart didn't answer. Gemelo slowed the car down and repeated loudly, "Jim, answer me, goddamn it! Did you tell her why Oswald was being set up?"

Hart started to say, "I was drunk," when Rose moaned loudly and a deep gurgle emerged from her throat.

"Jesus!" Hart said, eager to change the subject. "Do you think she'll live?"

"For your sake, she'd better not," Gemelo snarled. "Jesus Christ, what kind of a fool are you, sounding off to a junkie? Couldn't you get in her pants any other way? After that little episode in Miami where you spilled your drunken guts in that Cuban bar, it's lucky we all weren't picked up."

"Lay off, damn it," Hart pleaded. "No one would believe it anyway. We were all drunk to the eyeballs."

"And with Rose?"

"Don't rub it in," Hart said defensively. "I was drunker than a skunk and she was practically senseless."

"You must have made a beautiful pair. Well, figure out how the hell to get rid of her right now. We're only a few miles out of Eunice."

Hart had put his ear down to Rose's chest and could barely hear her breathing. "I think she's almost dead," he said.

Gemelo glanced in the rear-view mirror. "Great! I'll speed up to about fifty. When we hit a nice dark curve, get that goddamn door open and push her out. Make sure her bag goes with her."

"Jesus! You're just going to dump her out like that?"

"No, you are," Gemelo replied. "You sure don't want to get out in this rain and take the time to bury her. Dump her out and it'll look like a hit-and-run."

"I guess you're right. But I still hate to see that beautiful body all knocked to shit."

"In her condition, she ain't no good for nobody. Here comes a curve."

Lee Harvey Oswald had ridden to Irving with Wesley Frazier on the night of Thursday the 21st. His efforts to escape the plot had been in vain and he was resigned to going through with it. At least, when it was over, he'd have the money for an apartment and some nice furniture for Marina and the girls.

On Thursday the 21st, Hugh Ward flew Jack Ruby in the Aztec from Red Bird Airport in Dallas to a small field outside of Houston. Ruby went into town and stood for an hour a block away from the Rice Hotel, where the presidential motorcade was formed. He was able to observe how it was organized as the cars passed within thirty feet of where he was standing. He noticed, particularly, the lead car and the position of the motorcycles beside the president's car. Strangely, they weren't abreast of it but rolled along slightly behind, with the Secret Service car following about thirty feet to the rear. Other luminaries in individual cars and a press bus followed the Secret Service.

Ruby returned to the airport, boarded the Aztec, and Ward dropped him off at Red Bird Airport. He was back in his office at the Carousel little more than four hours after leaving Dallas. At the final orientation meeting that evening, he could report the exact posture of the motorcade. He was now convinced that even if the motorcade drove down Main Street, the job could be done without using team number three at the stockade fence.

President John Fitzgerald Kennedy now had less than twenty hours to live.

Chapter Fourteen

On November 22, 1963, Lee Harvey Oswald arose early, dressed quietly to avoid disturbing Marina and the baby, and slipped silently down the stairs. He drank a cup of coffee and then walked out the kitchen door to the garage. Carefully hidden there was a neatly wrapped package containing the 6.5 mm Mannlicher, which Lee had broken down and wrapped while the women were doing the dishes the night before.

Half a block down the street Linnie Mae Randle, to whom Lee owed his job at the Book Depository, was having breakfast with her brother, Buell Wesley Frazier. She was looking out the window at about 7:15 when Oswald crossed the street to her brother's car, parked in the driveway. As she said goodbye to Wesley at the kitchen door, she saw Oswald place the brown package on the rear seat of the car. Wesley joined Lee in the front seat and, as he glanced over his shoulder to back the car out of the drive, noticed the parcel.

"What's in the package, Lee?" he asked.

"Curtain rods," Oswald replied shortly.

Still making conversation, Wesley asked Lee why he hadn't

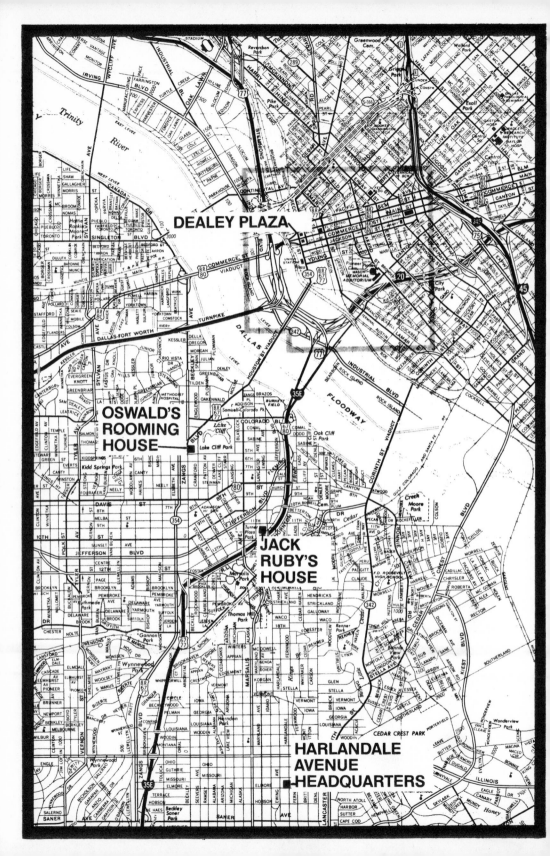

DEALEY PLAZA

OSWALD'S
ROOMING
HOUSE

JACK
RUBY'S
HOUSE

HARLANDALE
AVENUE
HEADQUARTERS

brought his lunch.

Lee hesitated before he replied, "With all the commotion going on downtown I thought I'd buy it."

A half hour later, when Frazier parked his car in the employee lot two blocks north of the Depository, Oswald got out, took the package from the rear seat, and walked hurriedly away. Frazier, locking the car, thought it odd that Oswald had not waited, as he always did, to walk with him to the building. Wesley followed about fifty feet behind, trying vainly to catch up, and was even more surprised to find when he entered the Depository that Lee was nowhere in sight.

Oswald had sprinted up the stairs to the second floor and down the short hall past the passenger elevator. Normally he entered Room 200, the Depository office, but today he avoided it, turning left past the Southwestern Publishing Company entrance. He continued through the building to the northwest stairway. Climbing the stairs with the Mannlicher under his arm, he reached the sixth floor moments after 8 A.M.

Kendricks had just stepped out of the shower and was putting on his terry cloth robe when the telephone rang. He walked into the bedroom to answer it and was surprised to hear Charles Cabell's voice on the line.

"Ed, have you seen a report—it should have crossed your desk about a week ago—concerning Lee Harvey Oswald?"

Ed thought for a moment, "No, Chuck, at least not one that I remember. Of course, I'm not caught up on everything, but I think somebody would have brought it to my attention."

"Not necessarily," Cabell said. "It was just a routine report, and of course I only heard about it second-hand. It appears that Oswald wrote a letter to the Soviet Embassy which the Company intercepted, copied, and passed along to the FBI. The Dallas Bureau office called him in for a routine interrogation and sent back a report, which just got through the computer analysis section for name identification. It's our Oswald, all right."

"What did the report say?"

"Oswald apparently told the FBI of a plan to assassinate the president on November 22, in Dallas. We passed the information on to the Secret Service, but it appears that the FBI treated it routinely as a 'crank' report—even though Oswald works for them as well as for Banister."

"Jesus Christ! The 22nd, that's today! Where's the president now?"

"At the moment, he's in Fort Worth."

"Where in Dallas is this supposed to happen?"

"The report has it that Oswald didn't know. The best guess, however, is that they'll try it at the new Trade Mart where Kennedy is scheduled to make a luncheon speech."

"My God, I'd better get hold of your brother immediately."

"That's what I was going to suggest. The report should be sitting on your desk. I wouldn't have known about it if I hadn't been tipped off by one of my old friends."

"Thanks, Chuck. You do keep your hand in, thank God!"

"I try to, but I don't really feel I can trust anyone there any more."

"I don't blame you. I'm not in much better shape—just a consultant. But at least I still have a desk."

"Call my brother now, would you?" Cabell urged. "I'm not sure that either the FBI or the Secret Service is taking Oswald's story seriously, and maybe he, as mayor, can do something to bring it to their attention locally. Much as I detest Kennedy, the country doesn't need an assassination right now."

"I'll call Dallas immediately. And Chuck, thanks."

"Don't mention it. I guess I wouldn't be taking the report so seriously myself, but the same information came out of Miami from another source about a week ago. A Cuban reported to the FBI that he heard a drunk in a barroom boasting about a plot to kill Kennedy in Texas."

"What?" Ed asked, shocked, but the line was dead. Cabell had hung up.

Kendricks placed a person-to-person call to Dallas and was informed that the mayor had already left for a breakfast function and would be unavailable for an hour. He stressed that his call was an emergency and left a message asking the mayor to call as soon as possible. Ten minutes later he was headed toward his office. He could shave when he got there.

On Harlandale Avenue the tension was mounting. The orientation meeting on the night of the 21st had been attended by all three teams. William Gemelo and Jim Hart were still shaken by their experience with Rose Chermi and had been quite apprehensive when they reported the event to Ruby. His reaction, unaccountably, had not been an angry one. He had simply said, "You did what you had to do." Banister, although perturbed, had agreed. He had suggested that they forget it and concentrate on the plans for the mission on the following day.

It had been agreed at that evening meeting that everyone would be in position by noon, and now, at shortly after 10 A.M. on November 22, Banister began the final indoctrination by relaying to Gemelo the instructions he had given Oswald.

"Lee is to make sure that the rear door beside the Houston Street loading dock is unlocked at twelve o'clock. You know what to do from there."

"Yes, Sir," Gemelo replied.

"Actually, you'll be about ten minutes behind the others getting into place, but Oswald should have everything set up for you, including the stack of boxes to shield your position." Turning to Ruby and Rigel, he continued.

"As team number two, you should have no trouble gaining access to the Criminal Courts Building. Your real problem begins when you reach the roof. It may be visible from some of the other buildings in the area. You could be spotted from one of them if you're not careful."

"We'll watch it," Ruby said confidently.

"Fine. It'll be your ass if you don't." Banister turned to Rigel and asked, "Carlos, have you got your stuff ready?"

"Right here, chief," Rigel said, hoisting a long toolbox that contained his Mannlicher. The weapon had been modified with a quick release clamp and knurled assembly bolts, so that he could break it down in ten seconds flat. "When I get to the roof, I'll leave the door open for Jack. If anybody asks what I'm doing there, I'll say I'm checking for leaks in the air conditioning plant."

"O.K. And I must say, you do look the part," said Banister, studying the outfit Rigel had on, "but you're awfully damn clean. Better go down to the basement when we get through and get some dirt on those work clothes if you're going to look like a real plumber."

"Will do, Guy," Rigel promised.

Banister continued with Roberto Navarro, "I guess I don't have to tell you what to do. I understand everything's in place."

"Yes, Sir."

"What about the getaway?"

"We'll have the station wagon warmed up and ready to go the minute we're sure that one of the teams has finished the job. Even if that has to be us, it'll only make a few seconds difference."

"All right. It's now 10:30. I want everyone to check his radio to be sure it's working. Bill, don't forget to check all the rounds to be sure they're fragmentary."

Preparing to leave, Bannister turned to Ruby and said, "Jack, before we take off I want to see you for a minute to give you some cash so you can pay everybody when it's over."

"All right, Guy. In fact, why don't I ride downtown with you?"

"I was going to suggest that. Well, gentlemen, it appears you're all ready, so I'd like to propose a toast." Banister raised his coffee cup. "To the success of our venture."

Navarro followed suit so violently that his coffee spilled down his arm.

"Vengeance for the betrayed of the 2506 Brigade who died at the Bay of Pigs," the emotional Cuban shouted.

"Amen," Banister added solemnly.

There was a moment of silence, broken by Ruby's rasping voice. "C'mon, you guys, we're running out of time. Let's get our ass in gear."

By 11:15 Oswald had neatly stacked a pile of boxes to shield the southeast corner window of the School Book Depository from any chance visitors to the sixth floor. Looking into the street, he calculated the approximate trajectory to the center of Elm and stacked a large carton and two smaller ones to serve as an arm rest. After placing another carton to act as a seat, he busily set about unpacking the Mannlicher and assembling it.

Once the weapon was assembled he checked it carefully and placed it against the wall between two pipes that would keep it from falling and protect the scope from getting knocked out of calibration. Then, picking up the clipboard he had stashed there the previous day, he stepped from behind the shield and walked down the aisle back toward the stairs he had come up at the northwest corner of the Depository.

The time was 11:37.

Kendricks had just finished talking to Cabell's brother and, as he leaned back in his desk chair, he had a queasy sensation in his stomach. Was this another case of someone crying "Wolf," or could it be the real thing? Ironically—if it was the real thing —feeling as he did about the president and his actions, why had he warned Cabell's brother? Then, realizing with horror the sinister implication of that thought, he said aloud, "My God, what's happening to me?"

Getting hold of himself, he reconsidered the situation. He had done what he could and probably, even if something was planned, it would be prevented. The mayor, when he had finally reached him, had described the massive security measures being taken at the Trade Mart. Apparently they had received some additional information themselves, or else they were taking Oswald's warning more seriously than Cabell had indicated.

Kendricks sat in his office and fretted over the impotence of his current status. He would still be sitting there at twenty minutes of two, when a distraught young secretary would burst into his office wailing, "Sir, the President's been shot."

At 11:15 Banister, driving a borrowed black Ford supplied by Ruby, pulled away from the curb at the Harlandale head-quarters. Ruby was beside him in the front, and Carlos Rigel, in mechanics dungarees and holding the toolbox containing the modified 7.35 Mannlicher, sat in the back. Roberto Navarro, Gemelo, and Hart followed them in the blue Olds.

The two cars proceeded north on Harlandale, then took Lamont to Ewing, which led them to the Houston Street viaduct. At 11:30 they halted for the light at the corner of Houston and Young, and Ruby got out in front of the Dallas Morning News building. He said, "Keep in touch!" to Banister, told Rigel, "I'll see you on the roof in forty-five minutes," and slammed the door.

When the light changed, both cars continued up Houston to Commerce. At Commerce, Banister turned right to Record and the Olds continued straight ahead up Houston. At Record, Banister turned north once more, crossing Main with the light. Just north of the corner, he pulled to the curb and Carlos Rigel got out, carrying his toolbox.

Banister said, "Good luck! And don't forget your radio."

By the time he had reached Elm, a glance in the rear-view mirror told him that Rigel had already disappeared into the Criminal Courts Building. Banister turned left into Elm and proceeded west, once more crossing Houston, and glanced to the right at the School Book Depository as he passed it. He followed Commerce Street west to Industrial Boulevard, where he turned south and drove to the entrance of the Union Terminal. Turning in, he drove toward the parking lot.

The blue Olds, meanwhile, had proceeded north on Houston to Elm, where Roberto stopped for a light. Crowds had started to gather for a view of the presidential motorcade. When the light turned green he crossed over and drove the short distance to the back of the Depository, where he entered the parking lot behind the pergolas next to the stockade fence.

The Rambler was still in position, and Hart jumped from the car to remove the Dallas Power & Light sawhorse that blocked the adjacent space. As Hart stacked it against the stockade fence several cars away, Navarro backed the Olds into the empty space next to the Rambler, angling it slightly so that the cars formed a "V."

Gemelo checked the area thoroughly while Hart raised the trunk lid of the Olds to help shield the team from anyone entering the lot. Roberto warmed up the engine of the Rambler so that it would start instantly when needed, and by 11:55 Hart and Navarro were ready and waiting behind the fence for the first call from Banister on the miniature transceiver. Meanwhile the crowds had begun to thicken at Main and Houston, and to the tense and expectant assassins the air seemed charged with electricity.

Gemelo, who had been patiently watching the other two, slipped his transceiver into his jacket pocket and said, "Well, it's about time I took off. That door should be open by the time I get to the Depository. Oswald's supposed to have it open by twelve."

Navarro agreed. "You only have five minutes, if that Hertz sign has the right time."

"According to my watch it's perfect," Hart said. Gemelo turned and walked away toward the School Book Depository.

At 11:45 Oswald placed three invoices for Scott Foresman books, which were located on the sixth floor, on the clipboard he was carrying. This would explain his presence there if questions were asked. Avoiding a floor-laying crew, which was working on the sixth floor that week, he walked down the stairs to the fifth floor a few minutes earlier than planned. He didn't want to be identified with the sixth floor anytime after twelve o'clock.

Oswald was standing near the fifth floor elevators at 11:50 when both cages descended with the floor-laying crew. Good, Oswald thought, they'll remember that it was the fifth floor I was on, clipboard in hand, obviously doing my job. As soon as the elevator was out of sight, he ran back up the stairs to the sixth floor to make one last check before going down to unlock the door.

Satisfied that nothing had been disturbed, he walked to the rear of the sixth floor and was stunned to see one of the floor layers emerge from an elevator.

"Damn, I forgot my cigarettes," the man said as he walked over to pick up his jacket, which was lying across some boxes. Picking it up he started back to the elevator, asking, "Are you going down? It's almost lunchtime."

"No Sir," Oswald replied. "But when you get downstairs

would you please close the gate to the elevator?"

"O.K.," the man said.

Oswald silently cursed himself as the elevator started down. He should have taken the elevator so a witness would know he had done so. Now he had to walk down. As he moved to the stairwell he dropped the clipboard between two stacks of boxes. He hurried down the stairs and unlocked the outside door that opened to the Houston Street loading dock.

A few minutes later Gemelo slipped inside, hurried up the stairs to the sixth floor, and by 12:20 was satisfied that everything was in order. The clip on the 6.5 mm Mannlicher was fully loaded and Banister, on the walkie-talkie, had just reported that the motorcade should be at Houston and Elm in seven or eight minutes.

Dave Ferrie had come up with the bright idea of rigging the walkie-talkies for aircraft frequency crystals. All that was needed was a slight modification of their transmitting and receiving coils and retuning of the antenna loading. It worked perfectly. With the three watts that each of the devices put out, Banister would be able to keep in clear and constant communication with the three teams. At the moment, however, he was a little upset. Number two team was having trouble getting into position on top of the Criminal Courts Building. The access door to the roof was locked, and when he made his first inquiry at 12 o'clock Carlos Rigel said he was picking it. Banister urged him to stay calm.

Rigel had just finished talking to Banister and had the door open when Ruby came down the hall from the elevator. They climbed to the roof together.

The day was sunny and clear and, although it was hot in the street, there was a nip in the air on top of the building. Remembering Banister's warning, they looked in all directions and were relieved to see that no adjacent building commanded a view of their position. If they kept below the parapets, they were out of sight of anything but helicopters. And, as Ruby had so aptly observed, the Dallas cops didn't have any of those.

Rigel had just finished assembling the rifle when Banister's second call came through, asking for a team status report. He heard Gemelo reply and then pushed the talk button down and reported that he and Ruby would be ready in five minutes. Hart, from his position behind the stockade fence, followed with a report that he and Navarro would also be ready in five minutes.

Glancing quickly over the top of the parapet, Rigel could see the crowd strung out down Main Street, with the motorcade in the distance. He also observed that the Olds and the Rambler were in position in the parking lot, the Rambler barely visible behind the foliage next to the pergolas.

He ducked back down behind the parapet just as the big Hertz sign on top of the Texas School Book Depository flashed 12:25. Banister's voice crackled through his earphone: "About five minutes."

After Banister pulled the car into the Union Terminal lot, he waited a few minutes to be sure he was not observed, then got out and started the walk back across the triple overpass to the pergolas next to the Depository.

On Elm, the crowd was not as thick as it had been on Main and Houston streets. In fact, it was rather sparse, which gratified Banister immensely. That meant fewer witnesses and a better view. Standing at the center of the pergolas on the adjacent lawn, he was in a perfect position to see the motorcade when it turned up Houston from Main.

He hoped that number three team would restrain themselves and act only as a last resort, because their position was so hazardous. His responsibility, as he had told Hart and Navarro repeatedly, was to observe the results achieved by the other teams and instruct Hart to fire only if the president survived the initial assaults. If they had to fire, and the Rambler got trapped, his Ford was parked across the underpass with clear access to Industrial Boulevard and adjacent freeways. If everything went according to plan, they would exchange vehicles on Harlandale Avenue, which would be relatively deserted at this time of day.

202

Gemelo and Navarro would take Roberto's old Ford. Ruby would pick up the '56 Olds after checking the stories at the *Dallas Morning News*. He was to stay free to plug any holes, since his Dallas police contacts made him the safest member of all the teams. His primary mission, however, was to place one of the expended bullets from Oswald's Mannlicher in a location where it was certain to be found. That would be the final link in positive identification of Oswald as the assassin.

Gemelo, Banister, Rigel, and Hart would all head for Harlandale, check on what was happening, and, if everything had gone according to plan, would head for Red Bird Airport. Maurice Gatlin would be waiting with the Aztec pre-flighted, engines running and ready, having received advance warning from Banister on the walkie-talkie frequency. Dave Ferrie, in New Orleans, would be available as a back-up pilot in case something went wrong.

Gemelo would still have work to do. Navarro would drop him off to meet Ruby's police contact and tell him where to find Oswald, then exchange the Rambler for his old Ford and come back to pick Gemelo up. After holing up at the Harlandale place overnight, Gemelo would get the '56 Olds from Ruby and drive it back to New Orleans. It was a complex series of maneuvers, deliberately confusing to any observers and calculated to confound potential pursuers.

The tense voice of Guy Banister brought all three teams to the alert. On the roof of the Criminal Courts Building, team number two, Ruby and Rigel, could hear the cheers as the motorcade came slowly down Main Street. Resting his arm lightly on the parapet, Rigel carefully aimed his rifle at the grass strip between Elm and the edge of the pergolas, making sure that the barrel did not extend beyond the edge.

By chance, for a moment the gun was pointed toward Abraham Zapruder, a clothing manufacturer who was anxiously waiting with his 8 mm camera to film the presidential motorcade. The amateur photographer was unaware that his face was appearing in Rigel's telescopic sight, or that he was about to take some of the most controversial footage of all time.

From his vantage point in the window of the School Book Depository, Gemelo could hear the crowd noises reverberating off the buildings on Main. After Guy's warning, he knelt and propped Oswald's Mannlicher on the box facing him. The ultrathin surgical gloves he wore would protect his hands from nitrite deposits in the event he was captured and keep his fingerprints off Oswald's weapon. As the lead car came into view at the corner of Main and Elm and started to turn the corner, he gave the settings a final check and glued his right eye to the four-power Japanese scope.

Roberto Navarro had been pacing nervously back and forth between the stockade fence and the bumpers of the two cars, smoking one cigarette after another.

Suddenly Hart put a hand up to the earphone connected to the unit in his pocket and said, "Get ready, they're damn near here. Banister says they'll be turning the corner from Main any minute now."

Navarro stopped pacing and peered cautiously through the brush on the outside of the stockade fence. "The lead car is just starting to turn," he reported.

Jim Hart needed no further warning. He was already centering his scope on Elm Street, just to the left of a large highway sign that faced in the opposite direction.

Roberto had hurried to his side and was watching the oncoming entourage through a pair of binoculars. "I can see everything," he said in a low voice. "Remember, don't fire unless I say so."

"I can see damn near as much as you," Jim whispered back.

"Sí, compadre," Roberto said, with a searching look at his unpredictable companion. "But remember, wait for the order. We are still the easiest for the cops to get to."

"Keep your voice down," Jim cautioned sharply. "They're coming around the corner."

Roberto returned to his binoculars, and both men watched eagerly as the dark blue presidential limousine trailed the lead car around the corner from Main into Houston Street and headed up the short block to Elm. Hart calmly cranked a round into the Mannlicher's chamber.

Guy Banister was standing less than one hundred feet in front of Navarro and Hart and even closer to Abraham Zapruder. He watched as Patrolman Joe Smith halted traffic at the corner as the motorcade proceeded up Houston.

The Hertz sign on top of the Depository, barely visible from his vantage point, was flashing 12:28. Banister instinctively glanced up at the Depository's sixth floor corner window. Gemelo was not visible, but he could see the muzzle of Oswald's 6.5 mm Mannlicher rifle and hoped fervently that everyone else was so absorbed with the motorcade that they wouldn't notice it. Gemelo had a perfect target coming up Houston, but he couldn't fire yet because the car was not in range of the backup teams—a vital detail, in case he missed. The Hertz sign now read 12:29.

As the lead car made the left turn into Elm, it was less than two hundred feet from where he was standing. Inexorably, the limousine carrying the president, Jackie, the governor, and Mrs. Connally turned and followed behind it.

Gemelo broke into a cold sweat as the limousine rounded the corner into Elm. As he squinted through the scope, he saw the lead car pass and began to apply gentle pressure to the Mannlicher trigger.

It had been agreed at the briefing the night before that he would fire first. That would pinpoint the Depository as the assassin's location. He was then to reload and fire again if he could, but under no circumstances was he to fire more than two rounds. After his first round, team number two—with Rigel at the trigger—could fire, but only then. If neither of them fired a fatal shot Navarro, observing the results through his binoculars, would decide whether Hart must expose team three by firing at near point-blank range from behind the stockade fence.

As the hood of the presidential limousine moved into the cross hairs of Gemelo's scope, partially obscured by the foliage of an intervening tree, he was startled to hear a shot off to his right. Hart must have had a clear shot and impetuously disregarded his instructions. Raising his scope slightly, Gemelo leveled the cross hairs just beyond the tree as the hood again came into view, this time with an unobstructed field. His abdominal muscles tightened as the cross hairs tracked slowly down the length of the big car, and he increased the pressure on the trigger.

The view through Hart's scope, as the long blue limousine rounded the corner at Elm, was breathtaking. The image was as large as if he were sitting on the hood. He had a completely unobstructed field to the left of the large highway sign and decided not to wait. Centering the cross hairs on the president's head, he slowly squeezed the trigger until the Mannlicher jerked in his hands. As Hart watched through the scope, a surprised expression appeared on the president's face and he instinctively reached for his neck as he disappeared from view behind the highway sign.

As the president's back came into view Gemelo shifted the cross hairs slightly until they were centered squarely on the president's spinal cord at the base of the neck. Holding his breath, he gently squeezed the Mannlicher's trigger and fired. Not bothering to see where his first shot had hit he jerked the bolt back, ejecting the empty shell, and slammed a new round into the chamber. Once again he found the elusive target in his scope and aimed hurriedly because the limousine had begun to accelerate. His scope once more found the huddled figure of the president, who was now holding his neck. Gemelo again squeezed the trigger as the elusive target receded. The whole action took less than three seconds and he knew instantly that in his haste he had missed. During the millisecond that his eye stayed glued to the cross hairs in the glass, he was astonished to see the top of John F. Kennedy's head shatter in a shower of red and gray matter that spread for twenty feet. That's it, he thought. Hart got him. He could never survive that one. Now to get the hell out of here. He ejected an empty shell onto the floor and put a new round into the chamber, more by instinct than purpose.

Gemelo's mind worked quickly. He had heard only three shots, so the devastating final shot must have been fired almost simultaneously with his. That makes it easy, he reasoned. Three shots mean three spent cartridges. Reaching into his pocket, he pulled out one of the three empty cases given him by Navarro and dropped it along with the other two on the floor. Then, pushing one of the boxes out of his way, he walked rapidly once more to the northwest stairway, letting the Mannlicher fall between a stack of cartons on the way. As he plunged down the stairwell, he pulled off and pocketed the surgical gloves.

From his vantage point atop the Criminal Courts Building, Carlos Rigel saw a flash and a puff of smoke near the stockade fence and realized that Hart had drawn first blood. Seeing the president grab his neck, he tracked his target through his scope, leading it slightly to compensate for the movement of the limousine. Governor Connally was turning to look at the president. At the precise moment that Gemelo fired his first shot from the Depository, Rigel jerked the trigger of his own carbine, spoiling his aim.

Governor Connally recoiled from the impact of the slug, which caught him in the right side near his right armpit. Through the scope, Connally's face and chest seemed to puff up and then collapse as the air in his right lung first compressed and then was exhausted through the hole in his chest. Stepping quickly back from the parapet to Ruby's side, Rigel said, "Let's get the hell out of here, Jack. I got Connally instead."

Without bothering either to work the bolt to eject the expended cartridge or to remove the clip, he broke the gun down, hearing another shot as he did so. Within twenty seconds the rifle was back in the toolbox and Rigel was following Ruby down the stairs.

Navarro, watching through his binoculars, was not certain that anyone had registered a fatal hit. Hart's first shot had already revealed their location, if anyone was paying attention, so they might as well buy some insurance. Tapping Hart on the shoulder lightly, to avoid spoiling his aim, he said, "Go!"

With the scope, the range was now almost point blank. Hart had a bead on the president's temple, and there was no way he could miss, even if the scope was off a degree or two. Connally had slumped down, and the limousine was speeding up. Hart's forefinger tightened on the trigger and the firing pin slammed home. John Fitzgerald Kennedy's head exploded in Navarro's face, or so it seemed when magnified by fifty-power binoculars.

"Magnifico," he muttered, transfixed for a moment. Then, remembering their precarious position, he turned as Hart dropped the rifle into the trunk of the Olds. He tossed the binoculars in as well, Hart slammed the lid, and they jumped into the Rambler.

"I even remembered to pick up the cartridge," Navarro said proudly.

"I noticed. Beautiful, wasn't it?" Hart exclaimed jubilantly.

"Compadre, I couldn't have done better myself. If only it had been Fidel!"

"Now, that may be possible," Hart replied, as Navarro eased the Rambler out of the slot and headed toward the Pacific Avenue entrance to the lot.

After unlocking the loading dock door, Oswald went to the men's room on the second floor, opened the window slightly, and sat quietly in a stall to wait. He could hear clearly the noise of the crowds outside. Within five minutes he heard the first crack of a rifle echoing across the Plaza. It was followed by a second shot, along with shouts and screams. He got up, walked to the men's room door, and peered cautiously into the hall. He saw no one but heard loud voices coming from the front hallway, so he waited a minute more. Satisfied that the voices were retreating, he slipped out of the men's room and walked through the swinging vestibule doors into the lunchroom. He was reaching into his pocket for a coin to place in the coke machine when a sharp voice commanded, "You, come here!"

Startled, Oswald looked up to see an officer with drawn pistol walking toward him from the doorway. As Lee responded to the command Mr. Truly, the Depository superintendent, also entered.

"Do you know this man?" the officer asked Truly. "Does he work here?"

"Yes, he's an employee," Truly replied.

Grudgingly, the officer removed his pistol from Oswald's stomach. He and Truly hurried back into the vestibule and up the stairs.

When they were out of sight, Oswald left the lunchroom and went to the Depository office. He walked through to its front entrance, where Mrs. R.A. Reid, the clerical supervisor, was just returning to her desk. As he passed her she said, "The president's been shot!"

Oswald mumbled, almost under his breath, "That's a damn shame," but didn't think she heard him.

Without pausing, Oswald walked down the front stairs to the main lobby. Encountering no one, he continued on to the first floor storage area at the rear of the building and entered the men's room, where he had earlier hung his shirt. He quickly put it on and went back into the storage room to check on whether anyone was in that area. Seeing no one, he went out the door to the loading dock that Gemelo had used earlier. He reached the edge of the ramp area just as the Rambler pulled up. Perfect timing, he thought, as he finished tucking in his shirt.

At the fifth floor, Gemelo stopped abruptly and peered cautiously out from the stairwell. He hurried down another flight and paused momentarily on the fourth floor, listening for voices. He could hear the excited gabble of some women approaching and ran down another flight.

At the third floor, he heard loud voices and running feet on the floor below. He cracked open the stairwell door and looked through a narrow slit, but saw no one. He stepped quickly into the aisle and hid behind a stack of boxes. Within seconds he heard the loud voices of two men, one obviously a police officer, who were racing up the stairs to the floor above. Sighing with relief over his split-second escape, he raced down the stairs.

Knowing that the police were now in the building and that it might be sealed off within minutes, Gemelo abandoned caution. He hurried to the front lobby through the second floor hallway and, curbing his fear, blended into the crowd standing outside. As more people returned to the building, he forced himself to walk nonchalantly down the concrete steps and across the street. There he stood between two parked cars and, like hundreds of others, scanned Dealey Plaza as an interested spectator. If all went according to schedule, he would be able to spot the Rambler turning off of Record onto Elm and reach it in seconds.

Officer Smith, who had left his post at the corner of Elm and Houston, ran up to Banister with his gun drawn and asked what he was doing. Banister said nothing but flipped open the Secret Service identification card and waved it at Smith.

"Sorry," the officer said and charged up the slope.

The encounter unnerved Banister and he walked to the far side of the pergolas, crossed the extension of Elm between the parked cars, and walked to the rear of the Depository. He was surprised to observe that the building had not yet been sealed off. Looking toward the street, he was shocked to see the Rambler, which had just picked up Oswald, disappearing down Pacific.

The plan had been that the Rambler would pick him up as it pulled out of the lot, but his encounter with Officer Smith had made him thirty seconds late. He now faced the added risk of going to the alternate rendezvous on Record Street. Donning a pair of horn-rimmed glasses and a raincoat he had been carrying over his arm, Banister stepped out from behind the loading dock of the Depository and walked rapidly down Houston Street.

Ruby emerged from the elevator of the Criminal Courts Building into the pandemonium of the main lobby. It was crowded with confused and frightened people talking excitedly, speculating on what had happened to the motorcade. As he walked through the Houston Street entrance fronting Dealey Plaza, he could see people running and hear the sirens blaring north on Elm.

Ruby paused for only a moment, then turned and walked the

few blocks south toward the building that housed the *Dallas Morning News*. He was jostled repeatedly by the crowds headed north, and it took him five minutes to reach his destination.

When he entered the newspaper office, he encountered a friend and asked what had happened. He was told that the president had been shot and taken to Parkland Hospital, where he was probably undergoing emergency surgery.

"Thank God," Ruby said. "I thought he might be dead."

His friend assured him that at last report Kennedy was still alive. It was the last thing Ruby wanted to hear, but he was careful not to show it. He now had to get his tail out to the hospital and complete his assignment there. He reached into his pocket to be sure that the little box containing the rifle slug was still there. Ten minutes later he was driving the Olds toward Parkland Hospital. It was thirteen minutes past one.

After confirming that things had gone as planned for Oswald, Hart and Navarro dropped him off at the corner of Griffin and Pacific. He hadn't said a word since the Rambler picked him up behind the Depository, but as he got out he mumbled to Hart, "I'll be in the third row close to the left-hand aisle. Make sure Jack has all the cash in small bills."

Hart nodded acknowledgment. Oswald jumped out, slamming the door, and the Rambler pulled away from the curb, turned right at the corner, and proceeded south on Griffin.

"I hope he doesn't do anything stupid," Navarro remarked as they crossed Main Street.

"You mean like think? Hell, no. He'll be an automaton as long as he expects that grand bonus this afternoon. He'll follow orders just like he has for the past four years."

"I guess you're right. As long as he doesn't hear his description on the radio or start thinking he's been set up, we should be home free."

"It's Bill's description, too, you know."

"Yeah, but even so. . . . "

Navarro slowed the Rambler at Commerce, then speeded up and crossed as the light turned green. "The traffic is already starting to jam up," he observed. "In another five minutes you won't be able to move west of this block. And for God's sake, Jim, don't worry about Oswald. He's already on a bus and won't know he's been had until Jack's buddy blasts him in the theater."

Nothing more was said as Navarro continued slowly south on Griffin. He was lucky and caught the light, then turned west on Jackson. They were almost at Record Street when Hart remarked, "Christ, listen to that."

From the distance the wailing sirens sounded like the start of a ten-alarm fire. At Record, Navarro executed a quick turn north and drove rapidly up the block, once more crossing Commerce. He pulled to the curb about fifty feet from the corner, across from the partially completed Dallas County Government building. The street was virtually deserted except for a few people running toward Dealey Plaza. After about five seconds, Jim said nervously, "Where the hell is he?"

Almost as though he had heard him, Guy Banister appeared around the corner of the building and stopped at the curb. He looked quickly around, crossed the street, and got into the back of the car. Navarro pulled away as Banister was closing the door and crossed Main on a yellow light. Out of the corner of his eye he saw several police cars on Main, racing toward the intersection at high speed.

Halfway up the block he again stopped the car and Carlos Rigel, complete with toolbox, emerged from the Record Street entrance of the Criminal Courts Building. He climbed into the back seat as Navarro again pulled away and veered into the far left lane. Speeding up slightly, he reached Elm just as the light turned green and made the left turn. It seemed to Hart like hours, but only six minutes had elapsed since they had pulled out of the parking space behind the fence.

At Houston Street Navarro eased into the right lane opposite the Book Depository, yelling to Banister, "Open the door; here comes Gemelo. I'm going to pick him up on the run."

Banister pushed the door open and, as the car swerved close to the curb, Gemelo, wearing dark trousers and a light rain jacket over his 5'10" frame, came running down the grassy slope and leaped through the open door. Navarro tramped down on the accelerator, pulling around several parked police vehicles, and roared onto the Commerce Street Expressway through the triple underpass.

Oswald glanced briefly at the retreating Rambler, then crossed Griffin and walked east on Elm at a normal pace. He was surprised to observe that traffic was already moving slowly. Had he turned around, he would have noticed that a motorcycle officer had begun diverting traffic north and south on Lamar, two blocks behind him.

He was in luck. An Oak Cliff bus was waiting for the light to change as he approached the corner of Murphy Street. Dodging traffic, he crossed against the light and rapped on the closed door. The driver admitted him and, as the light changed, maneuvered the bus into the crawling Elm Street traffic.

Oswald sat down behind the driver and watched the chaos created by the traffic diversion. When the thickening traffic brought the bus to a halt after crossing Poydras Street, he realized he would never make his 1:45 rendezvous with Ruby at the Texas Theater if he stayed aboard. He decided that if he hurried he could get another bus a few streets south that would take him down Ewing Street via the Houston Street viaduct. Once it crossed Jefferson he could either transfer or walk the rest of the way.

Oswald got up, asked for a transfer, and, as he waited for the door to open, glanced at the passengers in the rear of the bus. A sudden chill went up his spine when he saw a familiar face. It was that ill-tempered Mrs. Bledsoe, who had rented a room to him when he first moved to Dallas. Recalling his crudely critical parting comments to her, he was sure she recognized him. He swore to himself as he stepped from the bus.

Oswald hurried to Lamar Street, crossed to the opposite side, and walked rapidly south toward Commerce. His eardrums rebelled at the screech of countless screaming sirens, as police vehicles attempted to fight their way through the heavy traffic to Dealey Plaza.

Main Street was jammed solidly with traffic in both directions. He wondered momentarily whether the Rambler had managed to get through or was tied up in the snarled mass of immobilized vehicles. Growing more concerned by the minute about his own schedule, he almost ran toward Commerce, cursing himself. If only he hadn't stayed on that damn bus he could be in Oak Cliff by now.

Several buses were stopped in the curb lane at the corner of Commerce. As he passed one group of people, he was startled to hear a man who had just come out of the Dallas News Building exclaim loudly, "The president is dead, and the police are looking for an employee of the Book Depository!"

There was little traffic coming from the Plaza area, but the diverted flow from Lamar was starting to create problems. Crossing Commerce, Oswald walked rapidly toward Jackson in a state of panic, gripped by fear. Remembering the .38 pistol still buried in the yard on Neely Street, he had a sudden urge to retrieve it.

At the corner of Jackson, a lone taxicab driven by William Whaley was just pulling into the stand outside the Greyhound bus terminal. He crossed quickly, opened the door, climbed in, and was startled to discover that an older woman had opened the door on the opposite side. Not wanting to call attention to himself, he told her she could take the cab. But she refused, telling him politely, "No, that's all right. I'll get the next one." She would recall the incident later.

"Take me to 500 North Beckley," Oswald ordered.

"Right," Whaley said. "What the hell do you think happened?""

Oswald shrugged his shoulders but didn't reply; he was in no mood to get friendly with a cab driver. The driver looked curiously at him, pulled away from the curb and headed down Lamar to Jackson, where he turned right. At Austin a motorcycle officer was diverting all traffic south, and Whaley turned left. He continued to Wood and then turned again toward Houston Street. There, Oswald was relieved to see that traffic was being diverted south toward the viaduct.

"I've got it made," he gloated silently. Once on Houston it would be a straight shot for Oak Cliff.

As the Rambler turned south into the broad Industrial highway, Banister looked at his watch and said to Navarro, "We have plenty of time. Pull into the terminal parking lot next to the Ford."

"O.K., boss," Navarro replied, executing a left turn into the Union Terminal entrance. As they got out of the car, they could hear the scream of sirens across the triple underpass.

"You know, with all the furor over there, you'd think something important had happened," Carlos Rigel remarked.

Hart smiled grimly and said, "It did. We just elected the first Texas president, and the natives are celebrating."

Banister looked at his watch again and told Hart abruptly, "Quit the crap. We've got to stay on schedule." Then to Navarro and Gemelo he said, "It's already 12:50—you don't want to be late for your meeting with Ruby's friend. He might get nervous. And remember, Bill, he'll find you. Go south on Beckley. The main drag across the expressway is Eighth. Turn east, Roberto, and when you get to Patton let Gemelo out."

"Bill, when you get out, walk south on Patton to Tenth, turn left, and walk east towards Ewing. Roberto, you will continue east on Eighth and turn right on Marsalis or Ewing. Go to Harlandale and park anywhere within a block. We don't want all of the vehicles right in front of the house. Next, pick up your own car, go back for Bill, and then drive back past Ruby's to see if he made it home. He's on Ewing just east of the park— you know where."

Banister, Rigel, and Hart climbed out of the Rambler and into the '58 Ford. Banister started the engine, turned to the others, and said, "We'll leave after the Rambler turns onto the highway."

"Well, so far, so good," Hart rejoiced. "If our luck holds, Gatlin will be waiting for us at Red Bird Airport." Banister didn't comment. The time was 12:52.

Oswald got out of the cab at the corner of Neely. After paying the driver, he waited for him to pull away, then walked west for two blocks and, after crossing Elsbeth, stopped in front of 214, the apartment that he and Marina had shared before they went to New Orleans.

No one was in sight, so he walked around to the back yard and a few minutes later had dug up his Smith and Wesson .38 caliber Cobra and its cartridges, still well preserved in their plastic wrapping. He put them in his pocket, filled in the shallow hole, and returned to the street. After walking the two blocks back to Zangs, he turned north to Fifth and east on Fifth to Beckley. When he entered the front door of his rooming house, it was 1:14. It had taken him only six minutes to walk from Neely Street and, with the time he had saved in the cab, he could easily make his rendezvous with Ruby at the Texas Theater by 1:45.

After leaving the Terminal parking lot, Navarro drove rapidly north on the Industrial highway back to Commerce Street, where he turned left abruptly.

"Take it easy," Gemelo said. "You're starting to act like a nervous Latin."

There was little traffic going west on Commerce, and within a minute and a half they were turning south on Beckley. By now Navarro was concerned only about potential roadblocks. They had been rather conspicuous, picking Gemelo up in front of the Depository, but with the confusion around Dealey Plaza his concern was not great. When they drove past Oswald's boarding house, Navarro pointed it out to Gemelo with the comment, "I wonder where Oswald is by now?"

"Probably back in town stuck in traffic," Gemelo replied.

Actually, they had missed encountering Oswald by only thirty seconds.

At Eighth Street Roberto turned left and stopped at the corner at the intersection of Patton.

"O.K., chico, you're on your own," he said. "I'll pick you up just as soon as I switch cars."

"Do you think this guy will recognize me?" Gemelo asked as he opened the Rambler door.

"He's got your full description." Then, noticing the bulge in Gemelo's jacket, he said, "Maybe you'd better leave the gun with me."

Gemelo stared at him coldly. "You've got to be kidding," he snarled. "Don't be late."

As Navarro pulled away from the curb, he looked at his watch. He figured he could be back in approximately twelve minutes, maybe ten if the traffic wasn't too heavy.

William Gemelo reached the corner of Patton and Tenth at 1:08 and stopped, looking around. A cab was parked at the southeast corner and he concluded that the driver had stopped to have his lunch. A woman was standing nearby, apparently waiting for a bus, and two blocks down the street a police cruiser was driving slowly east on Tenth.

Gemelo was instantly alert, wondering if the patrol car was driven by the contact that Ruby had set up. He crossed diagonally to the southeast corner and waited until the police car reached the intersection of Crawford and Tenth. Then, slowly, he started walking east. He hadn't gone thirty feet when the cruiser pulled up and stopped a short distance ahead of him. The officer made no move to get out of the cruiser, so Gemelo walked up to the open window on the curb side, bent down, and said, "I assume you're waiting for me."

He was terrified when, staring at him with anger and disgust, Dallas Police Officer J. D. Tippit said, "You dirty rotten bastards. Ruby never said you were going to kill the president!"

Gemelo was stunned. He became almost incoherent. "We didn't . . . he didn't . . . the guy who did it . . . er . . . you want . . . is in the Texas Theater."

"That's a crock, buster," Tippit shouted. "You bastards planned the whole thing."

Gemelo stuttered, "Ruby . . . Ruby . . ." But he was interrupted with a rude "Ruby, Ruby, bullshit! You're not going to rope me into this. Stay right there."

Gemelo stepped back from the car and frantically reached into his jacket pocket, slipping the safety off his .38 Colt. Tippit slid out of the car and started toward him. Gemelo panicked, realizing that he was going to be arrested.

Roberto Navarro dropped off the Rambler wagon at Harlandale, picked up his '41 Ford coupe, and immediately started back to pick up Gemelo. He drove up Ewing to Eighth and cut west to Patton, where he turned south. Stopping at Patton and Tenth, he spotted Gemelo standing by a police cruiser parked around the corner. Turning the corner, he drove past it and parked about a hundred feet in front of the cruiser. As he switched off his engine, he glanced in the rear-view mirror and saw the officer getting out of the car.

He wondered if something had gone wrong and got out of the Ford to find out what was going on. He looked down the street to see Gemelo pull his gun from his pocket and fire five shots at the police officer at point-blank range. He watched with horror as the officer collapsed on the ground.

Gemelo didn't see him and took off at a fast trot towards Patton Avenue, cutting across a lawn at the southeast corner of Tenth. Navarro lost sight of him as he disappeared behind some bushes heading south. The woman who had been waiting for the bus was screaming hysterically. Navarro ran to the police car, made sure the officer was dead and raced back to the Ford. As he drove away the woman was still screaming, and in his mirror he could see others converging on the scene.

Gemelo cursed bitterly as he ran across a lawn, breaking open the Colt and ejecting the empty shells into some bushes along the way. With the cop out of the picture, he now had to get to Oswald before he got nervous and left the theater. If the cops picked him up, he might blow the whistle on everybody.

Heading down Patton, he ran across the street behind the parked taxi, swearing half audibly, "That poor dumb cop." Halfway down the block, he was debating whether to reload his pistol as he ran when a voice yelled at him from across the street, "Hey, man, what the hell's going on?"

He suddenly realized that in his haste he was calling attention to himself. He slowed down, looked across the street, and said, "Nothing, man," and continued on toward Jefferson Street.

He turned right on Jefferson and halfway between Patton and Crawford glanced back and saw two men crossing Jefferson, coming from a used car lot on the other side of Patton. Alarmed, he ran into a Texaco station at the corner of Crawford and hid behind some barrels stacked at the rear of the structure. While he waited he reloaded the Colt. He realized that if he stayed in the open it was only a matter of time before he'd be spotted. But if he could avoid being captured and get to the theater, the cop's death would be blamed on Oswald, as would the president's.

Gemelo abandoned all hope of getting to Oswald when he heard the scream of police sirens coming toward him down Jefferson. I'll give the gun to Ruby, he thought. He'll be able to fix it some way so that it will be connected to Oswald. Then, to change his appearance, he took off his jacket and tossed it under a car in the Texaco lot.

One of the exit doors in a church across the alley was slightly ajar. He ran into the building and hid in a closet in the basement. In the blackness the luminous dial on his watch read 1:18.

Oswald met Mrs. Earlene Roberts as he rushed through the hallway of the rooming house and started up the stairs.

"Oh, you are in a hurry," the housekeeper said.

Oswald continued up the stairs without replying, entered his room, grabbed his jacket, and slipped it on. He thought about washing his hands, dirty from digging up the pistol, but decided to wait until he got to the theater so he wouldn't miss Ruby. He headed back down and waved to Mrs. Roberts as he went out the front door.

He crossed the street and stood momentarily on the corner at the bus stop until he spotted a police cruiser headed north on Beckley.

"Uh, oh," he thought, "I'd better walk." He quickly turned about and walked west on Fifth, deciding to stay off the main thoroughfares by going down Madison to Jefferson. This would take him within a half block of the theater.

The uneventful walk took about eighteen minutes. However, when he arrived at the corner of Jefferson, he started to feel naked again as he heard police sirens roaring down West Jefferson toward Beckley.

"That should be over with by now," he thought, unaware that Officer Tippit had just been killed by his double, Bill Gemelo. Oswald stepped into the vestibule of a shoe store, pretending to look in the window until the patrol car had roared by. When he heard another siren in the distance, he was tempted to go into the store but didn't when he noticed someone inside looking out at him curiously. After the second patrol car had raced by, he stepped back onto the sidewalk and hurried toward the theater. He didn't know that he had aroused the suspicions of those in the store, and that they would report his whereabouts to the police who would mistakenly believe that he had killed Officer Tippit.

Worried now that a search might be on for someone of his description, he decided not to buy a theater ticket and resorted, instead, to a trick he had used often as a child. He pretended to be looking at the advertisements for coming attractions and, while doing so, inched slowly toward the lobby. When the ticket taker's attention was diverted by a commotion in the street, he slipped into the theater as a patron pushed open the handleless exit door to walk out.

Inside, Oswald walked directly to the men's room. He was annoyed to find that there were no towels or soap in the dispensers. He rinsed off his soiled hands as best he could, wiped them on his jacket, and then realized angrily, as he looked in the mirror that he had streaked his jacket with dirt. He removed it, entered the darkened theater, and moved down the aisle, counting the rows with his hand. He slipped into a seat, and as his eyes adjusted to the dim light he saw that the theater was almost deserted. He placed his jacket on the upturned seat beside him and waited. The theater clock said 1:43. Ruby should arrive in two more minutes.

Because of the heavy traffic, it took Ruby twelve minutes to drive the Olds to Parkland Hospital and park in a nearby lot. The place was cluttered with police cars and vehicles that had participated in the motorcade. Standing alone next to the emergency entrance was the presidential limousine, its pristine metallic blue paint glistening in the sun.

Ruby casually approached the vehicle, but his attention was riveted on the frenzied activity he could see through the open emergency room doors. He glanced momentarily at the interior of the limousine, which was covered with patches of blood.

Seth Kanter, a newsman he had met on several occasions, came out of a small building next to the drive and headed for the hospital's main entrance. Ruby followed, entered the front door, and walked up behind Kanter. He touched the reporter on the shoulder and, when he turned, asked, "Do you think I ought to close my places for the next three nights?"

Kanter shrugged his shoulders, raised one hand in the air, and mumbled something under his breath as he headed for a press conference on the status of the president.

Two minutes later Ruby knew that the president was dead. The report spread like wildfire through the hospital lobby and, as he hurried out the front door to get back to the Carousel, he stopped short.

"My God," he thought, "I almost forgot what I came for." He reached into his pocket, feeling for the little box containing the 6.5 millimeter slug. He had intended to drop it into the presidential limousine, but the interior was such a bloody mess that he was afraid it might go undetected, so he entered the emergency room door and joined a milling but now quiet crowd. He was surprised that no one challenged his presence. He saw no Secret Service personnel but heard someone mention that a blood-soaked stretcher, next to an elevator less than ten feet from where he was standing, was the one used for the governor. He reached into his pocket, removed the cotton-wrapped 6.5 mm slug from the box, and edged toward the stretcher. His hand darted under the soiled linen, and when he edged away again the slug was resting under the bloody sheets. He put the cotton in his pocket and tiptoed out the door as the announcement was being made to the hospital personnel that John F. Kennedy was dead.

Roberto Navarro sped across Tenth to Ewing and turned south. He passed Ruby's apartment but not seeing the blue Olds, concluded that he had arrived too early. He kept going. Somehow, Ruby must be contacted soon and told what had happened to Gemelo, but that was a job for Banister if he could reach him before he left Dallas.

Arriving at the Harlandale house five minutes later, he was relieved to find that the other team members were still there. The Rambler wagon was nowhere to be seen, but the black '58 Ford was in the drive. As he entered the house, he could hear Banister cursing into the telephone in the kitchen. Hart and Rigel were there too, having a late lunch of sandwiches and beer.

Banister greeted him with a complaint, "You'd think everybody and his aunt was trying to call New Orleans. I can't get through to save my ass."

"That's the least of our problems," Navarro said. As he told them what had happened to Gemelo, Banister's face turned white and he sank into a chair, muttering, "Oh, shit, that goddamn Ruby!"After a moment he got up and dialed the Carousel. The lines were busy. When he hung up the phone rang immediately. Banister gestured for Navarro to answer it.

Roberto did so, smiled, and handed the phone to Banister. "It's Gatlin. He wants to know what the hell we're doing."

Banister's instructions to Gatlin were brief: Their plans were changing but they'd be there sooner or later; keep monitoring the radio so that he could have the engines warmed up when they arrived. He hung up and asked Navarro to repeat his report on Gemelo. Then he shook his head and said, "We'll have to wait for Bill. He looks so much like Oswald that his only chance is to fly out of here with us. Maybe we ought to give the police a steer to the Texas Theater."

"I don't think you'll have to," said Hart, who had been listening to the radio. "I just heard a news flash that a man suspected of shooting a local police officer has been apprehended in a movie theater on West Jefferson. The description matched that of Oswald."

"Well, that really tears it," Banister said. "With all our planning, Oswald is still alive. We'll stay here and wait for Bill. Ruby got us into this and he'll have to get us out. I'll make him take care of Oswald."

It had been an hour since Gemelo had heard any sirens. Peering from the back door of the church, he saw that his jacket had disappeared from under the car in the Texaco lot. That could be a problem.

Wanting to avoid the Tenth Street area, he walked through the Texaco station lot to Crawford and proceeded north to Eighth and then east to Ewing. Forty-five minutes later he reached the Harlandale house. He was surprised to see Banister's Ford still there and the blue Olds parked a half-block up the street.

"What the hell happened?" Ruby exploded as Gemelo entered.

Ruby sat with a frown on his face while Gemelo went over the details of his encounter with Tippit. When he had finished, Ruby said, "That's one I sure pegged wrong. I figured the son of a bitch would kill his mother to get his name in the papers."

Banister's voice was heavy with sarcasm. "I wouldn't have worried about her, but I'm sure as hell worried about us. You screwed it up, so now you're going to unscrew it."

Ruby cringed. "Well, first I want Bill's gun. What caliber is it?"

"It's a .38 Colt."

"Switching a .38 should be simple enough. I'll arrange something. According to the radio, Oswald was carrying his cheapy .38 when they caught him."

Banister said, "The FBI will no doubt do the ballistics testing, so they can switch the cartridges or do whatever else is necessary to fix things up."

"I'll get the local cops to switch the jackets," Ruby said. "They're good at making evidence fit the crime. Remember, they've all got a hot potato on their hands—they'll have to cover up everything that doesn't fit to keep themselves out of a jam. O.K., I think I can handle it. Now, you guys better get your asses out of here."

When they were ready to leave Banister said, "One last question, Jack. What about Oswald? He'll squeal like a stuck pig to save his own skin. What the hell are you going to do? As long as he's alive, none of us is safe. Especially you."

"I'll think of something and fast. Don't worry. If there's no other way I'll do it myself."

Banister gave him an intense, cold stare. "O.K. Just so you

understand what you have to do. By the way, keep the money. You may need it for an emergency. Your defense will be provided for, if it cōmes to that."

Without even a handshake, Banister turned to Gemelo and said, "Bill, get going. You've got an airplane to catch. Do you have anyplace to hole up?"

"Yep, if Gatlin can fly me I can stay with some friends in Phoenix."

Banister reflected. "O.K.," he said at last. "Roberto, you've got yourself a new Oldsmobile. It's a damn nice car." He threw the keys to him. "The registration and signed title are in the glove compartment. In fact, you can drive Bill to the airport on your way out of town. Jack, I assume you're going to get rid of the Ford?"

"I'll return it to the guy I borrowed it from."

"Roberto, Hart's Mannlicher is in the trunk of the Olds, and Rigel's is here in this toolbox. You'd better bury them some-where."

Navarro nodded and said, "Yes, Sir. How about the middle of Lake Pontchartrain?"

Banister smiled in agreement, reached into his pocket, and pulled out an envelope. "This is yours. I damn near forgot. I've given the other boys theirs already. I'll see you back in New Orleans before long."

Then he turned to the others. "Well, that's it, then. Con-gratulations again, everyone. Clay will be pleased, assuming that Jack gets Oswald. God knows what Washington is up to at this point. They must be scurrying like hell to cover things up."

The phone rang again and Banister picked it up. It was the operator reporting that his station call to New Orleans had been completed. Dave Ferrie came on the line and said, "I was starting to get worried."

"Sorry," Banister replied, "but every damn telephone line in this city's been tied up for the last hour."

"I can believe it," Ferrie replied. "What's happening?"

"Well, I'm sure you've already heard the big news on the radio, but our own plans have changed. I'm going to have Maurice fly Bill to Phoenix some time this afternoon. If something goes wrong, I want you to be on tap in Houston in case we need the other plane. Our pigeon's still flying so we may have to go south for a while. I don't know yet, but for tonight we're going to sit tight here. If Gatlin gets back by noon tomorrow, we'll fly back in the Aztec. If he has problems, you can come and get us. Can you go ice skating tomorrow in Houston?"

"Sure," Dave replied. "Do you have the phone number at the rink?"

"I have it. I'll call between 3:30 and 5:30 tomorrow afternoon. If you haven't heard from me by then, you'll know something happened."

"O.K."

"Incidentally, if you have an opportunity call Clay and tell him so far so good."

"I will. I'll wait until I hear from you."

When he had hung up, Banister was silent for a moment. Then a satisfied smile began to cross his face. Picking up a can of beer, he turned to the others and raised it in a salute.

"Gentlemen," he said, "to Lyndon Baines Johnson, the new president of the United States."

Epilogue

At 11:10 A.M. on Sunday, November 24, 1963, *Jack Ruby*— a familiar figure around the Dallas police headquarters—was waiting in the basement when *Lee Harvey Oswald*, handcuffed to Detective J. R. Leavelle, was being escorted toward the car that was to carry him to the county jail.

At that moment Jack Ruby, his right hand extended, stepped between a newsman and a detective and fired a single .38 caliber bullet into Oswald's abdomen. For the second time in as many days millions watched murder—live—on TV. Shortly thereafter, without regaining consciousness, Lee Oswald died in the same emergency room at Parkland Memorial Hospital to which the mortally wounded President Kennedy had been taken two days before.

Ruby, probably expecting to be proclaimed a hero for eliminating the supposed presidential assassin, instead was indicted for Oswald's murder. He was tried, convicted, and sentenced on March 14, 1964, to die in the electric chair. Instead he died in prison, of lung cancer, before the sentence had been carried out.

Immediately after the assassination, *William Gemelo**** was flown to Phoenix by Maurice Gatlin, Sr., where he remained briefly before slipping across the Mexican border on or about November 25. He resurfaced in Dallas about three weeks later, in the company of Jim Hart.* Gemelo and Hart were arrested on narcotics charges that were later dismissed. Both men are believed to be alive, but their whereabouts are unknown.

W. Guy Banister returned to New Orleans on November 24 and shortly thereafter closed his detective agency at 544 Camp Street. In the summer of 1964, less than a year after the assassination, he died of an apparent heart attack.

Dave Ferrie also returned to New Orleans the morning following the assassination, stopping at Alexander, Louisiana, en route. On the 25th, he was arrested and booked as a fugitive from Texas. District Attorney Jim Garrison handed him over to the FBI, whose agents interrogated and released him. Garrison was within one week of indicting Ferrie for conspiracy in connection with the assassination when Ferrie died suddenly, on February 22, 1967. The cause of death was given as a cerebral hemorrhage.

Clay Shaw retired as president of the New Orleans International Trade Center in 1965. In 1966, he was accused by Garrison of being one of the conspirators in the assassination. He was indicted, went to trial, and was acquitted during the following year. He died of natural causes in New Orleans in 1974.

Rose Chermi survived being pushed from the speeding auto by Gemelo and Hart. The following day, November 21, 1963, she told the medical personnel who were treating her that President Kennedy was to be assassinated on the 22nd. On September 4, 1965, she was killed by a hit-and-run driver as she walked along a Texas highway near Big Sandy.

---

*Throughout the Epilogue, an asterisk denotes a pseudonym.

Hugh F. Ward died at the controls of a Piper Aztec when it plunged to earth near Ciudad Victoria, Mexico, on May 23, 1965. The cause of the accident is unknown.

*Richard Carson Filmore** was confined in several Texas jails and ultimately in Leavenworth Penitentiary. While there he was transferred on several occasions to the U.S. Medical Center in Springfield, Illinois, for psychiatric examination. In the spring of 1968 he was recruited back into the Central Intelligence Agency and performed missions in Europe, primarily in East Germany. He was still working for the Agency in 1971, living in the United States, but his present whereabouts are unknown.

*Carlos Rigel** left the United States immediately after the assassination and traveled extensively in Central and South America. He was last reported to be residing in Europe.

*Jim Hart** dropped out of sight after the president's death but was seen a few weeks later in Dallas in the company of William Gemelo. Recent reports have placed him in Europe and on the West Coast of the United States.

*Charles Hunter,** as recently as September, 1975, was reported to be living on the West Coast.

*Roberto Navarro** was reported killed in Havana in an abortive attempt on Fidel Castro's life in June or July of 1964.

Perry Raymond Russo lived to testify for Jim Garrison against Clay Shaw in the 1967 conspiracy trial. He died less than a year later, reportedly of a cerebral hemorrhage similar to that which ended the life of Dave Ferrie.

*Ross Allen** is currently running a small electronics manufacturing firm in Baltimore, Maryland.

Air Force General *Charles P. Cabell*, forced into retirement as deputy director of the Central Intelligence Agency in 1961, continued to work as a consultant to the clandestine services and for several CIA-related software firms in the metropolitan Washington, D.C. area. He later entered Fort Myers hospital in Virginia for a routine medical checkup, which he passed successfully. He collapsed as he left the hospital, on May 25, 1971, and died within hours.

Maurice Gatlin, Sr., who in addition to his duty as a transporter for the CIA was legal counsel to the Anti-Communist League of the Caribbean, died in a fall from the balcony of a hotel in San Juan, Puerto Rico, in 1964.

Marina Oswald Porter, in August, 1975, was living with her husband Kenneth on a farm near Dallas. She was employed as a clerk in a suburban department store.

*Manuel Rodriguez** is believed to be dead.

*Pepe Arnez** is alive and living in Miami.

*Ed Kendricks** died of natural causes in 1972.

Mario Garcia Kohly was tried for conspiracy to print counterfeit currency and a host of other charges in March of 1964. The charges were pressed by U.S. Attorney Henry Morgenthau, at the direction of Attorney General Robert F. Kennedy, and he was convicted. When his appeal was denied, he jumped bond and continued his anti-Castro efforts. He eluded the Justice Department for nine months, then turned himself in to serve his two-year concurrent sentence.

Kohly, the official de facto president-in-exile of the Cuban government, was sent to the federal penitentiaries at Lewisburg and Allenwood, Pennsylvania. Upon his release he returned to the Washington, D.C., area to continue his fight to free Cuba. He died on August 5, 1975, in Fairfax, Virginia, at the age of 76.

The author, *Robert D. Morrow,* code name Robert Porter, pleaded *nolo contendere* at his hearing on the counterfeiting charges before Judge Dorsey Watkins in February of 1964. His plea was accepted by the court and he was given a two-year suspended sentence before verdict. He has since worked as an independent electronics consultant and for a time operated an electronics development firm.

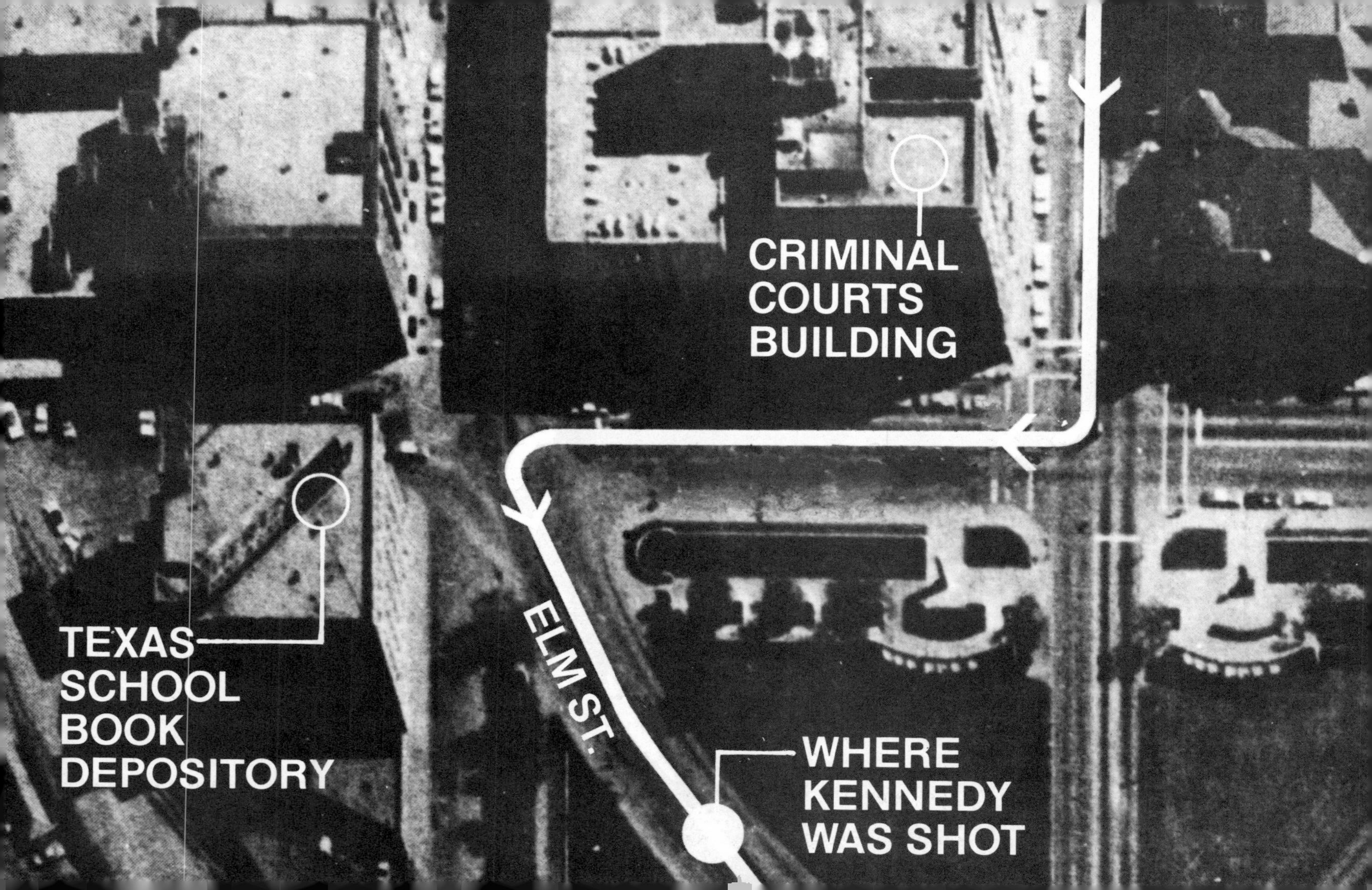
CRIMINAL COURTS BUILDING
TEXAS SCHOOL BOOK DEPOSITORY
ELM ST.
WHERE KENNEDY WAS SHOT